Kissinger and the
Yom Kippur War

Kissinger and the Yom Kippur War

DAVID R. MORSE

McFarland & Company, Inc., Publishers
Jefferson, North Carolina

LIBRARY OF CONGRESS CATALOGUING-IN-PUBLICATION DATA

Morse, David R., 1961–
    Kissinger and the Yom Kippur War / David R. Morse.
       p.   cm.
    Includes bibliographical references and index.

    ISBN 978-0-7864-9864-2 (softcover : acid free paper) ∞
    ISBN 978-1-4766-2077-0 (ebook)

    1. United States—Foreign relations—Israel. 2. Israel—Foreign relations—United States. 3. United States—Foreign relations—1969–1974. 4. Israel-Arab War, 1973—Influence. 5. Kissinger, Henry, 1923– I. Title.

E183.8.I7M67 2015
327.7305694—dc23   2015017145

BRITISH LIBRARY CATALOGUING DATA ARE AVAILABLE

© 2015 David R. Morse. All rights reserved

No part of this book may be reproduced or transmitted in any form or by any means, electronic or mechanical, including photocopying or recording, or by any information storage and retrieval system, without permission in writing from the publisher.

On the cover: Secretary of State Henry Kissinger speaking at a press conference (Thomas J. O'Halloran/Library of Congress)

Printed in the United States of America

McFarland & Company, Inc., Publishers
  Box 611, Jefferson, North Carolina 28640
    www.mcfarlandpub.com

In loving memory of my father,
Myron "Mike" Morse

Table of Contents

Preface   1

1. Nixon, Kissinger and the "Special Relationship"   5
2. The Prelude to War   23
3. The Inadequacies of Diplomacy and Bureaucracy   64
4. The Tide Turns   101
5. Negotiating a Ceasefire   120
6. The Failure to Avoid a Superpower Confrontation   137
7. Aftermath   165

Chapter Notes   173
Bibliography   193
Index   199

Preface

The Yom Kippur War of 1973 brought the United States and Soviet Union within arm's reach of a nuclear confrontation. Because of the war's centrality to Cold War politics, most existing accounts focus on strategic concerns and diplomatic maneuvers by the superpowers. However, recently declassified sources reveal the frequently ignored role of domestic politics on U.S. policy during the war and the impact that Watergate and a weakened Nixon presidency played in the decision making process. This book puts due focus on strategic and diplomatic influences, but it also gives proper attention to the influence of domestic factors, offering an improved, comprehensive narrative that weaves a new argument into the body of existing scholarship.

While Henry Kissinger did achieve his ultimate objective in the war, namely the securing of the United States—and himself—as the Middle East's chief peace broker, domestic challenges and strategically conflicting objectives vis-à-vis the Soviet Union provoked Kissinger, at times, into making costly mistakes. Kissinger was plagued by his own biases, misconceptions and errors of judgment. He missed opportunities to prevent the war, and, once it began, to reduce its duration. His first mistake, though Kissinger hardly stands alone, was to misinterpret and shrug off myriad signals of an impending attack. Secondly, Kissinger, in tandem with the Soviet Union, was unsuccessful in brokering a ceasefire in the early days of the crisis. It was a failure because war inevitably led to conflict between the superpowers, something that was not in the best interest of either side; rather, both sides had high stakes in the success of détente. Thirdly, for reasons still being debated, the United States delayed the rearming of Israel for four days, while the Soviet Union rapaciously pumped arms into Egypt and Syria via plane and ship. Fourthly, once a U.N. sponsored ceasefire was brokered, Kissinger unwittingly gave Israel a "green light" to carry the war forward, which nearly resulted in the destruction of the Egyptian Third Army. Lastly, Kissinger overreacted to a Soviet threat to intervene unilaterally in Egypt by moving the U.S. military to a state of nuclear alert, a move that unnecessarily brought the two superpowers within dangerous reach of a nuclear confrontation.

In Kissinger's own view, his handling of what he boastfully called "the best run crisis" during the Nixon presidency achieved his final objective. The Israelis, battered by the combined armies of Egypt and Syria, would within five years be willing to make concessions on land occupied in the 1967 War, the ultimate source of tension in the region. The Egyptians, humiliated in 1967, emerged from the Yom Kippur War confident and ready to negotiate. However, Kissinger's confrontational approach with the Soviet Union, exemplified by his overreaction to a Soviet warning that it might intervene in the crisis, led to a superpower confrontation that might have been avoided. As a result, relations with Washington's European allies were strained. Despite his efforts to lure the Arabs into the U.S. camp, the Arab oil embargo, which Kissinger had largely discounted, but which resulted following Washington's airlift to Israel, damaged the American economy and created a lasting negative impression in the collective American psyche of Arabs.

Chapter 1 evaluates the existing scholarship on the "special relationship" between the United States and Israel, with a focus on the Nixon Administration. The scholarship on the special relationship can be divided into three schools: the "strategic" school, the "domestic policy" school and the "special connection" school. While different scholars have focused on different schools, and each president has exemplified one philosophy or the other, under the Nixon Administration, geopolitical strategy has been unquestionably the focus of most prior scholarship

Chapter 2 examines the background of the war. The first section looks at the emergence of Kissinger as the *de facto* powerbroker for peace negotiations in the Middle East at the dawn of the 1970s, eclipsing Secretary of State William Rogers, who had worked diligently but unsuccessfully to create a Mideast settlement. Kissinger's "step-by-step" approach to Middle East negotiations offered Egyptian president Anwar Sadat no glimpse of hope that the crisis between Egypt and Israel would be resolved. The second section explores how Kissinger, convinced that Sadat lacked the military means to launch a successful invasion of Israel, opted for a strategy of diplomatic delay, which ultimately precipitated the war.

Chapter 3 focuses on the first week of the war, the diplomatic stalemate that resulted between the U.S. and the Soviets, and the bureaucratic impasse within the Nixon Administration, which resulted in no effective American military response. The first section examines how Kissinger sought to lessen, if not eradicate, the Soviet presence in the Middle East, while the Soviets, surprised by early Arab success on the battlefield, hoped to demonstrate the efficacy of Soviet military support and reassert itself into the Middle East peace process. The second section focuses on how infighting between the State Department and the Department of Defense prevented the Administration from countering a major Soviet airlift in support of Syria and Egypt. Nixon, distracted by the resignation of Vice President Spiro Agnew and Watergate, put Kissinger in the position of taking on an increasingly recalcitrant bureaucracy.

Chapter 4 analyzes the second week of the war with a focus on domestic politics. Though the airlift began to proceed at breakneck speed, the Administration was beset by allegations, led by Senator Henry Jackson and other conservatives, that Nixon, anxious to not alienate the Soviets in the interests of preserving a budding spirit of détente, was not doing enough to help the Israelis. In parallel, the American public was growing increasingly antagonistic toward the Arabs, a reaction that was as much fueled by media images of a besieged Israel as it was by incessant reports of an impending oil embargo. Ironically, such attitudes persisted despite vocal opposition from the Europeans over American involvement in the war.

Chapter 5 reveals the extent that Watergate had incapacitated Nixon and, as a result, emboldened Kissinger to take the substance of negotiations into his own hands. During talks in Moscow, Kissinger subordinated the wishes of Nixon, who wanted an overall settlement in the Middle East, by negotiating a simple ceasefire, which served to minimize, as Kissinger wanted, Soviet involvement after the war. In Jerusalem, Kissinger, unbeknownst to Nixon, gave the Israelis a "green light" to continue to encircle the Egyptian Third Army after a United Nations ceasefire resolution had gone into effect. The results of this green light ultimately led to a near crisis with the Soviets.

Chapter 6 contends that Kissinger's decision, in response to a Soviet threat to unilaterally send troops into Egypt, to place U.S. forces on DEFCON III, an alert which entails nuclear readiness, was a drastic and dangerous overreaction. It was fueled by Kissinger's concerns that the Soviets sought to take advantage of a weakened presidency that unnecessarily raised the stakes and brought the world within arms' reach of a global catastrophe. That Kissinger made the decision at all speaks to the impact of Watergate—a conversation between Nixon and Kissinger earlier that evening reveals a paranoid and virtually incoherent president obsessing that those that would have him impeached were trying to "kill the president." Yet having made the DEFCON III decision, the evidence suggests that Kissinger's motives were more to bolster the Nixon presidency in the eyes of the Soviets by showing that the Administration was still in charge, rather than to distract attention from Watergate, as much of the press clamored at the time.

The concluding chapter evaluates the Yom Kippur War's legacy. American relations with its Arab and European allies had been severely damaged and the energy crisis wreaked havoc on the American economy. Importantly, as a consequence of the DEFCON III alert, détente took a severe beating. Despite his mistakes, however, Kissinger had effectively ensured the exclusion of the Soviets from future negotiations in the Middle East peace process, as well as Israel's dependence on the United States for arms and financial support. In the eight months that followed the war, Kissinger made the Middle East his top priority, and his efforts arguably laid the foundation for the Camp David Accords, brokered by President Jimmy Carter and signed between Sadat and Israeli prime minister Menachem Begin.

CHAPTER 1

Nixon, Kissinger and the "Special Relationship"

The term "special relationship" has been used since the Johnson Administration to describe the close connection between the United States and Israel. This relationship reached new levels under the presidency of Richard Nixon, and many scholars have seen the Yom Kippur War of 1973 as a tipping point. Since that war, despite pretensions to evenhandedness, the United States has demonstrated unrelenting support for Israel.

In the words of Yaacov Bar-Siman-Tov, the special relationship thesis maintains that the United States and Israel have "a unique and unparalleled partnership, with high levels of friendship, amity, trust, and political and military cooperation, with each side occupying a special position in the other's domestic and foreign policy."[1] That this relationship is beneficial to Israel is clear. From 1948 to 1975, the United States transferred more than $6.5 billion in assistance to Israel, making it the highest per capita recipient of U.S. aid in the world during that time period.[2] Since 1976, Israel has been the number one beneficiary of American foreign aid, totaling an average of $3 billion a year (over $100 billion over the past forty years), an amount that is three times the annual foreign aid designated to all of Africa, Asia and Latin America. James Petras asserts that this number is misleadingly low as Israel receives numerous other benefits such as low or zero interest loans, loan guarantees and access to American intelligence and technology.[3] Additionally, from a diplomatic perspective, Israel has benefited immeasurably from American support in the United Nations.

Between 1972 and 2006, the U.S. vetoed forty-two Security Council resolutions that were critical of Israel, a number that is greater than the combined vetoes of all other Security Council members for the same period.[4]

Despite obvious benefits to Israel, many have argued that the special relationship is a one-way street, and that Israel brings little to the table when compared with American largess. As Bar-Siman-Tov has noted, the idea of a special relationship should only be considered from a U.S. perspective due to the asymmetrical nature of the relationship—namely that the benefits received by the United States are of a less tangible nature than those obtained by Israel.[5] Although much of the literature on the special relationship has focused on the consequences of the U.S.-Israeli alliance in global and Middle Eastern politics, much of the scholarly debate centers on offering explanations of American support and answering the question "What's in it for the U.S.?"

The scholarship on the special relationship can be divided into three schools. The first school, the so-called "strategic" or "national interest" perspective, focuses on "hard factors," such as the strategic value that Israel delivers to the United States in terms of geopolitics, first during the Cold War, and subsequently, as an ally in the fight against terrorism. The second school, the "domestic policy" point of view, emphasizes the role of domestic politics, particularly the influence wielded by the American Jewish community, and more recently, Christian Zionists. Included in this category is the body of scholarship focusing on the influence wielded by the pro–Israeli lobby and special interest groups such as the American Israel Public Affairs Committee (AIPAC). The third school, or "special connection" thesis, stresses the moral sympathy and sense of brotherhood or paternalism felt by Americans toward Israel.

Each of the three schools has its champions. Typifying the strategic school, historian Douglas Little writes in his book *American Orientalism*, "Cultivating Israel as America's geopolitical asset seemed more and more essential for U.S. policymakers as they struggled to prevent the Soviet Union from filling the vacuum created by Britain's slow-motion withdrawal from its empire east of Suez after 1945."[6] The strategic argument is perhaps best reflected in Henry Kissinger's articulation of the Nixon Administration's Middle Eastern strategy. "At the end of the day," Kissinger writes, "when confronted with the realities of power in the Middle East—after much anguish and circuitous maneuvers—he would pursue, in the national interest, the same strategy: to reduce Soviet influence, weaken the position of the Arab radicals, encourage Arab moderates, and assure Israel's security."[7] While many historians have acknowledged the impact of "softer" factors in America's Middle Eastern policy, volumes of analysis have focused on these "harder" concerns.⁸

Among the most vocal and popular advocates of the domestic policy perspective have been political scientists John Mearsheimer and Stephen Walt, who argue that Israel and the pro–Israeli lobby in the United States have consistently orchestrated an aggressive and well-funded campaign, directed at members of Congress and the American public, in order to promote Israeli interests. They write in *The Israeli Lobby and U.S. Foreign Policy* that in recent years "the lobby's political clout and public relations acumen have discouraged U.S. leaders from pursuing Middle East policies that would protect American interests and protect Israel from its worst mistakes."⁹ That the archives of Israel "bulge with information" about Israeli efforts to influence U.S. foreign policy is confirmed by research conducted by historian Peter L. Hahn. He writes, for example, that during the Truman era, Israeli envoys relied on David Niles, Eddie Jacobson, and other "friends" to provide indirect access to Truman and to relay insider information about U.S. policy making.¹⁰ Advocates of the domestic policy position argue that although the Executive branch has been less directly targeted than the Legislature, it has been anything but immune to the lobby's pressures.

According to political scientist Bernard Reich, AIPAC, undoubtedly the most influential of the pro–Israel lobbies, uses a number of direct and indirect methods to influence U.S. policy. AIPAC establishes contacts with politicians, congressional aides, administrative assistants, advisers, and bureaucratic officials. AIPAC personnel testify before Congress. It organizes letter writing and other public relations campaigns. Importantly, AIPAC has successfully formed coalitions with numerous domestic figures and organizations including prominent African American, Asian, and Hispanic leaders, scholars, and celebrities, which has been an important factor in strengthening the special relationship.¹¹

Describing the strength of the Jewish lobby, the chairman of the Joint Chiefs of Staff, George Brown, in October 1974, said during a lecture at Duke University:

> [The Jewish influence in this country is] so strong you wouldn't believe it now. We have the Israelis coming to us for equipment. We say we can't possibly get the Congress to support a program like that. They say, "Don't worry about Congress. We'll take care of the Congress." Now this is somebody from another country, but they can do it. They own, you know, the banks in this country, the newspapers ... you just look at where the Jewish money is in this country.¹²

Brown's statement was not politically acceptable, even in 1974, and it was retracted the following day.[13] Yet as political scientist Steven L. Spiegel observes, "that the chairman of the Joint Chiefs of Staff could make such a statement demonstrates that the pro–Israel forces were weaker than they had been before the [Yom Kippur] war." The war had changed assumptions of Israel as being invulnerable and boosted perceptions of Arab strength and effectiveness. Yet, as Spiegel notes, "along with enhanced Arab respectability and clout came resentment at the oil embargo and the increase in oil prices, acts widely seen as economic belligerence toward the United States."[14] While the special connection felt by many Americans toward Israel was fortified by the war, it was matched by a corresponding antipathy toward Arabs, particularly after the oil embargo.

Adherents of the third school of thought, the special connection school, have attributed American support for Israel to a sense of brotherhood and empathy felt by the American public. As political scientist Nadav Safron writes in *Israel: The Embattled Ally*, "Americans have felt a strong sympathy for Israel as a democratic nation and a society imbued with the libertarian values and humanistic culture of the West." Safron adds that Israel has evoked this sympathy because "it has been one of the rare working democracies among the scores of new nations that came into being since the end of World War II, and because its experience evoked echoes of America's own experience."[15]

The special connection stance was perhaps best expressed by Washington senator Henry "Scoop" Jackson, one of Israel's staunchest supporters during his six terms in the House and six terms in the Senate. When asked if the "Jewish lobby" was taking over Congress, Jackson retorted, "These people just don't understand. They refuse to realize that the *American people* support Israel. Americans, whether Gentile or Jew, respect competence. They like the idea that we are on the side which seems to know what it's doing."[16]

Historian Michelle Mart argues in *Eye on Israel: How America Came to View Israel as an Ally* that American perceptions of Israel underwent a drastic change in the years following World War II. In the aftermath of the war, the salient ideology of Americans was one of universalism; the United States had triumphed over the Nazis and the brutal totalitarian regime that Hitler's brand of fascism represented. She writes, "In the political narrative used by American policymakers as well as in contemporary popular culture, the proposed Jewish state came to embody universalism ... [and] the humanitarian imperative of caring for Jewish displaced persons."[17]

Another key work in the special connection camp is Elizabeth Stephens' book *U.S. Policy Towards Israel: The Role of Political Culture in Defining the "Special Relationship,"* which analyzes the role of culture in maintaining the "relative continuity" in U.S. policy towards Israel. She writes, "For many Americans, the history and culture of the United States is perceived to resonate with that of the Jewish state, which reinforces the feeling of moral responsibility for the preservation of Israel because of the role Washington had played in its creation."[18] Similarly, Abraham Ben-Zvi, a political scientist whose book *The United States and Israel: The Limits of the Special Relationship* is cut from the cloth of the strategic school, acknowledges

> [there is] a widespread fund of goodwill towards Israel that is not restricted to the Jewish community, and an equally strong and persistent commitment to Israel's continued national existence, integrity and security. Comprising a cluster of broadly based attitudes that underscore the affinity and similarity between the two states in terms of their pioneering nature and commitment to democracy, this paradigm emerged as a legitimate and pervasive precept.[19]

The special connection attitude is reflected in a speech delivered by President Bill Clinton in an address to the Israeli Knesset in October 1994:

> For decades, as Israel has struggled to survive, we have rejoiced in your triumphs and shared in your agonies. In the years since Israel was founded, Americans of every faith have admired and supported you.... In times of war and times of peace, every president of the United States, since Harry Truman, and every Congress, has understood the importance of Israel. The survival of Israel is important not only to our interests, but to every single value we hold dear as a people.[20]

While the strength of the U.S. commitment to Israel has vacillated with presidential administrations, one constant has been support from Congress. As Marvin C. Feuerwerger noted in 1979, "few ongoing foreign policy issues have sustained congressional interest as long as American policy toward Palestine." In 1922—twenty-six years before the creation of the Israeli state—Congress passed a joint resolution stating "the United States favors the establishment in Palestine of a home for the Jewish people." Congress initiated the first aid programs to Israel in the early 1950s, and throughout the 1948 to 1976 period, it frequently expressed its support for Israel by drafting letters and resolutions urging the president to support the Jewish state. When presidents asked for congressional backing for pro–Israeli programs, Congress overwhelmingly approved them.[21] Even today, censure of Israel by members of Congress is the exception rather than the rule.

Presidential support of Israel, by contrast, has varied with the exigencies and proclivities of each administration. Truman, for instance, who officially granted U.S. recognition to Israel in 1948, felt strong ideological sympathy for Israel in the wake of the Nazi holocaust, and was strongly influenced by Jewish concerns. Michael J. Cohen explains Truman's motivation as being described by two essential narratives. The first, what he calls the White House School, reflects Truman's goal of "dedication to the twin ideals of [honoring] international obligations and relieving human misery," as Truman wrote in his *Memoirs*.[22] The second, the State Department School, sees Truman as acting out of political interest in order to gain ground with the Jewish vote. This view is best articulated by James Forrestal, Truman's secretary of state for the navy and later secretary of defense, who repeatedly warned of the dangers of allowing electoral concerns to influence the course of foreign policy; he once opined that the Palestine lobby "bordered closely on scandal."[23]

As a point of contrast, in 1952, Eisenhower lost two-thirds of the Jewish vote to the Democratic candidate, Adlai Stevenson. Eisenhower placed no Jews in senior cabinet positions, and his administration boasted of maintaining a stance of total impartiality toward the Arabs and Israel. After his first election, articles in the press proliferated about a "new approach" to the Middle East. Henry Byroade, Assistant Secretary of State of Near Eastern, South Asian and African Affairs, declared, "If we are to be accused of 'pro' anything, let us make it amply clear that that prefix can only apply to one thing, and that is that our policy is first and foremost 'pro–American.'" In a 1954 speech, Byroade warned that the Israelis should look upon themselves "as a Middle Eastern state ... rather than ... a worldwide grouping ... [with] special rights."[24]

When Kennedy entered the White House, he signaled his intention to handle the Middle East situation in a "fair-minded and even-handed manner," which resulted in relations with Tel Aviv being smooth during his first year in office. Kennedy's inauguration in 1961 coincided with profound concerns, based on CIA estimations, that Israel might utilize a nuclear reactor it was secretly constructing with French help at Dimona in the Negev desert to develop atomic weapons. That January, Eisenhower had demanded that Israel "declare unreservedly" that it had no such plans, yet Prime Minister David Ben-Gurion refused. Other areas of tension followed. In the summer of 1961, Kennedy began a rapprochement with Egyptian president Gamal Abdel Nasser, and he supported a U.N. sponsored proposal by Joseph Johnson, the head of the Carnegie Endowment for Peace, calling for Israel to accept up to 100,000 Palestinian refugees.

In March 1962, after a deadly Israeli reprisal against Syria, Kennedy instructed U.N. Ambassador Adlai Stevenson to condemn Israel's action in the Security Council. Yet Kennedy was troubled by Soviet bomber shipments to Cairo, and during a visit by Israeli foreign minister Golda Meir just after Christmas in 1962, he likened Washington's "special relationship" with Tel Aviv to that with London, and he asserted, "in case of an invasion the United States would come to the support of Israel."[25]

Under Johnson, the special relationship took on new meaning. "The United States will continue its warm friendship with Israel," the new president declared to Golda Meir at the reception following Kennedy's funeral, adding, "Israel can count on this." Throughout his presidency he made good on this promise, placing friends of Israel in key positions in his cabinet, including the Rostow brothers, Walt and Eugene, whom he named respectively as his national security adviser and undersecretary of state.[26] Yet it was the Six-Day War of 1967—a war that transformed the Middle East in terms of its geography, politics and relationship with the rest of the world—that led to a fundamental change in the nature of the special relationship.

The crisis began on May 13, 1967, when Egypt received information from the Soviets that the Israelis were massing ten to thirteen brigades along the Syrian border for an attack that allegedly was to take place on May 17. The following day, Egypt began to move troops into the Sinai Peninsula, and on May 16, Egypt demanded withdrawal of the 3,400 men stationed there under the United Nations Emergency Force (UNEF). On May 22, Egyptian president Nasser stated that he would close the Straits of Tiran (Gulf of Aqaba) to Israeli ships, an announcement that was followed by official closure on May 23. On May 30, Jordan signed a mutual defense treaty with Egypt, joining the alliance already in place between Egypt and Syria. War broke out on June 5 when Israel launched a surprise attack on the Egyptian air force, destroying most of it within hours. Though there are different theories as to which country's actions most precipitated the war—Egypt, Israel, the United States or the Soviet Union—it was likely the subtle change in the communications of Johnson regarding Israeli preemption, from a red light to a yellow light, that resulted in Israel initiating a first strike against Egypt. According to William B. Quandt, the light "never turned green, but yellow was enough for the Israelis to know that they could take action without worrying about Washington's reaction."[27]

When the possibility of an Israeli first-strike initially became apparent, clearly the light was red. According to his memoirs, Johnson cabled Israeli prime minister Levi Eshkol on May 17 to urge restraint: "I am sure you will understand that I cannot accept any responsibilities on behalf of the United States for situations which arise as the result of actions on which we are not consulted."[28] A week later, on May 26, Johnson met with Israeli foreign minister Abba Eban, who was sent by the Israeli cabinet to ascertain the intentions of the United States. Eban conveyed the message to Washington that Egypt was preparing an all-out attack on Israel, and he wanted to ascertain the intentions of the United States. "All of our intelligence people are unanimous," Johnson said, "that if the U.A.R. attacks, you will whip hell out of them." He was referring to a CIA memorandum that stated "Israel could almost certainly attain air superiority over the Sinai Peninsula in 24 hours after taking the initiative or in two or three days if the U.A.R. struck first."[29] When Eban asked what the United States would do, Johnson said, "You can assure the Israeli cabinet we will pursue vigorously any and all possible measures to keep the Strait open." However, Johnson wanted to make his position absolutely clear. "The central point, Mr. Minister," he said, "is that your nation not be the one to bear the responsibility for any outbreak of war. Israel will not be alone unless it decides to go it alone."[30] Eban, who was returning to an Israeli Cabinet meeting the following day, needed a more definitive answer. He pressed the president, "Can I tell my Cabinet that you are going to use all measures in your power to get the Gulf and Straits open to all shipping, including that of Israel?" According to Eban, "the president stated with great emphasis: 'Yes.'"[31] When Eban left the room, Johnson turned to his advisers and said, "I've failed. They'll go."[32]

Johnson did have one card up his sleeve to prevent hostilities, a plan called "Operation Red Sea Regatta," which called for a declaration of maritime nations asserting the right of free passage through the Straits of Tiran. If Egypt rejected the declaration, an international convoy of freighters would sail through the Straits, escorted by American and British warships, rebuffing any Egyptian attempts to detain it. By the first week in June, however, plans for Regatta fell apart. A United Nations resolution calling on all countries to avoid violence also failed. During that week, Supreme Court Justice Abe Fortas, a close personal friend of Johnson who was considered to speak for the president, summoned Israel's minister in Washington, Eppie Evron, to a meeting. Fortas showed his cards: "If Israel had acted alone without exhausting political efforts, it would have made a catastrophic error. It would then have been almost impossible for the United States to help Israel and the ensuing relationship would have been tense.... The Israelis should realize that their restraint and well-considered procedures would now have a decisive influence when the United States comes to consider the measure of its involvement." Fortas added that time was running out and that it was now "a matter of days or even hours."[33]

When the Fortas message was communicated to the Israeli cabinet, several ministers who had been opting for restraint decided that Washington's red light had turned yellow. In Washington, Israeli ambassador to the United States Abe Harmon contacted Secretary of State Dean Rusk on June 2, just prior to returning to Israel for the cabinet meeting that would ultimately decide to go to war. Rusk reiterated that the issue of who fired first would be of the utmost importance. Harmon made one last visit prior to leaving for the airport, to Justice Fortas, who had spoken to the president earlier in the day. According to Fortas' law clerk, who overheard the conversation, Fortas told him: "Rusk will fiddle while Israel burns. If you're going to save yourself, do it yourself."[34] Three days later, the Israelis took him up on his advice. Fortas' comments to Harmon left no doubt that the shackles placed on Israel were being removed.

Despite Johnson's stated commitment of evenhandedness, his tacit support of Israel during the Six-Day War is unquestionable. His motivations, however, remain unclear. Political Scientist George Lenczowski offers four tentative explanations, each of which undoubtedly must have played a role:

1. Johnson was motivated by domestic calculations, namely pro–Israeli votes, dollars, and his desire to neutralize the protests of many Jews about his Vietnam policy.
2. It was during his presidency that the concept of Israel as a strategic asset vis-à-vis the Soviet took hold.
3. He was annoyed by Nasser's antics and wanted to see him punished.
4. He was influenced by the pro–Israeli sentiments of many on his staff.[35]

The Six-Day War marked a decisive shift toward a special relationship, and under Richard Nixon's presidency, it would be a relationship thoroughly dominated by Cold War concerns. Nixon, for all his notorious paranoia, was a pragmatist with a profound interest in foreign affairs, and the Middle East was no exception, though his top priorities remained the War in Vietnam, the Soviet Union, the threat of nuclear war, and restoring relations with China. He frequently referred to the Middle East as a powder keg, and he was worried about the global ramifications of the Arab-Israeli conflict, particularly as a potential catalyst of open hostilities between the superpowers.[36] Though largely supportive of Israel, Nixon generally pursued what he perceived to be the national interest, which he viewed to often be in stark contrast to the unnecessary distractions of domestic politics.

Nixon complained frequently about the pro–Israeli lobby, which he regarded as being shortsighted in its unrelenting advocacy of Israel. Writing in his memoirs, Nixon complains:

> One of the main problems I faced ... was the unyielding and shortsighted pro–Israeli attitude prevalent in large and influential segments of the American Jewish community, Congress, the media, and in intellectual and cultural circles. In the quarter century since the end of World War II, this attitude has become so deeply ingrained that many saw the corollary of not being pro–Israeli as being anti–Israeli, or even anti–Semitic. I tried unsuccessfully to convince them that this was not the case.[37]

Liberals and the "intellectual and cultural circles" were an obsession of Nixon. It bothered him that that many of the same people "who were urging that we send more military aid to save Israel were opposing our efforts to save South Vietnam from Communist domination."[38] In a March 1970 memorandum to Kissinger he wrote:

> What they must realize is that these people are very weak reeds. They will give Israel a lot of lip service, but they are peace at any price people. When the chips are down they will cut and run, not only as they are presently cutting and running in Vietnam, but also when any conflict in the Mideast stares them straight in the face.
> On the other hand, their real friends (to their great surprise) are people like [Barry] Goldwater, [William F.] Buckley, RN [Richard Nixon] et al., who are considered to be hawks on Vietnam but who, in the broader aspects, are basically not cut-and-run people whether it is in Vietnam, the Mideast, Korea, or any place in the world.
> They must recognize that our interests are basically pro-freedom and not just pro–Israel because of the Jewish vote. We are *for* Israel because Israel in our view is the only state in the Mideast which is *pro*-freedom and an effective opponent to Soviet expansion.... This is the kind of friend that Israel needs and will continue to need, particularly when the going gets very tough in the next five years....[39]

Kissinger, in his memoirs, supports Nixon's contention that strategic concerns, rather than domestic politics, dominated his motives. He contends:

> For on almost all practical issues his unsentimental geopolitical analysis finally led him to positions not so distant from ones others might take on the basis of ethnic politics.... He would make gestures to demonstrate—in part to himself—that he was free of the traditional influences that had constrained other Presidents. But at the end of the day, when confronted with the realities of power in the Middle East—after much anguish and circuitous maneuvers—he would pursue, in the national interest, the same strategy: to

1. Nixon, Kissinger and the "Special Relationship"

reduce Soviet influence, weaken the position of the Arab radicals, encourage Arab moderates, and assure Israel's security.[40]

Nixon saw the Middle East in starkly Cold War terms. As Lenczowski observes, Nixon seemed to "accept as an axiom that confrontation with the U.S.S.R. was virtually inevitable in case of an Arab-Israeli war." As a result, he had a "tendency to oversimplify, if not actually to distort" complexities in the region by accepting the idea that "the Soviets are the main cause of Middle East tensions."[41] Nixon was encouraged in this view by Israeli prime minister Golda Meir, who, for example, told him on September 18, 1970, that "Israel's problems were not caused primarily by the Arabs. They were the direct result of the Soviet presence and Soviet military equipment."[42]

Despite Nixon's focus on foreign affairs, he drew firm and unyielding distinctions between his friends and his enemies, and he continuously brooded over ways to exact revenge on the latter. Historian Noam Kochavi, in his book *Nixon and Israel: Forging a Conservative Partnership*, astutely argues that traditional geostrategic interpretations of the special relationship ignore the role of "ideational and psychological factors" and the emotional impact that certain decisions made by Israel had on Nixon and Kissinger *outside* the context of the Middle East. Kochavi argues that in the beginning of the 1970s, Meir and her ambassador to the United States, Yitzhak Rabin, led a "conservative turn" in Israeli policy that ingratiated Israel to the White House. "Coupled with a purposeful courtship of the evangelical movement," he writes, "Israel's public support for the Administration's approach in Vietnam and for Nixon's reelection campaign won appreciation and sympathy in the White House, and fostered a sense of common purpose that went well beyond a strict strategic calculus."[43] However, Kochavi contends that Israel's discreet backing for the Jackson-Vanik amendment, which linked U.S.-Soviet relations to the issue of Jewish emigration and thereby threatened the Administration's efforts to achieve détente, "undermined Nixon's and Kissinger's perception of Israel as a trusted, like-minded ally, since they both strongly opposed the amendment and placed great stock in the unswerving loyalty of friends." Though Nixon squarely put Israel in the category of "friend," the basic "DNA" of the U.S.-Israeli relationship under Nixon's tenure could best be characterized as cooperation with bouts of friction.[44]

Despite the friction, however, the special relationship reached new heights during Nixon's first term as president. According to journalist Seymour Hersh, Rabin "had a special entrée into the White House because he had been among the few foreign leaders who paid attention to Richard

Nixon on his 1966 world tour as a private citizen. At a time when others were shunning Nixon, Rabin invited him to Israeli army headquarters and provided ... red carpet treatment." In June 1972, Rabin was criticized for excessively praising Nixon's address to Congress following the president's summit in Moscow. Additionally, Rabin was accused of supporting Nixon for president and interfering in U.S. politics. Rabin responded that he was only stating "a fact." Kissinger, who was finely attuned to the bents of the president, quickly established a special relationship with Rabin, who soon had a direct telephone line to Kissinger's desk.[45] Kissinger once quipped, "I'll tell you one thing about Yitzhak Rabin. You always know what he wants. He wants more."[46]

In Nixon's reelection bid in 1972, his staffers began to boast that his close working relationship with Israeli leaders and his record of aid to Israel had been higher than any other administration to date. During the general election, McGovern's dovishness frightened many Jews, particularly his criticism of Israel's reliance on military force. To counter perceptions that the Democratic Congress had played a substantive in pushing for increased aid to Israel, the Nixon reelection campaign warned that Nixon, unlike McGovern, would strongly support Israel in another Arab–Israeli crisis.[47]

For all of Nixon's avowals that he operated above the fray of domestic politics, there is compelling evidence that domestic public opinion was a constant concern of the president. "PR is terribly important," Nixon told Kissinger in the midst of the crisis that erupted following the execution of Israeli athletes during the 1972 Munich Olympics. Nixon brooded obsessively over public opinion—Kissinger referred to him as having a "monomaniacal preoccupation with public relations"—especially criticism from pro–Israeli hawks.[48] Political scientists Lawrence R. Jacobs and Robert Y. Shapiro write that public opinion was a "guiding concern" of the Nixon Administration from the beginning; for example, just days after his inauguration, the president told his staff to track "what moves and concerns the average guy."[49]

There has been much written in the press about Nixon's anti–Semitism. In White House tape recordings, Nixon lashed out repeatedly at the Jews, whom he believed to be the source of many of his problems. "The Jews are all over the government," Nixon complained on one occasion to his chief of staff, H.R. "Bob" Haldeman, adding, "Generally speaking, you can't trust the bastards. They turn on you. Am I wrong or right?" Haldeman agreed: "Their whole orientation is against you.... And they are smart. They have the ability to do what they want to do—which is to hurt us."[50]

Nixon's adversarial, paranoid relationship with the media is legendary, and to him, the media and the Jews were nearly inseparable. A February 1, 1972, conversation with Reverend Billy Graham, following the National Prayer Breakfast, an annual event hosted by members of Congress, makes it clear that Nixon viewed the media as being dominated by Jews. Nixon refers to a remark made my comedy writer and producer Paul Keyes that "eleven out of the twelve writers [in Hollywood] are Jewish." He continues: "Now, *Life* is totally dominated by the Jews. *Newsweek* is totally, is owned by Jews, and dominated by them, their editorials. The *New York Times, The Washington Post*, are totally Jewish." Nixon asks rhetorically:

> Now, what does this mean? Does this mean that all the Jews are bad? No. It does mean that most Jews are left-wing, particularly the younger ones like that.... They're way out. They're radical. They're for peace at any prices, except where the support of Israel is concerned.... The best Jews, actually, are the Israeli Jews.... Because Israel, the reason Mrs. Meir supports me, which she does, is for a very fundamental reason. They know the Democratic candidates will be catering to the domestic Jewish vote, but she supports me. Because she knows the greatest danger to Israel is Russia. And she knows that in the [1970] crisis involving Jordan that I faced the Russians down for 'em. She knows that I am the only one that will do it. She knows that any Democrat will cave to the Communists, to the Russians. See, that's the point. She's tough.

Graham, responding to Nixon's comments about Jewish control of the media, exhorts, "But this stranglehold has got to be broken or this country is going to go down the drain!" Asks Nixon, "Do you believe that?" "Yes, sir," responds Graham. Nixon exclaims, "Boy! I can never say it though, but I believe ..." Graham cuts Nixon off. "But if you've been elected a second time, you might be able to do something."[51]

Nixon biographer Conrad Black observed, "As was not uncommon to people of his generation, Nixon had absurd ideas about the solidarity and conspiratorial proclivities of people with any Jewish ancestry."[52] Kissinger, himself a Jew, wrote, "The president was convinced that most leaders of the Jewish community had opposed him throughout his political career. The small percentage of Jews who voted for him, he would joke, had to be so crazy that they would probably stick with him even if he turned on Israel. He delighted in telling associates and visitors that the 'Jewish lobby' had no effect on him."[53]

Yet this was hardly the case. As historian Salim Yaqub observes, "In denying any interest in the Jewish vote, Nixon was, of course, protesting too much. He cared deeply about what he saw as the ingratitude of American Jews and worked assiduously to reverse it." According to Yaqub, Nixon

Kissinger speaking at a press conference in January 1974.

1. Nixon, Kissinger and the "Special Relationship"

attempted to achieve this by "demanding recognition from Jewish groups for every pro–Israel action he took" and currying favor with American Jews. In September 1969, after shipping fifty F-4 Phantom jets to Israel, Nixon wrote a memorandum to Kissinger pressing for an explanation of "the absolute failure of the American Jewish community to express any appreciation by letter, calls or otherwise." Additionally, he sought to win over American Jews by insisting that the evenhanded peace talks engaged in by Secretary of State William Rogers did not have full presidential backing. Yaqub writes, "While such assurances helped to reduce Jewish opposition to Nixon, they also hampered his administration's ability to promote a settlement of the Arab-Israeli conflict."[54]

Nixon's preoccupation with American Jews was starkly evident during the 1972 Munich Olympics crisis; Jewish reaction weighed heavily on the president. "The trouble with the Jews," he told Kissinger, "is that they've always played these things in terms of outrage. You've got the Jewish Defense League raising hell and saying we ought to kill every Arab diplomat." He added, "We've got to show we care on this one because ... you don't really know, Henry, what the Jewish community will do on this. It's going to be the goddamnedest thing you ever saw."[55] Kissinger pulled out his Jewish credentials to argue for an approach that balanced both domestic political concerns and America's weakening position with Arab countries. "God, I am Jewish. I've had thirteen members of my family killed. So I can't be insensitive to this. But I think you have to think also of the anti–Semitic woes in this country if we let our policy be run by the Jewish Community...."[56]

Nixon, however, needed no reminder that Kissinger was a Jew, and he referred to it constantly. When Kissinger was awarded the Nobel Peace Prize in October 1973 for his role in the Vietnam negotiations, Nixon, jealous, offered advice on how to donate the award money. "I would not put any in for Israel," said Nixon. Kissinger responded, "Absolutely not. That would be out of the question. I never give to Israel." Nixon reiterated, "You should not." Kissinger insisted, "No. That is out of the question."[57]

Though Nixon's relationship with Israel was fraught with ambiguity, during the Yom Kippur War, Cold War concerns assumed center stage, and the Administration's support of Israel, its client state, was unqualified. By November 15, just five weeks after the war began, the United States had flown nearly 700 sorties into Israel, equipping it with 11,000 tons of military equipment.[58] Congress had approved a request by Nixon to supply Israel with $2.2 billion in emergency aid, which set an important precedent. By 1974, Israel became the largest recipient of U.S. foreign assistance, a tendency that continues to this day—Israel has only been recently superseded by Iraq and Afghanistan in terms of aid.[59]

Yet the war also coincided with a series of domestic crises that virtually incapacitated the president and left his new secretary of state, Henry Kissinger, the undisputed architect of U.S. foreign policy. On October 10, Vice President Spiro Agnew resigned and pleaded no contest to charges of tax evasion and bribery. On October 12, the U.S. Court of Appeals ordered Nixon to release a series of tapes to Archibald Cox, the Watergate special prosecutor. On October 20, Attorney General Elliot Richardson and his deputy William Ruckelshaus resigned because of their refusal to follow Nixon's orders to fire Cox. Their resignations left Solicitor General Robert Bork as the highest-ranking member of the Justice Department; insisting that he had to obey the president's orders, he dismissed Cox. Termed the "Saturday Night Massacre," the House of Representatives immediately introduced 22 bills calling for the impeachment of the president or an investigation into impeachment proceedings. More than a million telegrams demanding impeachment poured into congressional offices. In fact, Watergate exploded while Henry Kissinger was in Moscow negotiating a ceasefire to the Yom Kippur War.

During the nearly three week duration of the war, Kissinger's influence reached its zenith, while that of the president declined, as he moved from a state of distraction to one of emotional paralysis. Kissinger's status within the administration had already risen with the resignation in April 1973 of Nixon's two chief gatekeepers, H.R. "Bob" Haldeman, White House Chief of Staff, and John Ehrlichman, Assistant to the President for Domestic Affairs, a result of their involvement in Watergate. In August, Secretary of State William Rogers, tired of being marginalized and the incessant squabbling with Kissinger for control of foreign policy, resigned. On September 22, only two weeks before the outbreak of the Yom Kippur War, Kissinger became both secretary of state and national security adviser.

As political scientist Asaf Siniver notes, "Ironically, Kissinger's ascendancy had an adverse effect on the formal process of decision-making. His dual position in the administration made formal NSC procedures even more cumbersome, as he now reviewed and recommended policies to the president as the national security advisor as well as the secretary of state. This created an absurd situation of bureaucratic politics in which one person argued at the same time for different policy preferences while representing the interests of his two respective institutions." Siniver quotes William Quandt, who served as a staff member in the National Security Council at the time:

1. Nixon, Kissinger and the "Special Relationship" 21

Nixon meeting with Secretary of Defense James Schlesinger in June 1974. Kissinger faulted Schlesinger with delaying the shipment of arms to Israel in the early stages of the war.

> [Kissinger] would let his bureaucracy produce a draft, and he would sometimes then sign it as Secretary of State, come over to the White House, and NSC staff would say "here is what the Secretary of State recommends, but in your role as National Security Advisor here is what you wrote," and put another memo on top to Nixon. It is amazing.[60]

With Kissinger at the helm of foreign policy on October 6, 1973, when the Yom Kippur War began, there was little doubt that gaining the upper hand over the Soviets in the Cold War political game would be Henry Kissinger's greatest concern. As Jussi Hanhimäki incisively argues in his 2004 book *The Flawed Architect: Henry Kissinger and American Foreign Policy*, Kissinger saw each event through the prism of the Cold War, and his preoccupation with the Soviet Union frequently led to a distorted perspective. Notes Hanhimäki, "He operated, essentially, in the same bilateral framework as his predecessors had, taking it as a given that containing Soviet power—if not communist ideology—should be the central goal of American foreign policy. Almost every initiative he pursued ... was aimed at serving this goal."[61] While other factors did come into play, it was this unswerving mindset that determined Kissinger's strategy, and in some cases, caused him to err.

The centrality of the Cold War to Kissinger's thinking during the Yom Kippur War is made clear in Richard Ned Lebow and Janice Gross Stein's *We All Lost the Cold War* and Raymond L. Garthoff's *Détente and Confrontation: American-Soviet Relations from Nixon to Reagan*. Lebow and Stein incisively argue that the war escalated because the United States and the Soviet Union, despite having the same goal, namely détente, attempted to achieve unilateral gain at the expense of the other. Similarly, Garthoff argues that the superpowers shared responsibility for inflating the conflict into a superpower confrontation by maneuvering for political advantage while at the same time attempting to diffuse the crisis and end the war.[62]

However, on the whole, scholars have tended to underplay the role of domestic factors, specifically Watergate, pro–Israeli factionalism and bureaucratic battles within the Administration as determinants of policy during the war. As Kissinger walked a diplomatic tightrope with the Soviet Union during the crisis, he was besieged by conservative critiques, fronted by Senator Henry Jackson, with charges that he was not doing enough to help Israel. Jackson, bolstered by pro–Israel and anti–Arab public sentiment, argued that Kissinger's desire for détente with the Soviets was leading to an excessively conciliatory posture. Additionally, the Department of Defense stymied Kissinger's attempts to facilitate a rapid rearming of Israel, which could have led to a quick end to the war. Evidence shows that Secretary of Defense James Schlesinger was preoccupied with the specter of Arab reprisals; Assistant Secretary of Defense William Clement was a Texas oilman with close ties to big oil and much to lose should the moderate Arab oil producers turn hostile. The result—a delayed but massive airlift of military supplies to Israel—led to a dangerous confrontation between the U.S. and Soviet Union which would have lasting repercussions.

In the long term, the war had detrimental consequences. Following the confrontation with the Soviet Union, domestic criticism of détente mounted in the U.S. In December, the House of Representatives passed the Jackson-Vanik amendment, which linked détente to Soviet Jewish emigration, thereby defeating an attempt by the Administration to confer most-favored-nation status to Moscow. Rapprochement between the superpowers would become increasingly elusive in the coming years, beginning with the Carter Administration, and reaching an all-time low under Reagan. Israel did make peace with Egypt, but the long-term result of the Yom Kippur War was an obdurate and emboldened Israeli policy vis-à-vis the Palestinians, Syria and Lebanon.

CHAPTER 2

The Prelude to War

Although the October War caught the U.S. by surprise, there was no lack of evidence that the combined forces of Egypt and Syria intended to attack Israel in the fall of 1973. The war was a consequence of the American inability to resolve what had become a crisis in the Middle East, one precipitated by the Israeli occupation of Arab land taken in the 1967 War, and a failure by the Nixon Administration to acknowledge the myriad warnings from Egyptian president Anwar Sadat that he regarded war as the only solution. In both regards, no one's actions were more consequential than those of Henry Kissinger, who emerged as the orchestrator of Middle Eastern policy early in Nixon's second term, supplanting a role that had previously been occupied by Secretary of State William Rogers. While Rogers had worked diligently but unsuccessfully to create a Mideast settlement, Kissinger favored a gradual "step-by-step" approach to negotiations, a process that ultimately pushed Sadat over the brink. Despite Sadat's vociferous threats to settle the matter promptly, by military means, Kissinger, as well as senior intelligence officials in the U.S. and Israel, mistakenly dismissed them as shows of bravado and political expediency.

This chapter analyzes events that led to the breakout of war from an American perspective. It traces the ascendency of Kissinger and his gradualist approach to resolving the Mideast crisis, which prevailed over Rogers' efforts to broker a ceasefire. Ultimately, the ensuing standstill and inactivity due to these two divergent strategies provoked Sadat into launching the war. Once Sadat began to prepare for battle, Kissinger continuously misread the signs, a consequence of what he himself has deemed "a failure of intellect as opposed to intelligence."

The Internal War: Kissinger Battles Rogers

During his first term as president, Nixon's handling of the Arab-Israeli situation was schizophrenic. At times it was confrontational toward the Arabs and the Soviets; at other times, it was even-handed, reflecting a belief that the United States could best lessen Soviet influence by being perceived as impartial in the Arab-Israeli conflict.[1] This schizophrenia reflected the foreign policy team that Nixon put together when he assumed office in 1969. The president was determined to wrest control of foreign policy from the State Department bureaucracy, which he saw as a bastion of the Democrats, and he created an invigorated National Security Council, placing Kissinger at its helm. Kissinger was a Harvard professor and foreign policy expert with whom Nixon shared the view that the United States needed to wed strength with diplomacy in order to minimize the dangers of a nuclear war.[2] As secretary of state, Nixon chose a close personal friend, William Rogers, a lawyer who had served as attorney general under Eisenhower when Nixon was vice president. Nixon placed Rogers in charge of the Middle East. Yet it was Kissinger to whom the president turned in order to develop the broader workings of his overall foreign policy.

Investigative journalist Seymour Hersh writes that an NSC staff member who had worked closely with Kissinger told him that Kissinger had "a real hesitancy" about being involved in Middle East negotiations when Nixon entered office in 1969. He was acutely aware of his own lack of knowledge of the politics and the personalities in the region. As the staffer told Hersh, "He just didn't see how [the negotiations] were going to work, and his attitude was: So why jump in and not be successful and make a lot of enemies in the process?" However, by the end of 1969, Kissinger was working behind the scenes to undercut Rogers, whom he saw as floundering.[3]

When it came to articulating Middle Eastern policy, Nixon at times appeared to back Kissinger, who believed in supporting Israel and the moderate Arab states; at other times, he supported Rogers, who felt that the United States, together with other major powers, particularly the Soviet Union, should adopt an active diplomatic role in promoting a political settlement based on UN Resolution 242 which called for an Israeli withdrawal from territory occupied during the 1967 Six-Day War in exchange for an Arab commitment to peace.[4]

As might be expected, given the convolution of strategies, there was incessant conflict and suspicion between Kissinger and Rogers. Kissinger remembers:

> During his first term, Nixon never formally chose between the two strategies: my recommendation of stonewalling radical [Arab] pressures or State's view of defusing them by offering compromise solutions. He leaned toward my analysis, but he implemented it not by making a decision but by simply letting State Department initiatives run their futile course. My relationship with Nixon, never easy, was in any event more complex with respect to the Middle East than with most other issues.[5]

Nixon's own conflicted feelings toward Kissinger are clear from a conversation he had with Chief of Staff H.R. "Bob" Haldeman in February 1971, while the two were waiting for Kissinger to join them in a meeting. Nixon complained:

> [The trouble] with Henry's personality, Bob, is it's just too goddamn difficult for us to deal with. I mean, let me just put it out there for a minute, for this reason. If we—you know, I have, I beat him over the head time and again, you know, to get him to—you see, he's trying to get involved in the Mideast again. I said, "Don't do it."
>
> You've got to remember that Henry is a terribly difficult individual to have around, you know, in terms of our, just our whole general morale. I mean, he just really is, Bob. It's too damn bad. But he's making himself so, and I think it's because of his, this psychotic hatred that he has for Bill [Rogers]. What the Christ is the matter with him? What the hell is it? I mean, he—hardly anybody believes that—is Rogers out to get him? Is that it? ... Every day. It's something or other ... the way State's cutting him out, cutting us up, the things they are doing, the horrible things they are doing.[6]

Kissinger's focus on Rogers bordered on the obsessive, and accounts of squabbles between the two are ubiquitous. The diary of Haldeman is replete with examples[7]:

August 29, 1969: "E (Ehrlichman), K (Kissinger) and I had a long session with Mitchell, primarily about Rogers problem."[8]

March 10, 1970: "I learned from Haig this morning that K had really battled with Rogers on phone yesterday about Laos, and the whole deal is really building up. P [President]'s refusal to see K today won't help, but it is just because he doesn't want to get into Middle East with K."[9]

June 23, 1970: "K in for long talk, about his worries about very adverse stories about his dating [actress] Jill St. John. He thinks Roger is planting them to destroy him. May be."[10]

July 13, 1970: "K in to see me for his periodic depression about Rogers. This time he's found Rogers is meeting Dobrynin tomorrow, and K is absolutely convinced he's going to try to make his own Vietnam settlement, plus get a Summit meeting, and take full credit for all. K's temptation is to confront Bill [Rogers] and insist they have it out with P, or else one will have to leave. Thinks he can scare him out. I urged against it on grounds he might not scare out and P can't follow through, especially before elections. Actually it would be counterproductive for K, and hurt him badly with P, and solve nothing."[11]

July 15, 1970: "K is building up a new head of steam about Rogers.... K still feels this is all part of plan to do him in and to take over foreign policy by State from White House. Talked to me several times and kept repeating his charges and complaints but has no real alternative except to fire Rogers, which isn't very likely.... Then tonight Haig called, P had called K at a party to say he'd called Rogers to congratulate him on his press conference today. K really distressed by this..."[12]

September 10, 1970: "K got me at end of staff meeting to plead that Rogers be kept out of meeting with Golda Meir next week, on grounds he's most hated man in Israel and would be a disaster."[13]

An important factor behind Nixon's decision to put Rogers at the helm of negotiations in the Middle East was that he worried that Kissinger's Jewishness would create the perception that the United States favored Israel. In an Oval Office discussion on March 9, 1971, with Haldeman and Ehrlichman, Nixon discussed Kissinger's outrage over an article in *Newsweek* which referenced his being Jewish. Said Nixon:

> What apparently set him all off on this.... Anybody who is Jewish cannot handle it. Even though Henry's, I know, as fair as he can possibly be, he can't help but be affected by it. You know, put yourself in his position. Good God! You know, his people were crucified over there. Jesus Christ! And five million of them, popped into bake ovens! What the hell does he feel about all this?

Haldeman responded, "Well what he ought to recognize is even if he had no problems at all on it, it's wrong for the country, for American policy in the Middle East, to be made by a Jew." Nixon agreed as Haldeman continued, "And he ought to recognize that. Because, then if anything goes wrong ... they're going to say it's because a goddamn Jew did it rather than blame Americans."[14]

Rogers was confident, with some reason, that a Middle East settlement might be achievable. There had been several diplomatic initiatives put forth by the Soviet Union in the last months of 1968 for an Arab-Israeli agreement. These proposals, though unworkable as they stood, demonstrated a considerable distance from the former Soviet positioning as one-sided defenders of the Arab cause. In December, the Soviets proposed bilateral talks with the United States in order to attempt to find a diplomatic solution. Nixon was doubtful of the Soviets' intentions, but willing to give them a try as a test to see if they truly wanted peace.[15]

Likely fueling the president's interest in new solutions was the failure of the diplomatic mission of Dr. Gunnar Jarring, Swedish ambassador to the Soviet Union, a mission that had been mandated by United Nations Resolution 242. Despite Jarring's efforts to broker a settlement, heavy fighting, named the "War of Attrition," continued along the Suez Canal, and on the Syrian border with Israel.

In addition to the Soviet proposal, French president Charles de Gaulle, whom both Nixon and Kissinger greatly admired, had pushed for talks on the Middle East between France, Britain, the United States and the Soviet Union. When de Gaulle first proposed the meeting between the "four great powers" during the Johnson Administration, the former president is reputed to have asked sarcastically, "Who are the other two?" and didn't give the matter much consideration.[16] In February 1969, however, Nixon approved Rogers' recommendation for two sets of parallel talks, the first between the four powers, which the president saw as being largely for show, and the second between the Americans and Soviets, where the serious business could be done.

Despite Nixon's apprehensions, Rogers remained at the center of nego-

Soviet ambassador to the United States Anatoly Dobrynin and Richard Nixon.

tiations. He appeared to be making some initial progress, and the Soviets, particularly Anatoly Dobrynin, Ambassador to the U.S., seemed to be acting in earnest. It was not long, however, until Kissinger, who felt that the time was not ripe for substantive and detailed negotiations, began to undercut the negotiations in his discussions with Nixon and the Israeli ambassador, Yitzhak Rabin, who was concerned that the talks excluded Israel.[17] According to Rabin, during this time, "the erosion in the United States' position [with Israel] reached such proportions that our minister in Washington, Shlomo Argov, asked ... that Israel denounce the current American moves—even at the risk of sparking a confrontation with the United States."[18]

On October 28, 1969, Rogers presented a policy statement to the Soviets that would ultimately be known as the "Rogers Plan," after the secretary announced the details publicly in a December 9, 1969, speech. In this plan, which was rejected by Israel, Egypt and the Soviet Union, Rogers articulated an American policy of evenhandedness, one embracing "friendly ties with both Arabs and Israelis." In a well-publicized speech, Rogers announced:

> To call for Israeli withdrawal as envisaged in the U.N. resolution without achieving agreement on peace would be partisan toward the Arabs. To call on the Arabs to accept peace without Israeli withdrawal would be partisan toward Israel. Therefore, our policy is to encourage the Arabs to accept a permanent peace based on a binding agreement and to urge the Israelis to withdraw from occupied territory when their territorial integrity is assured as envisaged by the Security Council resolution.[19]

While the press raved about the Rogers Plan, within the Administration it was met with overwhelming opposition. The day after delivering his speech, Rogers attempted to defend it during a meeting of the National Security Council. Nearly everyone present objected to the strategy, including Nixon, who believed that the State Department was losing ground in the region. Nixon pointed out that in the eleven months since he had taken office, the Soviets had strengthened their position in the Middle East, while the American position with the moderate Arab states had worsened. The president felt by calling on Israel to withdraw from the Arab territories with only vague reassurances of peace, the Soviet Union would "come out looking good."[20]

Kissinger was the most vocal critic of the plan. He argued that Rogers was headed down a "slippery slope" by pressuring Israel to withdraw from the occupied territories. He predicted, "The longer Israel holds its conquered Arab territory, the longer the Soviets cannot deliver what the Arabs want." In time, he argued, the Arabs would conclude that friendship with the Soviet Union was "not very helpful," and they would ultimately turn to the U.S.[21]

In the end, Rogers' plan appealed to neither the Israelis nor the Arabs. His call for "Israeli withdrawal" alienated the Arabs since he did not insist on *total* withdrawal. By contrast, the Israelis saw the speech as favoring the Arabs, since Rogers allowed for only "insubstantial" changes to the borders as they existed before the 1967 War—Israel saw the old borders as not providing adequate security. Additionally, his call for a "just settlement" of the refugee problem sparked Israeli fears of being flooded with hostile Palestinians who would upset the demographic balance. Finally, his stipulation that Jerusalem should be a "unified city for persons of all faiths and nationalities" was unacceptable to both sides.[22]

When the plan was released, Israeli prime minister Golda Meir fumed. "Nobody in the world can make us accept it. We didn't survive three wars in order to commit suicide."[23] According to Seymour Hersh, on December 17, Nixon ordered White House aide Leonard Garment, a Jew and frequent intermediary with the Israelis, to give private assurances to Meir that the Rogers initiative would not have his full backing. Garment also quietly passed the word to leaders in the American Jewish community.[24]

Still, the Israelis protested. On December 20, Israeli Ambassador Yitzhak Rabin flew to Washington with an angry letter from Meir and approval to launch a public campaign against the plan. According to Rabin's memoirs, in a private meeting with Kissinger, Rabin warned, "Let me tell you in complete frankness, you are making a bad mistake. In taking discussion of a peace settlement out of the hands of the parties and transferring it to the powers, you are fostering an imposed solution that Israel will resist with all her might. I personally shall do everything within the bounds of American law to arouse public opinion against the administration's moves!"[25]

Kissinger had a warning of his own:

> Under no circumstances, I beg you, under no circumstances should you attack the president. It would mean a confrontation with the United States, and that's the last thing Israel can afford. The president has ... given Rogers a free hand; but as long as he himself is not publicly committed, you have a chance of taking action. How you act is your affair. What you say to Rogers, or against him, is for you to decide. But I advise you again: Don't attack the president![26]

Opposition to the plan was pervasive. Egyptian president Nasser said that he would not negotiate with the Israelis. Ambassador Dobrynin announced that the Soviet Union would not distance itself from Egypt. The plan catalyzed the Israeli lobby, and in February 1970, 70 senators and 280 representatives demanded that the Nixon administration stop bullying Israel at the peace table and start selling Israel arms for use in battle.[27]

The Rogers plan was effectively dead on arrival. William Quandt cites three reasons. First, he argues, it was based on the mistaken assumption that the United States and Soviet Union could "deliver" their respective clients. Second was the marginal involvement of the White House. Lastly, Quandt writes, was that Rogers underestimated Israel's "will and ability to resist American pressure."[28]

Of the Rogers Plan, Nixon wrote in his memoirs:

> I knew that the Rogers Plan could never be implemented, but I believed that it was important to let the Arab world know that the United States did not automatically dismiss its case regarding the occupied territories or rule out a compromise settlement of the conflicting claims. With the Rogers Plan on the record, I thought it would be easier for the Arab leaders to propose reopening relations with the United States without coming under attack from the hawks and pro–Soviet elements in their own countries.[29]

In the aftermath of the Rogers Plan, the situation moved from bad to worse, and fighting between Israel and Egypt raged on. As a stopgap measure, in the summer of 1970, Assistant Secretary of State Joseph Sisco convinced Meir and Nasser to reopen discussions with U.N. Ambassador Jarring. In late July, Israel, Egypt and Jordan agreed to accept a 90-day ceasefire. Though not foreseen at the time, the ceasefire was to have deleterious consequences. It unleashed powerful forces among the Fedayeen, who were appalled that King Hussein of Jordan and Nasser would sell them out by reducing hostilities.

In late August 1970, an emergency session of the Palestinian National Council was convened in Amman, and some of the more radical groups called for the overthrow of King Hussein. Before any consensus could be reached, on September 6, the Popular Front for the Liberation of Palestine (PFLP), led by George Habash, hijacked three commercial jet liners. A fourth plane was hijacked three days later. Altogether, the PFLP had nearly five hundred hostages, many of whom were American.[30]

Nixon was determined to take a tough stance. On September 10, he placed the 82nd Airborne Division at Fort Bragg on semi-alert and six C-130 transport planes were flown to Turkey, where they would be available for the possible evacuation of Americans from Jordan. On September 11, units of the Sixth Fleet left port and four more C-130s, escorted by twenty-five F-4 jets, were flown to Turkey. That same day, the Fedayeen blew up the jets and moved the remaining fifty-four hostages, over half of whom were Americans, to an undisclosed location.

On September 15, King Hussein announced that he was forming a martial government. The following day, in what came to be known as Black September, civil war broke out in Jordan, which threatened to overthrow Hussein and lead to a possible superpower confrontation. Nixon and Meir met on September 18. Though they never discussed the possibility of Israeli intervention, this prospect became less remote on September 19, when the first reports of a Syrian armored incursion into Jordan arrived in Washington.[31] Nixon recalled:

> One thing was clear. We could not allow Hussein to be overthrown by a Soviet-inspired insurrection. If it succeeded, the entire Middle East might erupt in war: the Israelis would almost certainly take pre-emptive measures against a Syrian-dominated radical government in Jordan; the Egyptians were tied to Syria by military alliances; and Soviet prestige was on the line with both the Syrians and Egyptians. Since the United States could not stand idly by and watch Israel being driven into the sea, the possibility of a direct U.S.-Soviet confrontation was uncomfortably high. It was a ghastly game of dominoes, with a nuclear war waiting at the end.[32]

On September 20, Hussein issued an urgent appeal for American help. Later that evening, Hussein requested intervention from any quarter against heavy attacks from Syrian tanks.[33] With the United States in crisis mode, Kissinger stepped to the forefront. He was Nixon's go-to man, and unlike Rogers, he held the trust of the Israelis. After meeting with Nixon, Kissinger reached Ambassador Rabin who was at a fund raising dinner in New York with Golda Meir, and announced that King Hussein had requested that the Israeli air force attack the Syrians. "Are you recommending that we respond to the Jordanian request?" Rabin asked. Kissinger replied that he needed more time to answer. He returned an hour later to unequivocally state, "The request is approved and supported by the United States government." "Do *you* advise Israel to do it?" Rabin asked. "Yes," replied Kissinger, "subject to your own considerations."[34]

At 11:30 p.m. Rabin called with Meir's reply—Israel would fly reconnaissance planes at dawn and then pass judgment. At 5:15 a.m., Alexander Haig, Kissinger's deputy, who had just received a call from Rabin warning that ground action might be necessary, awoke Kissinger with news from the president. Nixon had decided that morning to tell Israel that the United States agreed to Israeli ground action "in principle," subject to consulting with King Hussein.[35] As negotiations over specifics unfolded, the situation on the battlefield changed. The Jordanians had halted the Syrian advance and Israeli intervention was no longer required. A possible Arab-Israeli and superpower confrontation had been avoided.

On September 25, Kissinger phoned Rabin, conveying a message from Nixon to Meir: "The president will never forget Israel's role in preventing the deterioration in Jordan and in blocking the attempt to overturn the regime there.... These events will be taken into account in all future developments."[36] Nixon would be true to his word. When war broke out in October 1973, Kissinger would be secretary of state, and the United States would play a crucial role in supporting Israel.

The years between the Jordanian crisis and the October War were uninspired ones in the Middle East, and the attentions of Nixon and Kissinger were focused in other directions. In 1971, the Vietnam War fumed, and in May, Kissinger began a series of secret talks with the North Vietnamese. In July, Kissinger made a secret visit to China to prepare the way for Nixon's momentous trip the following year. Serious discussions were underway with the Soviet Union regarding détente. And 1972 was an election year. The Middle East was low on the list of the Administration's priorities.

Not that it was completely out of mind. On September 28, Nasser died, and Egypt had a new president, albeit one who was seen as relatively powerless and temporary—Anwar Sadat. Elliot Richardson, then Nixon's secretary of health, education and welfare, was sent by the president to attend Nasser's funeral, and reported back to Washington that Sadat would not be president for any more than four to six weeks before someone more fitting was elected or selected.[37] Facing Sadat were the social, economic, political and military challenges awaiting anyone who succeeded the iconic Nasser. Sadat wrote in his autobiography:

> We [Nasser and I] both shared the same fears about what might happen in Egypt after Nasser's departure. Nasser concurred with me that great burdens were waiting his successor, and I laughed and told him: "Allah will have to help the poor fellow".... It certainly never crossed our minds that Nasser would die in the very same month, or that I would be taking over in a new process of transferring power. But that was the will of Allah.[38]

As Sadat biographer Joseph Finklestone has noted, one factor that played to Sadat's favor was a remarkable gift for oratory, a unique ability to win over audiences with rhetoric that often did not give away his true intentions. Writes Finklestone:

> Speaking of war and peace, Sadat used the complex language which led to so much misunderstanding. It has to be remembered that hardly any of Sadat's speeches had the preciseness that people in the West expect from their lead-

ers in addresses to Parliament. They were rambling and discursive. They might last for four hours and might consist of stories and anecdotes. His experiences as a soldier and earlier as a boy in a village provided him with a fund of homilies. In Egypt, as in every Arab country, where the oratorical and homiletic have a special attraction, giving them almost the significance of real events. Sadat's long discourses were widely appreciated by the masses.[39]

While the Nixon Administration kept an eye on Sadat, its attention was subsumed by other events. In November 1971, radical Palestinian factions assassinated Jordan's prime minister Wasfi al–Tal in Cairo. In September 1972, Palestinian guerrillas massacred eleven Israeli Olympic athletes in Munich. However, with Kissinger distracted with Vietnam, the opening to China and détente with the Soviets, Rogers reemerged as the chief negotiator in the Middle East. At least for the time being.

Rogers attempted to resurrect the suspended peace talks. Senator Henry Jackson had succeeded in passing a bill that provided Israel with unprecedented access to arms, all on credit; in fiscal years 1971, 1972, and 1973 Israel received nearly a tenfold increase in military aid above the prior three-year period.[40] To Rogers, the need could not have been greater for renewed efforts toward negotiations, especially since the U.S. had adopted a policy that so clearly benefitted Israel.

In May 1971, he made the first visit by a secretary of state to Egypt since 1953. It was interesting timing, given that just forty-eight hours earlier, Sadat had arrested his vice president, Ali Sabry, a Soviet favorite, when he learned of a possible coup against his government. Rogers saw this as a possible sign that Sadat intended to lessen his dependence on the Soviets. He was reassured after meeting with Sadat, who seemed to desire a closer relationship with the United States. Roger's subsequent visit to Israel, however, proved to be far less satisfactory, hampered by Israeli perceptions that he was pro–Arab, and a deep Israeli skepticism about Sadat's intentions.[41]

Though Rogers continued to explore avenues for negotiations, his differences with Kissinger were far from over. Kissinger wanted to delay the settlement process until such time as the Arabs realized that peace would be unattainable without the United States. In Kissinger's words, "the longer the stalemate continued, the more obvious would it become that the Soviet Union had failed to deliver what the Arabs wanted. As time went on, its Arab clients were bound to conclude that friendship with the Soviet Union was not the key to realizing their aims."[42] Rather than pushing for an overall agreement, which Kissinger felt would require applying extraordinary pressure on Israel, Kissinger favored a limited agreement that would not outline a final settlement.[43] Unlike Rogers, Kissinger believed that only a self-confident Israel would be willing to make the necessary concessions for a peace agreement.

Yet by 1971, for Rogers, the beginning of the end was in sight. In March, Missouri Democratic Senator Stuart Symington made headlines by declaring in a Senate speech that Kissinger was "secretary of state in everything but title" making Rogers an object of ridicule. "It is rather sad," Symington said, "that wherever one goes in the afternoon or evening around this town, one hears our very able secretary of state laughed at, because they say he's only the secretary of state in name." In a press conference, Nixon called Symington's comments a "cheap shot," and referred to Rogers as "my oldest and closest friend in the Cabinet." Writes Seymour Hersh, "Salvaging Rogers became an important crusade for the president, and that decision reflected an astute judgment: Rogers would go along, and be content to be secretary of state in title only, as long as he did not suffer too much humiliation in public. Nixon's goal was not only to protect Rogers but to hold on to the White House's ability to make policy on its own."[44]

In the end, the third Rogers initiative failed, and Kissinger assumed the mantle of chief Middle East negotiator. Middle East policy would now be directed by Nixon and Kissinger, and would follow the basic tenets of what came to be known as the "Nixon Doctrine," a term coined in July 1969. Its structure may be summed up in a February 18, 1970, address that Nixon made to Congress:

> Its central thesis is that the United States will participate in the defense and development of allies and friends, but that America cannot—and will not—conceive all the plans, design all the programs, execute all the decisions, and undertake all the defense of the free nations of the world. We will help where it makes a difference and is considered in our interest.[45]

In other words, the Administration would play an active role in supporting its allies, but it was not willing to directly shoulder the responsibility of their defense, as it had done in Vietnam. Rather, the United States would support proxy allies, such as Israel and Iran, but it would draw the line at American military intervention.

On November 23, 1971, in anticipation of a visit by Meir to Washington and in an effort to put pressure on the Nixon administration, the Senate, in a vote sponsored by Senator Henry Jackson, voted by 81 to 14 in favor of providing $500 million in military credits for Israel, with half the sum earmarked to cover the purchase of F-4 Phantom jet fighters. That same day, a group of eight senators from both parties met with Rogers to urge acceptance of the measure. Roger argued that providing the Israelis with the Phantoms would "only make them more stubborn" in negotiations.[46] One senator, incensed, threatened Rogers that he would take the matter to the president. A confident Rogers responded, "That is your privilege, but I am sure that the president will back me up."[47]

It would prove to be one more argument that Rogers would lose. During Meir's visit, Kissinger eclipsed Rogers in closed-door meetings. The United States agreed to supply Israel with new Phantoms and Skyhawk missiles over a three-year period, marking the first long-term arms deal ever between Washington and Jerusalem. Both sides agreed to focus on a limited settlement with the Arabs with the understanding that Israel would not be bound by the Rogers plan. Additionally, it was agreed that talks on an interim settlement would be conducted on two tracks. The first track would be spearheaded by Assistant Secretary of State Joseph Sisco and would be between Egypt and Israel. The second would consist of secret meetings between Kissinger and Dobrynin with the promise that these talks would not result in any pressure on the Israelis to accept a deal concocted by the superpowers. Also, it was agreed that Rabin and Kissinger would hold secret discussions.[48] Notably absent from the picture was Rogers.

In the end, it would be Kissinger's strategy of militarily bolstering Israel while dangling the carrot of negotiations to the Arabs that would triumph. It fit nicely with the Nixon Doctrine. Importantly, with Nixon's upcoming visit to Peking in February 1972, the last thing the White House wanted was to rock the boat. And with a presidential election in November, Middle East negotiations would be disruptive politically. The White House explicitly told the State Department not to push any Middle East initiatives until after the coming elections.[49] For the time being, the strategy in the Middle East amounted to a policy of delay, one of pursuing Kissinger's deliberate, gradual course. While optimum for the Israelis, it was not yet clear to the U.S. just how unacceptable the status quo was to the Arabs.

The Failure of Intellect

With Kissinger advocating a gradualist approach to negotiations in the Middle East while focusing his energy on Vietnam, China and the Soviet Union, and Rogers' attempts to broker a peace settlement bearing little fruit, the new Egyptian president, Anwar Sadat, became convinced that war was his only alternative to retrieve lost Egyptian territory. In retrospect, it is difficult to imagine how the signs of war were missed. In the

Nixon meeting with Kissinger regarding the resignation of Vice President Spiro Agnew on October 10, 1973. Agnew's resignation due to allegations of tax fraud occurred during the first week of the war.

fall of 1973, warnings, sometimes indirect, often unequivocal, came from multiple directions, including Egypt, Jordan, Saudi Arabia, Iran and the Soviet Union. Additionally, evidence of an Arab military buildup from U.S. and Israeli intelligence continued to mount. Yet as Nixon recalled in his memoirs, "the news of the imminent attack on Israel took us completely by surprise."[50]

While Nixon and Kissinger realized that the Israeli occupation of Egyptian and Syrian territory was unsustainable, they misinterpreted the signs of war that were emanating with increasing frequency from the Middle East. Despite the immense numerical superiority of the Arab armies—Israel's population of 3.2 million paled to the 55.2 million Egyptians, Iraqis, Jordanians and Syrians combined—this had never stopped Israel from victory in the past. In 1956, allied with Great Britain and France, Israel quickly defeated Egyptian forces in the Sinai. In 1967, Israel launched a brilliant preemptive strike and routed the forces of Egypt, Syria and Jordan. Additionally, the qualitative differences were seen as insurmountable. The discipline, training, and dedication of the Israeli Air Force and Army were seen as decisively important factors in the past that would serve to guarantee future Israeli victories. The Israeli Army was bolstered by a "never again" philosophy stemming from the Holocaust.[51] In part due to hubris, in part due to a lack of foresight in imagining that Sadat might stage a limited attack with narrow objectives in order to break the diplomatic stalemate, as opposed to total war which would clearly lead to an Egyptian defeat, both Israel and the United States allowed themselves to be lulled into a precarious state of complacency.

It was not because Egypt and Syria lacked sophisticated weaponry. Following the 1967 War, both countries had procured highly advanced Soviet arms, especially air defense and anti-tank capabilities aimed at undermining the Israeli air and tank superiority By the early 1970s Egypt and Syria boasted the world's densest networks of SA-2, SA-3, and cutting-edge SA-6 Soviet surface-to-air missile batteries. They integrated modern Soviet bloc anti-tank weapons, such as the SAM-7 shoulder-fired missile, the RPG-7 rocket launcher, and the AT-3 Sagger wire-guided missile. Yet the idea that the Arab countries would attempt another military excursion after their sound beating in the Six-Day War seemed, at the time, preposterous, and the specter of these capabilities were discounted by Israeli intelligence.[52]

As early as 1971, Sadat had threatened to go to battle. In an address at the Naval Academy in Alexandria, on June 22, 1971, he declared, "I fully understand my duty towards my homeland, towards national problems and towards our courageous armed forces.... I am telling you in all sincerity and clarity that the year of 1971 is a decisive one, for we cannot wait forever."[53] However, the year passed with limited hostilities.

Despite the Egyptian president's seemingly direct warnings, he was sending mixed signals, particularly when his action are viewed through a Cold War lens. The divide between Egypt and the Soviets deepened early in Sadat's presidency. In July 1971, he condemned a Communist coup d'état in Sudan, claiming he did not want a Communist regime on Egypt's doorstep. On October 11, he visited Moscow and was promised shipments of military equipment, including aircraft, after he argued, "I don't mind, my friends, if you keep me one step behind Israel, but I find it a bit too much to be twenty steps behind her!"[54] By February 1972, the arms had yet to arrive. Soviet general secretary Leonid Brezhnev blamed it on the Soviet bureaucracy and red tape. "I am not convinced of that," was Sadat's reply, "and if this is repeated, I will have to act—a decision will have to be taken."[55] Given these developments, it was easy to imagine that an unbridgeable gulf was developing between Moscow and Cairo, and potentially, an easing of tensions between Cairo and Jerusalem.

A source of the conflict between Sadat and the Soviets was that as much as Sadat saw war as the only solution to the impasse of regaining the Sinai from Israel, Moscow continued to emphasize the desirability of a negotiated settlement. Speaking of his meeting with the Soviet leaders on March 1, 1971, Sadat declared in a radio speech: "The Soviet Union's viewpoint was that a peaceful solution was the only solution."[56]

According to Kohler, Gouré and Harvey, Moscow realized that it had to tread carefully. On the one hand, they did not want to jeopardize détente; on the other hand, they were reluctant to alienate their Arab allies. They observe:

> Although Brezhnev in a speech on March 21, 1972, warned that "Arab cooperation is expanding and the defensive military strength of the Arab countries has greatly increased," the Soviet Union seemed too involved in developing its détente policy with the U.S. to seriously consider supporting Sadat's insistent calls for a renewal of military action. Nevertheless, Moscow also recognized that to ignore this problem threatened to alienate not only Sadat but also Syria's President Assad.[57]

The same Soviet position was evident in its critique of the Syrian Communist Party Program in May 1971. According to the transcript, the Soviet representatives rejected a military solution to the Arab-Israeli conflict because a new war could "lead to a confrontation between the Soviets and the Americans." The transcript continues:

> We do not conceal the fact that we are not in favor of this except in the case of extreme necessity. Our opposition is not to a military solution per se, but arises only because we are realistic. This does not prevent us from working to increase the military fighting capability of the Arab countries.[58]

In late May 1972, Nixon made his historic first trip to the Soviet Union for a series of talks with Brezhnev, focusing on détente. The joint Soviet-American statement that followed made scant reference to the Middle East. Only a mild statement calling for "military relaxation" was included. Sadat was infuriated. He felt abandoned by the Soviets, whom he saw as capitulating to Israel, which was receiving arms from the United States in growing numbers. Writes Craig Daigle, "There can be no mistaking the fact that the Middle East agreements at the summit 'proved the last straw' for Sadat. By telling the Egyptian president, who had promised his people 1971 would be the year of decision, that 1972 would also pass without a decision of any kind, and by calling for a 'military relaxation' in the area for the benefit of détente, Soviet and American leaders left Sadat in an untenable position."[59]

On July 6, Sadat received the official Soviet analysis of the talks with

Nixon. It explained that no progress had been achieved on the Middle East question. Worse, no mention was made of the promised weapons, which had yet to arrive. Sadat ordered the immediate withdrawal of the 15,000 Soviet military advisers from Egypt, and demanded that all Soviet equipment be either sold to Egypt or withdrawn to the Soviet Union. By July 16, Sadat had made good, and an estimated 10,000 to 20,000 advisers and four Soviet MIG 25 aircraft had been returned to the Soviet Union.[60]

Journalists Isabella Ginor and Gideon Remez argue that the normally used term "expulsion," regarding the withdrawal of Soviet advisers is misleading and inaccurate. "We contend," they write, "that the withdrawal of Soviet troops from Egypt in 1972 was by prior consent." They continue: "Actually the personnel withdrawn in the summer of 1972 consisted mainly of the integral Soviet units which had been stationed in Egypt since 1969–70, while at least the bulk of the genuine advisers remained—and continued preparing the Egyptian forces for the cross-channel offense.[61]

However, Sadat does not support this view in his memoirs. He writes:

> One of the reasons behind my decision was the Soviet attitude to me; but another important reason was that within the strategy I had laid down, no war could be fought while Soviet experts worked in Egypt. The Soviet Union, the West, and Israel misinterpreted my decision to expel the military experts and reached an erroneous conclusion, which in fact served my strategy, as I had expected—that it was an indication that I had finally decided not to fight my own battle. That interpretation made me happy; it was precisely what I wanted them to think....
>
> Yet another reason for my decision was that I wanted to put the Soviet Union in its place—in its natural position as a friendly country, no more, no less. The Soviets had thought at one time that they had Egypt in their back pocket, and the world had come to think that the Soviet Union was our guardian. I wanted to tell the Russians that the will of Egypt was entirely Egyptian; I wanted to tell the whole world that we are always our own masters. Whoever wished to talk to us should come over and do it, rather than approach the Soviet Union.[62]

Additionally, at the time of the expulsion, a war of words erupted between Egypt and the Soviets. On August 19, the Egyptian newspaper *Akhbar al–Yom* charged that the Soviet Union did not supply enough arms to Egypt to enable it "to eliminate the traces of the [Israeli] aggression." A week later, the Soviet newspaper *Izvestia* countered that the U.S.S.R. had fulfilled its commitments to Egypt and that "the only basis for peace in the Middle East is the total liberation of Arab territories from the Zionist invaders."[63]

By the end of the month, Sadat made diplomatic overtures to the

White House. Significantly, backchannel communications were established between Cairo and Washington. A secret meeting between Kissinger and Hafiz Ismail, Sadat's national security adviser, was set for early in 1973.

Kissinger was baffled by Sadat's decision to expel the Soviets. Why had he not consulted the U.S. first and asked for a quid pro quo? It seemed to him, at the time, to be the epitome of diplomatic naiveté. In retrospect, Kissinger acknowledged that Sadat had used an "extraordinary tactic that no one fathomed." He writes in his memoirs:

> If a leader announces his real intentions sufficiently frequently and grandiloquently, no one will believe him. Sadat had first declared 1971 as the "year of decision." We had believed him.... Sadat made no military move that year or in 1972. Ominous threats continued to issue from Cairo, but ... our assessment was that Sadat had few if any military options. Israel's military superiority appeared unchallengeable. Sadat could not escape his dilemmas by launching an all-out military offensive since it was bound to fail.... There seemed no rational military purpose for it.... Thus it would follow that Egypt had no choice but to await the American diplomatic initiative.[64]

At some point in 1972, Sadat began to prepare for war. According to Badri, Magdoub, and Zohdy, the decision was made in November, when Egyptian political and military leaders reached agreement that "Egypt could never escape from the stagnated state of no war, no peace, without recourse to armed force."[65] Sadat biographer Raphael Israeli writes that beginning on July 12, 1972, Sadat began in earnest to execute a plan of disinformation when he leaked a report saying that the Egyptians had not been able to use the sophisticated weaponry that had been left by the Soviets. "Such a leak was calculated to indicate to the West and to Israel," says Israeli, "that Egypt could no longer man and operate her most advanced weapons, therefore she was unlikely to wage war in the foreseeable future." This leak was followed by more detailed "reports" about the Egyptians having insufficient and badly maintained arms as well as poorly trained personnel to operate them. According to Sadat, Israeli writes, "both Israel and the West 'swallowed' these reports and 'went to sleep,' assuming that Egypt was technologically doomed and that all the sophisticated weaponry in her possession had become useless."[66]

On January 2, 1973, Kissinger received a report stating that on December 17, a representative of King Hussein, Zayd Rifai, met with Sadat, who proposed that Egypt and Jordan resume diplomatic relations and work together to force a political settlement on Israel. Sadat told Rifai that he had become convinced that the only way to regain Egyptian lost territories was to start a war with Israel. Only by hitting "hard and deep" in Israel,

Sadat said, and inflicting a sizable number of civilian casualties, could Egypt convince Israel that it would be best for them to surrender occupied territories.[67]

Warnings continued to mount. On January 28, Dobrynin handed Kissinger a message, which emphasized the urgency of the United States and Soviet Union working together to settle the Middle East conflict. It read:

> It is necessary to emphasize that time is passing while the situation in the Middle East remains complicated and dangerous. If effective measures are not taken, the events there can get out of control. There is no doubt that if hostilities in the Middle East erupt once again then—taking into account existent ties with this area of other states including major powers—there could develop quite unwelcome consequences for the cause of international security, and it is difficult to envisage what would be the end of it and for how long these complications would persist.[68]

Kissinger was unfazed. Meanwhile, Nixon was growing impatient with Kissinger. High on his agenda was achieving what he saw as the dual objectives of détente with the Soviets and diminishing Soviet influence in the Middle East. Additionally, Nixon was sensitive to the growing restlessness and antipathy of the Arab world to the status quo. It was his last term in office, and the president, who had yet to feel the sting of Watergate, wanted results. Nixon noted in his memoirs of February 3:

> I hit Henry hard on the Mideast thing. He now wants to push it past the Israeli elections in October, but I told him unless we did it this year, we wouldn't get it done at all in the four-year term. I spoke to Henry about the need to get going.... I am pressing him hard because I don't want him to get off the hook with regard to the need to make a settlement this year because we won't be able to make it next year, and of course, not thereafter with '76 coming up. He brought that up himself so apparently the message is getting through. What he's afraid is that Rogers, et al. will get ahold of the issue and will try to make a big public play on it and that it will break down. On the other hand, Henry has constantly put off moving on it each time, suggesting that the political problems were too difficult. This is a matter, which I, of course, will have to judge.[69]

Nixon also acknowledged the challenges to reaching a settlement posed by American Jews. He continues:

> He [Kissinger] agreed that the problem with the Israelis in Israel was not nearly as difficult as the Jewish community here, but I am determined to bite this bullet and do it now because we just can't let the thing ride and have a hundred million Arabs hating us and providing a fishing ground not only for radicals but, of course, for the Soviets.[70]

On February 6, Nixon and Kissinger met with King Hussein and his advisor and future Jordanian prime minister, Zaid al–Rifai, in the Oval Office. Hussein had been having secret meetings with Israel, and the president asked him for an appraisal of the Middle East situation. Hussein felt that while the expulsion of the Soviet advisors was a significant event, it also increased the danger of Sadat agitating the situation on his own, which could perhaps lead to all-out war. Rifai, according to Kissinger's notes, felt that Sadat was "certain to start another war of attrition." Additionally, the Saudis had offered to pay Jordan a subsidy if the king would let the Fedayeen return, a proposal that Hussein refused.[71]

In his memoirs, Kissinger wrote, "The February 6 meeting with Hussein was my first direct exposure to what turned out to be a tragedy for the peace process in the Middle East: the personal distrust between Sadat and Hussein.... The pity was that these two moderate leaders failed to give each other the support that might have speeded up Middle East diplomacy; they wound up in an impasse from which the sole exit was war."[72]

By mid–February, there were indications that Egypt and the Soviet Union were moving closer together. Early in the month, Ismail had spent three days meeting with Brezhnev and a joint statement released after his visit stated that the Soviet Union gave its "full understanding" of the Egyptian position in opposing a partial settlement with Israel. The reference to a partial settlement was a direct reference to a proposal that had been made by Rogers to couple the reopening of the Suez Canal, which had been closed since the 1967 War and had been the front line in the War of Attrition, with a partial Israeli withdrawal from the Sinai Peninsula.[73]

In an ominous development, on February 21, Israeli fighter planes shot down a civilian Libyan jetliner over the Sinai desert, killing 74 passengers and crewmembers.[74] While the Arab street "seethed with anger" over the incident, one article in *The Washington Post* noted the restraint shown by Arab leaders, who "appeared to be restraining popular anger."[75] Two days later, Ismail met with Nixon and his staff in the Oval Office. As the meeting began, Ismail handed the president a message from Sadat with a threat: "Circumstances lend themselves now to exerting further efforts to achieve a full and just settlement"; otherwise, "the situation in our region has deteriorated almost to the point of explosion." Nixon, who according to Kissinger was "always uncomfortable with detailed negotiation," regretted that more progress had not been made and promised to "see where we stand to explore the possibilities that [there] might be some movement which could take place."[76]

There is some debate as to the impact that the February meeting had on Ismail. Stein writes, "These disappointing conversations reaffirmed President Sadat's decision to go to war."[77] Yet according to Mohamed Heikal, the former Egyptian minister of information, Ismail felt Nixon was "eager to play a personal role in solving the Middle East problem." However, he adds, "any good effects these contacts might have produced were largely nullified by the visit of Golda Meir to Washington." She had met, amidst much fanfare in the press, with the president on March 1 as part of a ten day visit to the United States, and a deal was struck to supply Israel with Phantom jets and begin co-production in Israel of Super Mirage aircraft. Though the deal was made in secret, news quickly leaked to the press. Heikal recalled, "It was clear from the size of the deal that the United States was once again underwriting Israel's offensive strike capacity. There was great disillusionment on the Egyptian side."[78]

Heikal was correct that Nixon wanted to play a role in a Middle Eastern settlement, and he was willing to pressure Golda Meir into coming to the table. In a conversation on February 23, the president told Kissinger, "We've got to take a very strong line with the Israelis. I know that. We've got to take a very strong line with these people." However, Kissinger wanted to delay. He was fuming that Rogers, overenthusiastic about a possible breakthrough following the talks with Ismail, was "running like crazy without knowing where [he's] going." He warned the president, "Now, my worry is ... it took us 18 months to get these guys [the Egyptians] coming to us. If we now act like over-eager puppies, pleading with them to be permitted do something, we're dead." However, Nixon was adamant. Referring to Meir's upcoming visit, he told Kissinger:

> We're going to move.... I'll propose the toast and the rest, but I want you to be sure Rabin knows that she must not come here and say, "Well, we're ready to wait." Henry, understand. Publicly, I don't want to say anything. I don't want to embarrass the Israelis. The Israelis privately have got to know if we're going to play this game with these people, they got to play a more conciliatory game with us. They can't, because they've given nothing—the Israelis.[79]

In a memorandum that day, Kissinger reiterated to Nixon his position that it might be best to "stand back and let the two sides reflect further on their position." The president wrote in the margins, "Absolutely not. I have delayed through two elections and this year I am determined to move off dead center. ... I totally disagree. This thing is getting ready to blow."[80]

Following his visit in Washington, Ismail met secretly with Kissinger in New York. Nixon's goal for the meeting was that the two men set some long-term goals that would lead to a "phased" settlement with Israel.[81] Despite Nixon's instructions to "move on the Middle East," Kissinger arrived in New York determined to slow things down until after the Israeli elections.[82] "My strategy with Ismail will be to say next to nothing, or to speak at such a level of generality that it doesn't mean anything," he told Yitzhak Rabin. Notes Daigle, "In part, Kissinger believed that he had to distinguish his approach from that of Rogers and Sisco, who were willing to dive into the heart of Arab-Israeli negotiations at the first opportunity. But he also felt that his newfound celebrity stature, produced by the successful negotiations with China, the Soviet Union, and Vietnam, made it such that he should 'sell' his involvement in an Arab-Israeli negotiating process only for something concrete in return." Kissinger insisted, "I will make no proposals to them, no promises. Nothing will come out of this meeting unless they come in with a new proposal. And if they do that, I will tell them I will study it. My guess ... is that they will not have a new proposal."[83]

On the evening of March 1, Palestinian terrorists struck again. Eight members of the Black September Organization seized the Saudi Embassy in Khartoum, Sudan, taking hostage U.S. Ambassador Cleo Noel, Deputy Chief of Mission George Curtis Moore, the Saudi ambassador and the chargés d'affaires of Belgium, Japan, and Jordan.[84] The terrorists demanded the release of numerous individuals, mostly Palestinian, who were imprisoned in Jordan, Israel, and the United States, including Sirhan Sirhan, the killer of Senator Robert Kennedy. At 11:30 a.m. on March 2, during a press conference, Nixon, despite advice to say nothing from Golda Meir, his staff and the State Department, rejected the demands outright. That afternoon, at 3:06 p.m. on March 2, Washington time, five bursts of sub-machine gunfire were heard coming from the Saudi Embassy in Khartoum. Noel, Moore, and the Belgian diplomat Guy Eid had been killed.[85]

Kissinger wrote in his memoirs that Khartoum complicated the budding relationship with Egypt. He remembers:

> Egypt found itself in a quandary about what position to take on the Khartoum murders. It was torn between personal revulsion at the killings, the need to maintain radical support for the war planning even then going on (of which we were ignorant), and the desire to involve us in the peace process. The contemplation of its dilemmas increased Egyptian irritability. A senior Egyptian official in Cairo cautioned us that some in his government opposed the peace effort and that the press leaks of our sale of jets to Israel were "not making things easier for us."[86]

The State Department dispatched a telegram to the U.S. Interests Section in Cairo, stating that if Egypt tried to link the subject of terrorism to the new U.S. arms contracts with Israel, "it should be made clear to the Egyptians that the United States was committed to Israel's defense and survival, and therefore had an ongoing military supply relationship with it." The telegram stressed the importance of Egypt taking a firm stand against Black September terrorism. If any support were allowed to continue, it would drive a wedge between Arab states and the "entire civilized community which considers such methods anathema."[87]

On March 30, in a two and one-half hour speech, Sadat declared that Egypt had reached a "prominent landmark," entering a stage of all-out confrontation. He accused the United States, particularly Secretary of State William Rogers, of carrying on psychological warfare against Egypt by building up Israel military superiority. He referred to the talks between Ismail and the U.S. as a guise for allowing Israel to remain in occupation of Egyptian territory indefinitely.

In a now familiar pattern, Kissinger downplayed the speech's significance. He told Nixon that Sadat "seems to be pondering the idea that the concept of restoring Egyptian sovereignty might allow for some [U.S.] arrangements that address Israel's security concerns."[88] In other words, Sadat would tolerate the U.S. arming of Israel.

On April 9, *Newsweek* published an interview between Sadat and reporter Arnaud de Borchgrave, in which Sadat said, "The time has come for a shock," and that the battle was now "inevitable."[89] A week later, James Schlesinger, then director of the CIA, informed Kissinger that the Egyptians had moved SA-6 surface-to-air missiles within 20 miles of the Suez Canal and 30 Mirage jets had been transferred from Egypt to Libya. Additionally, there were reports that the Egyptians were trying to organize an oil boycott by the Arab producers against the U.S. and Western Europe in the event of war. Yet the Israelis doubted that aggression was likely. Schlesinger concurred:

> Taken in the sum of their content, they do not seem to indicate an Egyptian intention to renew hostilities. They do, however, seem to indicate an element of bluff, to suggest the intention to either increase pressure on Israel, or the United States, to be more responsive to Egyptian wishes in connection with a peaceful settlement of the Middle East problem, or to divert Egyptian public opinion from focus on dissatisfaction with conditions in Egypt, or both.[90]

During that time, Americans were becoming increasing antipathetic toward Arabs, and images of growing Arab economic control proliferated in the press. By mid–April 1973, the U.S economy was drowning in inflation, a severe trade imbalance, and an international monetary crisis fueled by a plummeting dollar, a process that had begun in the early 1970s. On August 15, 1971, the president took the drastic step of implementing wage and price controls for ninety days and removing the convertibility of the dollar to gold.[91] Complaints of the "Arab cartels" strangling Americans with high oil prices and holding the United States hostage to its agenda were a constant in the media.[92]

Tim Jon Semmerling describes the mood of Americans in 1973, who were disconcerted about the rising wealth of the Arab oil nations. In his words, "some imagined the future of the International Monetary Fund as being not "run by the suave, dark-suited Americans and Europeans, but by white-robed sheiks from the Middle East.... There was a fear that the Arabs were likely to be irresponsible and untrustworthy with this new monetary wealth, maybe even using blackmail against America, and, thus, it was feared that America was funding its own demise."[93] This image combined with the image of Palestinians, which according to R. S. Zaharna, had undergone dramatic changes, from that of refugee following the Six-Day War to that of "terrorist," created the general impression of an Arab menace, which directly threatened the United States, and indeed, civilization itself. Zaharna writes:

> Whereas the refugee was a helpless victim of the powers that be, the terrorist "equipped with nothing more complex than guns, dynamite and airline schedules, render some of the most advanced nations impotent."
>
> During this period, Palestinian became synonymous with terrorists, skyjackers, commandos, and guerrillas. The Fedayeen was often used but rarely translated. This added to the mysteriousness and deviousness of the Palestinian groups. Fedayeen means "freedom fighter."
>
> While the main goal of the Palestinian groups was to gain international awareness of the plight of the Palestinian people, the hijackings got the world's attention but did little to garner the world's sympathy or understanding in the American media. Palestinians were viewed as "dedicated, vicious political fanatics" and "unpredictable terrorists," and their acts were seen as "insensible terror," and "savage and irrational."[94]

Not that Israel was without its critics. On April 15, Senator J.W. Fulbright (D–AR), Chairman of the Foreign Relations Committee, said that the Nixon Administration was unable to apply pressure on Israel for a Middle East settlement because the United States Senate was "subservient" to Israel. In an earlier interview on the CBS program *Face the Nation*, Fulbright had said, "The Senate is subservient much too much. We should be more concerned about the United States' interest, rather than doing the bidding of Israel. This is a most unusual development."[95] In response, Meir told the press, "This is a man who hasn't slept nights for years," referring to Fulbright's opposition to donations to the United Jewish Appeal being tax deductible. "Charity contributions are free of tax," she added.

Fulbright knows the law. He has been searching for years. Maybe one day he'll find something."[96]

However, in April 1973, it was the image of the wealthy, avaricious Arab that most completely captured the American imagination. On April 18, Rogers met with Saudi Arabia's minister of petroleum, Sheik Ahmad Zaki Yamani, and requested that the Saudis increase oil production to help ease the price burden on Americans. The sheik responded that his country would find it difficult to comply with the secretary's request for more oil, unless the U.S. helped to bring about a political settlement in the Middle East that was satisfactory to Arab states.[97] Yamani also presented Kissinger with a threat that the Saudis would be less than cooperative should the U.S. continue to tolerate the Arab-Israeli status quo. Kissinger, writes journalist Donald Neff, urged Yamani to keep the threat a secret.[98]

On April 19, *The Washington Post* ran a story with the message that had been delivered to Kissinger and Rogers, namely that Saudi Arabia would be willing and able to increase its production of oil to the United States provided that the "U.S. creates the right political atmosphere" regarding its policy toward Israel. The sheik, said the article, stated that the Saudi economy was already having trouble absorbing all the money it was obtaining from petroleum sales. Ominously, the article noted that this was the first time that Saudi Arabia publicly linked the flow of oil to the U.S. with Washington's Middle East policy.[99]

In May, King Faisal summoned Frank Jungers, Chairman of the Board of the Arabian American Oil Company, to his palace in Riyadh and warned him about the possibility of an oil embargo. Jungers passed the word to both the White House and the State Department. That same month, Faisal told four other leading oilmen about the seriousness of his threat. All were ignored by the Administration.[100]

On May 3, the new Israeli ambassador to the United States, Simcha Dinitz, met with Kissinger and relayed the contents of a message that King Hussein had sent to Meir. The king cautioned:

> A major international military fiasco in the area is inevitable. Algerian ground units will soon be in Egypt. The Sudanese will also be in Egypt. Morocco will send forces to Syria. Libyan Mirages are already in Egypt. Considerable Iraqi forces will be in Iraq very close to our borders under a united command. If Jordan's fate were in the hands of the Iraqi Commander, Iraqi Lightning's would be in Jordan now, but probably they will end up in another theater. This is the alarming outline I see.

Dinitz warned that Israeli sources had confirmed the information, and added that the Syrians had begun military preparations. Kissinger responded that he would have U.S. intelligence look into the matter.¹⁰¹ As it had done in the past, the CIA concluded that it was unlikely that Sadat would initiate any military activity in the near future. Rather, Schlesinger speculated that the Arab moves "have the objective ... of bringing maximum psychological pressure on the U.S. and Israel." However, his memorandum warned, "there is danger that these moves will in the future develop some momentum of their own.¹⁰²

During the first week of May, Kissinger traveled to Zavidovo, the Politburo hunting preserve about ninety miles northeast of Moscow, to discuss Brezhnev's upcoming visit to the United States in June. It would mark the second summit between Brezhnev and Nixon. During his talk with Kissinger, on May 7, Brezhnev accused the United States of taking a "tranquil attitude" towards events in the Middle East. He warned that "all sorts of committees are being formed and all sorts of military meetings are being held—not just to have a few drinks, but to discuss military matters."

Brezhnev surmised that the Nixon administration felt that the Soviet Union could control the Arabs. He counseled:

> We can tell the Arabs not to fight. All that has been done until now and the direction of urging restraint has had its positive results in the sense of contributing to such restraint. And our influence could go on having a positive effect in that direction, provided the Arab states could see prospects ahead for a basis being found for a peaceful solution to the problem. But the mistake of the U.S.—and obviously ourselves too—may lie in fact that neither side can count on its influence being effective if the sides there don't see prospects for a peaceful settlement.... Because the Arabs have before them the task of returning their lands and ... if Israel, counting on the success achieved in the short war [of 1967] remains in place, we might not be able to maintain the status quo in the situation, and then we may be confronted by events that will prevent us both—the U.S. and the Soviet Union—with complex problems.¹⁰³

In Cairo, Sadat was sounding increasingly bellicose. On May 15, he called on the Arab nations to use their oil to apply pressure on the United States to abandon its support of Israel. He rallied the Egyptian parliament: "The case is one of a protracted struggle and not only the Suez Canal battle. This is the battle of America's interests, the battle of energy, the battle of the Arabs. These are big battles for which we must plan and coordinate." That same day, four Arab countries—Libya, Iraq, Kuwait and Algeria—in a "symbolic protest against Israel's continued existence as a nation," temporarily halted the flow of oil to the West.¹⁰⁴

A memo in the president's briefing book of May 16 stated that Mohamed Hassanein Heikal, editor-in-chief of *Al-Ahram*, Egypt's most widely circulated paper, warned that an armed conflict might be imminent and that oil would be another weapon in the Arab arsenal. The memo stated:

> After a lengthy period during which Heikal has written [only] on other topics or been silent, this week he returned to the Arab-Israeli problem.... He does strike several noteworthy themes: The use of armed force must be backed by a strong domestic Arab front.... The Arab world continues to be divided and Arab leaders have not recognized important changes in the international system.... The focus of interest in the Middle East is shifting from the Suez Canal to the Persian Gulf ...Heikal is warning his readers ... that Egypt must develop a long-term strategy to mobilize the Arab world to use its unparalleled oil resources and financial reserves to bring about a change in the current situation."[105]

On May 20, Kissinger met with Ismail in a French farmhouse between Paris and Chartres. Ismail stated that the status quo was intolerable to Egypt, and that the only alternative seemed to be war. He warned:

> So if this is not the solution that Egypt wants, what is left for her? To accept status quo? Or go to war? I don't call it war; it is not war. We have been in a state of war for 25 years. As I said to you in Washington, the ceasefire is a burden to everybody, even to the Israelis themselves. There will come a point when we say that whatever positions we have offered are in the past tense, and have no meaning.[106]

In a memorandum to Nixon, Kissinger noted that in private conversations, Ismail had said he felt military action would be "too adventurous" for the present; Kissinger surmised that he was thinking that such action would be for the "longer term future."[107] Yet Ismail's reaction to Kissinger is striking in its contrast. Ahmad Maher El-Sayed, one of Ismael's advisors who was present at the meeting, later said, "What we heard from Kissinger was 'don't expect to win on the negotiating table what you lost on the battlefield.'"[108]

On May 31, Director of the State Department's Bureau of Intelligence and Research, Ray Cline, presented a memorandum to Rogers which presciently declared that should a United Nations debate on the Middle East the following week produce no movement in the Israeli-Egyptian impasse, a resumption of hostilities by autumn "will become a better than even bet." Cline's memorandum continues:

> Sadat's national security adviser has recently been saying ... that the no-war, no-peace situation is more dangerous for the future of Egypt than war itself ... [and this] probably accurately stated Sadat's feeling.... Sadat has long preferred a political settlement to renewed combat ... [but] mounting evidence indicates that he is becoming ever more strongly tempted to resort to

arms.... Although he has no illusions that Egypt can defeat Israel militarily, he seems on the verge of concluding that only limited hostilities against Israel stand any real chance of breaking the negotiating stalemate by forcing the big powers to intervene with an imposed solution. Should he shed his last doubts about whether military action is essential to achieve this American shift, the only remaining decision would relate to the timing and scope of his move.[109]

By June, any illusion of a break between Moscow and Cairo evaporated when military deliveries of arms from the Soviet Union to Egypt resumed. Sixty MIG-21s that had been operated by the Soviets in Egypt had been turned over to the Egyptians following the expulsion. Following that, seven MIG-21s, 15 SU-17 fighter bombers and two helicopters were delivered, in addition to SA-6 missiles, tanks, armored personnel carriers, artillery, vehicles and support equipment. In the assessment of a CIA memorandum, such deliveries were only "designed to maintain Cairo's arms inventories rather than to introduce new weapons systems." The memo did note, however, that the Egyptians viewed "the present stalemate [with Israel] as intolerable and more difficult to change with each passing day."[110]

On June 16, Brezhnev arrived in Washington for a series of meetings with Nixon at the White House and Camp David. Discussions focused on

Nixon (center) with Henry Kissinger (right) and Secretary of State William Rogers in August 1972. Kissinger and Rogers were frequently at odds over Middle Eastern policy.

SALT, European security, Vietnam, Most Favored Nation status, and other economic issues. Though little concrete progress was made during the summit, it did result in the unveiling of the Agreement on the Prevention of Nuclear War. Ironically, four months later, the two superpowers would reach the brink of a nuclear confrontation. It wasn't until June 23, during the last evening of the summit at the "Western White House" in San Clemente, that the talks with Nixon moved to the Middle East. Nixon had retired for the night and was in his pajamas. At 10:30 p.m. there was a knock on his door. It was a Secret Service agent. In what Kissinger describes in his memoirs as a "gross breach of protocol," Brezhnev wanted to talk. Nixon recalled of the meeting:

> For the next three hours we had a session that in emotional intensity almost rivaled the one on Vietnam at the dacha during Summit I. This time the subject was the Middle East, with Brezhnev trying to browbeat me into imposing on Israel a settlement based on Arab terms. He kept hammering at what he described as the need for the two of us to agree, even if only privately, on a set of "principles" to govern a Middle East settlement.... Brezhnev was blunt and adamant. He said that without at least an informal agreement on such principles he would be leaving this summit empty-handed. He even hinted that without such an agreement on principles he could not guarantee that war would not resume."[111]

In the minutes of the meeting that he sent to Nixon, Kissinger quotes Brezhnev as warning, "We must put this warlike situation to an end.... If there is no clarity about the principles, we will have difficulty keeping the military situation from flaring up." By "principles," Brezhnev meant guarantees of an Israeli withdrawal from the Arab land occupied in the 1967 War. Nixon, frustrated and tired, replied that there was nothing to be done that night. Kissinger noted in the minutes, "Typical of Soviets to spring on us at last moment without any preparation."[112] He writes in his memoirs:

> In other words, twenty-four hours after renouncing the threat of force in the Agreement on the Prevention of Nuclear War, Brezhnev was in effect menacing us with a Middle East war unless we accepted his terms And he was vehement as he did so. Dobrynin told me afterward that he had told Sukhodrev to refrain from translating some of Brezhnev's more pointed remarks. But what got through was clear enough. Brezhnev wanted to settle the Middle East conflict that summer and the terms he proposed were the Arab demands. The facts were that there was no chance even of launching a serious peace process before the Israeli election four months away, and there was no possibility at any time of achieving the terms Brezhnev was proposing.[113]

Regarding the Administration's insouciance, Daigle observes, "Brezhnev's dramatic presentation should have alerted Nixon and Kissinger that events in the Middle East would soon spiral out of control, but neither took the Soviet warning seriously." He adds that it "is all the more surprising when considering that in the weeks leading up to the summit, the White House received numerous intelligence reports suggesting that Egypt and Syria were in active preparation for war and that the danger of hostilities would rise if the Nixon-Brezhnev talks passed without any results Sadat considered useful."[114] Yet the Administration remained unmoved.

In July, the United Nations Security Council took up the issue of the Middle East conflict. It was the meeting that Cline had warned might exacerbate tensions, should a resolution condemning Israel not be a result. As often proved the case, Cline was spot on. The ensuing draft resolution, proposed by the "non-aligned" nations on the Council—Guinea, India, Indonesia, Panama, Peru, Sudan, and Yugoslavia—called for a reaffirmation of UN Resolution 242 and the safeguarding of rights of the Palestinians. It was a position that the U.S. was unprepared to accept. Rather, the Americans called for language that was less harsh on Israel, and more of a "consensus" approach that was less specific on the wording of Resolution 242. John Scali, U.S. Ambassador to the U.N., argued that the proposed resolution would cause "irrevocable and permanent damage" to any prospects of peace in the Middle East.[115]

In his July 23 Revolution Day speech, Sadat "reacted with considerable emotion and anger" to the U.S. position, and said that Egypt was preparing for a confrontation with Israel and the United States.[116] On July 24, the draft resolution came to a vote. It stated that the United Nations

- expressed deep regret that the secretary-general was unable to report any significant progress by him or by his special representative in carrying out the terms of resolution 242, and that nearly six years after its adoption, a just and lasting peace in the Middle East had still not been achieved;
- strongly deplored Israel's continuing occupation of the territories occupied as a result of the 1967 conflict;
- expressed serious concern at Israel's lack of cooperation with the special representative of the secretary-general;
- expressed its conviction that a just and peaceful solution of the problem of the Middle East could be achieved only on the basis of respect for national sovereignty, territorial integrity, the rights of all States in the area and for the rights and legitimate aspirations of the Palestinians;
- declared that in the occupied territories no changes which may obstruct a peaceful and final settlement or which may adversely affect the political and other fundamental rights of all the inhabitants in these territories should be introduced or recognized;

- requested that the secretary-general and his special representative resume and pursue their efforts to promote a just and peaceful solution of the Middle East problem.

Australia, Austria, France, Great Britain, Guinea, India, Indonesia, Kenya, Panama, Peru, the Soviet Union, Sudan, and Yugoslavia voted in favor. China abstained. There was only one veto: the United States.[117] The veto was only the fifth ever cast by the United States. It was the second time that the U.S. was to be the only country on the Security Council to veto a resolution that was critical of Israel. From 1972 through 2011, the United States stood alone in its support of Israel forty-three times.[118]

In late August, U.N. Secretary-General Kurt Waldheim, despite the U.S. veto, left on a tour of the Middle East. He told U.S. Ambassador John Scali that his purpose was not to find a solution to the problem, but to consult with the parties, assess the situation, and "contribute modestly to efforts for peace." In a memorandum to Kissinger on August 23, Harold Saunders, Kissinger's advisor, warned that there were reports that Waldheim had "much more activist intentions in mind," that he might be proposing a Middle East peace conference. "Our main interest," wrote Saunders, "is in not having him raise Egyptian hopes unrealistically about what he can and cannot deliver."[119]

Waldheim returned from his trip early in September with a "deep sense of foreboding." He writes in his memoirs, "I had no crystal ball premonition of what was about to happen. But I am still astonished that the Israelis and the Americans, with all the intelligence resources at their disposal, so completely misjudged the situation."

Sadat, in his conversations with Waldheim, was deeply critical of the U.N.'s inability to achieve a comprehensive settlement. "Does it help," Sadat told him, "if the Security Council adopts one resolution after another, and none of them are implemented? If it does not act as is its duty, we shall have to take other measures to restore our legitimate rights." Waldheim attended the Non-Aligned Summit Meeting in Algiers on September 5, and was struck by the "close collaboration and collusion" between Sadat and Syrian president Hafez al–Assad, who were "sitting together in a corner of the lounge outside the main conference hall, their heads together in deep conversation for a long time."

Waldheim recalls that of all his meetings, he was most disturbed with the attitude of Golda Meir. She told him in a private discussion over lunch:

Dr. Waldheim, we know you are always saying the situation in the Middle East is dangerous and explosive, but we don't believe you. The Arabs will get used to our existence and in a few years they will recognize us and we shall have peace. So don't worry. It is a disagreeable situation, but we do not believe that there is real danger for us.[120]

While the situation in the Middle East intensified, the White House was becoming increasingly distracted by Watergate, which by August was growing to a fever pitch. On July 13, Alexander Butterfield, a former presidential appointments secretary, informed the Senate Watergate Committee of the existence of a White House taping system. On July 23, the Senate Committee and Watergate Special Prosecutor Archibald Cox demanded that Nixon hand over a range of White House tapes and documents. Two days later, Nixon refused. On July 26, the Committee subpoenaed several tapes, and on August 9, it took legal action against Nixon, who would claim executive privilege for failing to comply with the subpoena.

Still, on August 9, the *New York Times* published the results of a worldwide survey that indicated that foreign leaders and public figures overall supported the president, though they were taking the crisis more seriously than they had several months earlier. In the Soviet Union, news of Watergate had been suppressed so as not to weaken the public standing of Brezhnev, who had become closely tied to Nixon and the policy of détente. Notably, the study concluded that concern did not "match the apprehension voiced in Washington," singling out Henry Kissinger, who had "openly expressed foreboding recently that if Watergate seriously weakens Mr. Nixon's standing at home over a long period, foreign confidence in the implementation of Mr. Nixon's foreign policy goals will inevitably be undermined."[121]

On September 3, frustrated by the Watergate scandal and tired of fighting bureaucratic battles, Rogers resigned. Nixon named Kissinger as secretary of state—in addition to his role as national security adviser. The infighting between the NSC and the already beleaguered State Department would come to an end. Other than the ailing president, Kissinger became the sole architect of American foreign policy.

In public statements, Nixon continued to paint a façade of evenhandedness regarding U.S. policies in the Middle East, despite his private support for Israel following the Jordanian crisis. During a well-publicized press conference on September 5, a reporter asked Nixon if the Arab threat of limiting the oil supply would cause moderation in U.S. support for Israel. Nixon responded:

> Both sides are at fault. Both sides need to start negotiating. That is our position. We're not pro–Israel; and we're not pro–Arab. And we're not any more pro–Arab because they have oil and Israel hasn't. We are pro-peace. And it's in the interest of the whole area for us to get those negotiations off dead center. That is why we will use our influence with Israel; and we will use our

influence—what influence we have—with the various Arab states, and non-Arab state like Egypt to get those negotiations on. [The White House later acknowledged that this was an error and noted that Egypt was an Arab state.][122]

Nixon said, during the press conference, that he had directed Kissinger to assign "the highest priority" to settling the Arab-Israeli dispute. Kissinger, on the other hand was lowering expectations. In a September 10 meeting with Israeli Ambassador Simcha Dinitz, Kissinger assured him that there "won't be any big initiative when I come in." He acknowledged to Dinitz that he was getting pressure from the public to take some action in the Middle East. "As I told your Prime Minister and as I have told you before," Kissinger said, "the trend here to do something is getting overwhelming." He added:

> The trouble is, the U.S. public doesn't understand what it really is that the Arabs are proposing—that as a precondition for a negotiation you give up all the territory in exchange for an "end to the state of belligerency," which is indistinguishable from the ceasefire that exists. They think the issue is Israeli intransigence. Most people don't understand.[123]

Public pressure for some kind of resolution of the Middle East conflict was indeed mounting. Inflation, particularly at the gas pump, continued to take its toll. As Americans would find out in October, the worst was yet to come. The media tended to blame the Arabs. However, as Kissinger stated, Israelis were not immune to criticism.

Despite the increasing visibility of the Middle East in the minds of Americans, largely driven by the ensuing economic strife, and no shortage of warnings from Sadat and other sources, the Administration continued to discount the signs of war. Much of the fault rested with U.S. intelligence. On September 26, during a visit to the Golan Heights, Israeli defense minister Moshe Dayan claimed that Syria had massed hundreds of tanks and artillery along Israeli lines. Still, on September 30, Ray Cline sent a memorandum to Kissinger that, though granting that the possibility of a limited Syrian strike could not be excluded—on September 13, in an air battle over the Mediterranean, Israel had downed 13 Syrian MIG jets—stated that Syrian military activity was more likely "part of a contingency plan for defense" rather than steps toward offensive action.[124]

The U.S. placed excessive faith in the estimates of Israeli intelligence, which was remarkably complacent. On October 1, Kenneth Keating, U.S. Ambassador to Israel, sent a telegram to Joseph Sisco, Assistant Secretary of State for Near Eastern and South Asian Affairs, stating that Israel "did not perceive a threat at this time" from either Syria or Egypt. Keating, a former senator and seasoned diplomat—prior to his assignment in May 1973 in Israel he had been the U.S. Ambassador to India—concluded that the purpose of Dayan's comments was to reassure troops that had not been given leave to spend Yom Kippur with their families that remaining at their posts was for "solid reason."[125]

Keating's comments could not have been further off the mark, and warnings continued to mount. On October 3, in a conversation with Assistant Secretary of State Joseph Sisco, Israeli ambassador Dinitz expressed a "growing concern" in Israel about an increased supply of military equipment entering Arab countries from the Soviet Union. Most disturbing was the deployment of Soviet Sukoi 20 and Mirage 5 planes which could fly under the Israeli radar net and penetrate population centers, thereby giving the Arabs strategic strike capability. Dinitz questioned whether the Soviets were reacting to the escalation of weapons being provided to moderate Arab countries—it was speculated that France had just sealed an agreement with Saudi Arabia for Mirage aircraft—or if it represented a policy of deeper Soviet penetration into the Persian Gulf. Sisco promised to investigate the situation.[126]

On October 4, in a hardly undisguised move, the Soviets executed an airlift of dependents, basically family members, from both capitals. Kissinger later admitted that perhaps the Soviets intended to send the Americans a signal. In an interview, he told Lebow and Stein:

> I do find it credible now that Brezhnev tried to warn us at San Clemente and through their open airlift. The warnings were probably meant. We missed those warnings. I regard [our flawed evaluation of the meaning of the airlift] as one of our biggest intelligence failures. We thought there was another quarrel between the Soviets and their Arab allies. But, why should they take their dependents out from both [Cairo and Damascus] at the same time. We missed it.[127]

On Friday, October 5, the Israelis raised the final red flag. At 5:30 p.m. Mordechai Shalev, Deputy Chief of Mission at the Israeli embassy in Washington, called General Brent Scowcroft, National Security Council Deputy, and relayed to him a message from Golda Meir. The message warned that Syria and Egypt were in a state of alert and poised for battle. The only possible conclusion, Shalev said, was either they felt that Israel intended an offensive military move, or that they themselves were planning an attack. Meir stated that should Syria or Egypt attack, it would be important to make it clear to them that Israel will "react militarily, with firmness and in great strength." She asked Kissinger to convey the information to the Arabs and Soviets.[128]

Meir had assumed a misunderstanding, because Israel felt, despite strong indications to the contrary, that it would be an act of lunacy for the Arab countries to attack. AMAN, the Israeli military intelligence organization, had concluded that the overwhelming military might of Israel would deter an Arab offensive, at least until 1975, when Egypt and Syria would have better military capacity. This was despite several ominous signals known to Israeli intelligence. When the Soviet evacuation began, a high level Soviet source had warned the Israeli intelligence agency, Mossad, of the possibility of an impending attack. Israeli aerial reconnaissance had detected an increase in gun deployments along the Suez Canal. The following day, AMAN shared these concerns with the United States, concluding that there was a "low probability of war."[129]

Meir, who had opted against a full-scale mobilization at the time, despite her better judgment, wrote in her memoirs:

> Today I know what I should have done. I should have overcome my hesitations. I knew as well as anyone else what full-scale mobilization meant and how much money it would cost, and I also knew that only a few months before, in May, we had had an alert and the reserves had been called up, but nothing had happened. But I also understood that perhaps there had been no war in May exactly because the reserves had been called up. That Friday morning, I should have listened to the warnings of my own heart and ordered a call-up. For me, that fact cannot and never will be erased, and there can be no consolation in anything that anyone has to say or in all of the common-sense rationalizations with which my colleagues have tried to comfort me.[130]

Despite her personal remorse, Meir hardly shoulders the blame for Israel's being caught by surprise. Rather, her confidence was shared widely by members of the Israeli leadership, not in a small way due to hubris, following the stunning victory in the war of 1967. As historian Alistair Horne remembers:

> In Tel Aviv shortly after the 1967 victory, I recall that disturbing encounter with General Ezer Weizman, the larger-than-life architect of the air force triumph, and later to be president of Israel. A massive, swaggering figure who with his close-cropped blond hair and blue eyes could almost have doubled for a 1940s Luftwaffe ace. He commented on the great military triumph Israel had just won; then asked, rhetorically, what should they do now? Sticking my neck out, rashly, I replied I thought Israel had about a year in which to make a "good peace." He cut me off at the knees, lambasting me as a "Limey armchair historian," and he then proceeded to boast, in disquieting, and unashamedly racist terms, that Israel "can lick any combination of Arabs that come against us."[131]

Much of the blame for Israeli complacency can be laid on the shoulders of its iconic defense minister, Moshe Dayan. According to Brecher and Raz, during the pre-crisis period, Dayan, "like almost all his colleagues in the high policy elite ... seemed mesmerized by the appearance of security."[132] During a meeting of Meir's so-called Kitchen Cabinet on October 3, Dayan dismissed the potential consequences of not mobilizing the troops as minor. Israel's leading military correspondent paraphrased Dayan's argument: "If they [the Egyptians] cross the Suez Canal, they will sustain heavy losses, and in the second stage, the IDF will hit from all sides. They won't solve anything, and will be in a more difficult situation after the crossing, while at present—the Suez Canal protects them."[133] Dayan was convinced, given Israel's uncontested prowess in prior wars and its perceived military supremacy at the time, that a Sadat venture into Israeli occupied territory would be inconceivable.

Michael Brecher writes that Dayan's perception changed during the night of October 4, when news arrived that the Soviets were evacuating dependents from Damascus and Cairo. The next day he approved a proposal, at the General Staff Meeting, by Chief of Staff, General David Elazar, to move to a level "C" alert, the maximum, of the permanent army and air force. However, he chose not to mobilize the Israeli reserves. Brecher posits that Dayan's decision was motivated by three perceptions: (a) that the defensive deployment of Arab forces could quickly become offensive and that Israeli mobilization could not prevent an attack by Egypt and Syria; (b) that Israel's mobilization would be interpreted by the Arabs and the world as an aggressive act; (c) that Israel's "secure" borders and second-strike capability would enable them to absorb an Arab attack without excessive cost.[134] In other words, the decision not to mobilize the reserves was based on the assumption of overwhelming Israeli defensive capability, coupled with a desire to avoid any semblance of Israeli aggression. Israel was determined to avoid the worldwide censure it had incurred following its preemptive strike in the 1967 War.

Some of Kissinger's critics claimed during and after the war that he had tied Israel's hands and prevented them from initiating a first strike. According to a memorandum drafted by the State Department's Middle East Task Force on October 7, immediately after the war began, Meir informed Dinitz that General Elazar had asked for permission to strike first, because the Israelis were "sitting like eggs." Meir responded, "No, I don't want to have a preemptive strike and then have to spend the rest of my life explaining why we struck first." She told Dinitz, "Dr. Kissinger had always told me, whatever happens, don't be the one that strikes first," adding, "You think I forget?"[135]

During a cabinet meeting on October 18, Kissinger explicitly denied that he had in any way tied Israeli hands. He told the group:

> There is a story going around that we held Israel back from a preemptive attack. All our intelligence said there would be no attack. Why did Israel not figure there would be an attack? Because we for four years had been telling them they had to make diplomatic moves. Therefore they developed the posture that there was no need to move, there was no threat; the Arabs are too weak, so they interpreted the intelligence this way. We did the same, but we figured that because they were so good, the Arabs wouldn't dare to attack.[136]

Kissinger's claims are supported by Dayan, who affirms in his memoirs that not striking first was a political move designed to garner American support. He writes: "I feared that such moves would burden our prospects of securing the full support of the United States ... and if American help was to be sought, then the United States had to be given full proof that it was not we who desired war—even if this ruled out preemptive action and handicapped us in the military campaign."[137]

That Dayan was strongly against an Israeli first strike for political reasons is supported by his remarks at a press conference on October 6, just hours after war began. He stated:

> We were faced with the dilemma of whether to open fire first, and of course, thereby to obtain a very important advantage, or not to do so and lose this military advantage, but make sure that the picture will be known, the true one, that the Egyptians and Syrians started the war.... It was a decision of the government not to strike first ... in order to have the political ... advantage at the expense of the military advantage.... I think it was the right decision ... unlike six years ago [when] we couldn't have taken such risks; but after all, Sinai is far away and we can allow ourselves such a tactic or strategy ... even if we shall have to evacuate or lose some positions, it is far away.[138]

In large part a reaction to Israeli complacency, U.S. intelligence sources concurred that the chances of an Arab attack were slim, trusting the superiority of Israeli intelligence. Philip H. Stoddard, an official with the State Department's Bureau of Intelligence and Research (INR), later recalled that the prevailing view was "if the Israelis aren't nervous, why should we be nervous?"[139]

Kissinger wrote retrospectively:

> Policymakers cannot hide behind their analysts if they miss the essence of an issue. They can never know all the facts, but they have a duty to ask the right questions. That was the real failure on the eve of the Mideast war. We had become too complacent about our own assumptions. We knew everything but understood too little. And for that the highest officials—including me—must assume responsibility.[140]

Some have argued, in Kissinger's defense, that the intelligence he received was fraught with noise and contradictions. In the estimation of INR Deputy Director Phillip Stoddard, "We didn't alert the policymakers in time to do something about it: 'On such-and-such a date, this is going to happen, and here's why we think so, and here are the sources.' We didn't shake them up in such a way that would say, 'Good God,' and start getting geared up." Significantly, analysts underestimated Sadat. According to Roger Merrick, the author of the INR analysis presented by Cline to Rogers on May 31 that gave 50–50 odds of an Arab attack: "Looking at Sadat throughout his career, he appeared to be a classic 'maxi-max' leader who identified his alternatives and systematically pursued lower risk options, but when unsuccessful, progressively accepted higher risks." It would only be later, notably during the Camp David Accords, that it became clear that Sadat was willing to take big risks. Still, the interpretation of intelligence ultimately fell on Kissinger's shoulders, and the evidence that Sadat would attack was overwhelming.

According to Brecher and Raz, the misinterpretation of available intelligence can be reduced to two mistaken assumptions about the Arabs. Firstly, that Egypt would not launch a war against Israel without superior air power to launch an in-depth attack against Israel and dislocating its air force and principal airfield. Secondly, that Syria would not initiate a war against Israel without the active participation of Egypt.[141] As subsequent events would show, Egypt was more than willing to engage in a war with limited military objectives. Yet the U.S. and Israel both drastically underestimated Sadat's unwavering resolve to break the status quo. The Israelis clearly had no intention of entering into negotiations, let alone relinquishing territory occupied in 1967, without sufficient prodding from the United States. Kissinger's stalling and gradualist approach to the Arab-Israeli peace impasse became a direct cause of Sadat's decision to launch an attack. Moreover, had he been keener in reading the signs of an impending Arab attack, the war might have been avoided.

As Kissinger writes in his memoirs, "The breakdown was not administrative, but intellectual."[142] Grappling with his failure, he adds:

> There were questions crying to be asked that would have rapidly reached the heart of the matter. That they occurred to no one, including me, seems inexplicable in retrospect. What crisis could possibly occur in Soviet-Arab relations that involved *both* Egypt and Syria simultaneously? Why would the Soviets evacuate dependents but not advisers if there was a political crisis? Why would they undertake an emergency airlift if they were not working against a deadline? What could that deadline be other than the opening of

hostilities? The Israeli view that the Soviets might fear the outbreak of war should have given us pause. For if we had reflected, it would have been clear that the Soviets could not be fearing an Israeli attack. Had they done so they would have made urgent representations in Washington to get us to dissuade Israel, and perhaps added public threats. If the Soviets evacuated dependents because they feared a war, they must have had a very good idea that it would be started by the Arabs.[143]

Adding insult to injury, during September and October 1973, the CIA's analytical capabilities were in a state of disarray. A number of significant personnel changes had been made and some of the most knowledgeable Middle East analysts had moved to other jobs. According to a CIA report, in the Agency's Office of Current Intelligence, the office principally responsible for presenting current intelligence analyses to the White House, the chief was new and had just returned from a one year sabbatical. Additionally, his boss was away on leave the week before October 6. Also, at the time, most of the CIA's Directorate of Intelligence officers "had not had firsthand experience in the field, or the opportunity to gain the up close 'feel' so necessary where available evidence is ambiguous."[144]

Additionally, evidence shows that Kissinger did not share much of the intelligence regarding the likelihood of an Arab attack with CIA Director William Colby. In a memo written by Colby to Kissinger on October 27, the CIA chief admonished: "I fully understand the need for secrecy in our government on these delicate subjects, although it is clear that the backchannel in many instances is becoming the main channel, causing lost and even counterproductive motion, aside from anguish, among many not in the circuit."[145] Included in the backchannel talks was the record of the earlier warnings from Brezhnev about the Arabs' intent, private dialogues between Kissinger and Soviet Ambassador Dobrynin and private messages from Sadat.[146]

A post-mortem report prepared for the CIA Director on December 20, 1973, states that "[intelligence] community analysts were provided with a plentitude of information which should have suggested, at a minimum, that they take very seriously the threat of war in the near term." However, the report further states, "the assessments which appeared in various intelligence periodicals, spot reports, and memoranda did not sufficiently utilize the information available and consequently did not provide a warning of impending hostilities." Rife are examples of indicators of an imminent war, accompanied by "rather timid cautionary advice" or even "reassurances" that the Arabs would not resort to war.[147] Some examples include the following:

> The movement of Syrian troops and Egyptian military readiness are considered to be coincidental and not designed to lead to major hostilities.
> —Defense Intelligence Agency, Intelligence Summary, October 3, 1973

> The exercise and alert activities under way in Egypt may be on a somewhat larger scale and more realistic than previous exercises, but they do not appear to be preparing for a military offensive against Israel.
> —Central Intelligence Bulletin, October 5, 1973

> Both the Israelis and the Arabs are becoming increasingly concerned about the military activities of the other, although neither side appears to be bent on initiating hostilities.... For Egypt, a military initiative makes little sense at this critical juncture.... Another round of hostilities would almost certainly destroy Sadat's painstaking efforts to invigorate the economy and would run counter to his current efforts to build a united Arab political front, particularly among the less militant, oil-rich states. For the normally cautious Syrian president, a military adventure now would be suicidal, and he has said so.
> —Central Intelligence Bulletin, October 6, 1973

> The Watch Committee met in special session at 0900 on October 6, 1973, to consider the outbreak of Israel-Arab hostilities.... We can find no hard evidence of a major, coordinated Egyptian/Syrian offensive across the Canal and in the Golan Heights area. Rather, the weight of evidence indicates an action-reaction situation where a series of responses by each side to perceived threats created an increasingly dangerous potential for confrontation. The current hostilities are apparently a result of that situation.... It is possible that the Egyptians or Syrians, particularly the latter, may have been preparing a raid or other small-scale action.
> —Special Report of the U.S. Intelligence Board Watch Committee, October 6, 1973[148]

The report concludes: "The hindsight of the post-mortem process bestows an element of wisdom which is denied those—in this instance, intelligence analysts—who must deal in foresight. Indeed, what may seem so clear now did not, could not, seem so clear then. Still, there is no gainsaying the judgment that ... the principal conclusions concerning the imminence of hostilities ... were—quite simply, obviously, and starkly—wrong."[149]

When the final and unequivocal warning did arrive from Israeli sources, Scowcroft immediately wired Kissinger who was in New York attending a United Nations conference. His staff, however, saw no reason to interrupt him, and he did not receive the message until the following morning. He admitted in his memoirs: "Nor am I sure I would have done anything immediately with the messages had I received them. It was now the middle of the night in all capitals concerned; nothing menacing seemed afoot. We were not informed that Israel had taken any special precautions—and it had not called up reserves."[150]

Ultimately, the fault for not anticipating the attack was not in the quantity or quality of intelligence, but rather in the Administration's interpretation of the information. Kissinger, indeed the machinery of the American intelligence community, relied too much on Israeli intelligence, which was considered to be among the best in the world, and without equal in its ability to track Egyptian plans and motives. Additionally, Sadat had yet to prove his mettle as a brilliant strategist who was not afraid to take calculated risks. Kissinger firmly believed that it would be foolhardy for him to undertake a war that they could not possibly win. It was his belief in Israel's unquestionable military superiority that blinded him to the intensity of Egypt's frustration with the status quo. The thought that Sadat would be willing to undertake a limited war to break through the diplomatic impasse never took hold.

Chapter 3

The Inadequacies of Diplomacy and Bureaucracy

The first week of the war marked the most precarious crisis in Israel's twenty-five-year history as a nation. As Egyptian and Syrian troops rolled across the Sinai desert and the Golan Heights, bolstered by Soviet missiles and tanks, for the first time since declaring independence Israel feared for its very existence. In Washington, the week was fraught with diplomatic stalemate and bureaucratic infighting. Kissinger, now the undisputed architect of U.S. foreign policy, initially anticipated a rapid Israeli victory, one that would signal to American allies the success of an important U.S. client state. As a result, at the war's onset, he was reluctant to offer Israel any tangible support, either militarily, or diplomatically in the United Nations. At the same time, he feared that an overly confident Israel would be intractable in future negotiations, and that a badly bruised Egypt might be resentful towards the United States. Mistakenly confident in Israel's ability to quickly turn the battlefield situation around, he initially opted for a policy of patience, while at the same time halfheartedly pushing for an early ceasefire, an illusory prospect given that both belligerents were equally confident of victory.

Both Washington and Moscow walked a tightrope as the crisis intensified. War was not in the best interest of either country; both sides worried that war in the Middle East would jeopardize a budding spirit of détente and instigate a possible superpower confrontation. At the same time, the two sides had diametrically opposed objectives. Kissinger sought to lessen, if not eradicate, the Soviet presence in the Middle East. The Soviets, surprised by early Arab success on the battlefield, sought to demonstrate the efficacy of Soviet military support and reassert themselves into the Middle East peace process. The result was a diplomatic stalemate, the brunt of which was borne by Israel, which suffered catastrophic battlefield defeats during the first days of fighting.

At the same time, stalemate gripped the bureaucracy of the Nixon Administration. Once the Soviets began a major airlift to the Arabs, infighting between the State Department and the Department of Defense precluded any substantive American military response, and Israeli pleas for assistance on a massive scale essentially fell on deaf ears. While Kissinger and Nixon sought a speedy rearming of Israel, the DOD, wary of alienating the Arabs, constructed roadblocks. Nixon, however, was distracted by the resignation of Vice President Spiro Agnew and Watergate, and he thereby put Kissinger and the State Department in the position of taking on a recalcitrant bureaucracy. Once the president did exercise clear and unequivocal leadership, a massive airlift took place with breathtaking speed and efficiency. Still, Nixon remained virtually absent from the decision making process while the country found itself in the grips of a major foreign policy crisis.

Diplomatic Stalemate

When Kissinger received news that war was imminent, he characteristically sprang into action, grabbing the telephone in an effort to circumvent what by then was inevitable. Despite his best efforts, in tandem with Soviet ambassador Anatoly Dobrynin, to preempt the war, and later, to facilitate a ceasefire, Kissinger would be unsuccessful. It became quickly evident that the Arabs were making marked gains on the battlefield, and both they and the Israelis were too confident in their military abilities to contemplate any ceasing of hostilities. However, the situation was far more complicated. Both the Soviets and Americans had everything to gain by a victory by their respective client state. While maintaining peace was the immediate need, and averting a superpower confrontation was the overall goal, each side stalled, hoping to have the dominant hand at the negotiating table. It was a fatal confluence of directly opposing goals that prevented any kind of meaningful diplomatic exchange from taking place.

At 6:15 a.m. on Saturday, October 6, 1973, Assistant Secretary of State Joseph Sisco awoke Kissinger in his New York hotel room with the shocking announcement: Israel, Egypt and Syria were on the brink of war. Sisco had just received an urgent message from Kenneth Keating, U.S. Ambassador to Israel, whom Israeli prime minister Golda Meir had summoned two hours earlier. "We may be in trouble," she said.[1]

The Israeli government had received word that a coordinated Egyptian and Syrian attack would be launched later that afternoon, on the Jewish holy day of Yom Kippur, the Day of Atonement. Clearly, Meir thought, there was a misunderstanding of Israeli intentions. She requested that the United States urgently convey a message to both the Soviet Union and the Arab nations that Israel, under no circumstances, would attack either Syria or Egypt. The Israelis would call up "some" reserves, but would stop short of a general troop mobilization as evidence of its good intentions.

Kissinger's first move was to immediately call Dobrynin, at 6:40 A.M, "obviously waking him up." He told a "sleepy and confused" Dobrynin that the United States had "information from the Israelis that the Arabs and Syrians are planning an attack within the next six hours and that your people are evacuating civilians from Damascus and Cairo." Dobrynin responded with a barrage of questions to which Kissinger injected, "If this keeps up, there is going to be a war before you understand my question."[2] He asked Dobrynin to convey to the Soviets a U.S. request that they use their influence to curb the attack. Dobrynin agreed to convey the message and take "all measures necessary."[3]

The last thing that Kissinger wanted was a Middle Eastern war. Rather, his strategy had been to opt for a gradual approach to negotiations. He had been confident that the Egyptians would come to believe that only the United States could compel Israel to make concessions on the Arab territory it had occupied since 1967. Time, he felt, was on his side. Egypt would ultimately turn to the U.S. and the Arab world would come to move away from the Soviet Union. He correctly assumed that the Soviets, like the United States, did not want war.

Kissinger may have been accurate in observing that Dobrynin was confused. According to Dobrynin, Kissinger's call was "a complete surprise." He writes:

> I knew that the Middle East was tense, but I did not know the war was so close. Our embassy was not informed of the conversation Anwar Sadat had with our ambassador in Cairo on the eve of the war, when the Egyptian president rather clearly hinted at hostilities but did not name an exact date. Neither were we informed about evacuation of Soviet families from Egypt and Syria.[4]

Kissinger's next call, at 6:55, was to Mordechai Shalev, Deputy Chief of Mission at the Israeli Embassy—Ambassador Dinitz was in Israel fol-

3. The Inadequacies of Diplomacy and Bureaucracy

lowing his father's death. After chiding him for delivering the message to Washington rather than directly to his hotel room in New York, Kissinger informed Shalev that he had obtained a promise of cooperation from the Soviets and that he was urging restraint on the Egyptians. "We would like to urge you not to take any preemptive action because the situation will get very serious if you move," Kissinger said.[5]

At 7:00 a.m., Kissinger called Egyptian foreign minister Mohamed El-Zayat, who was in New York attending the same United Nations General Assembly meeting, and told him that he had warned Shalev that

Soviet leader Leonid Brezhnev during his June 1973 visit to Washington. Brezhnev had repeatedly warned the White House of the danger of war.

should Israel attack first, the United States would take a "very serious view of the situation." He asked the foreign minister to convey to his government a U.S. request to "show restraint."[6] Kissinger then tried in vain to reach the Syrian foreign minister, Mohammed Zakariya Ismail, who was also in New York.[7]

In an effort to circumvent the inevitable, a flurry of phone calls ensued between Kissinger and Dobrynin, Shalev and El-Zayat. At 7:15 a.m., Shalev called back to reiterate Meir's assurance that Israel would not launch a preemptive strike. Twenty minutes later, Kissinger called Dobrynin, who informed him the U.S. request had been conveyed. The United States would "play no games," Kissinger asserted. At 8:15 a.m., Zayat called back with Cairo's reply. There had been an Israeli "provocation," Zayat told him. Israeli naval units supported by aircraft had attacked the Egyptians in the Gulf of Suez, Zayat asserted. Ten minutes later, Kissinger called Israeli foreign minister Abba Eban to convey Zayat's claims. Eban knew nothing, but both he and Kissinger thought it "inconceivable" that Israel would attack on the Jewish holiest of days. Eban agreed to check with Jerusalem.[8] At 8:29 a.m., Kissinger received a call from Shalev. For a half hour, Egyptian and Syrian planes had been attacking Israel on all fronts.[9] Kissinger immediately sent messages to kings Hussein of Jordan and Faisal of Saudi Arabia asking them to use their influence to avert hostilities.[10]

In a revealing foreshadowing of Kissinger's behavior in the coming weeks, it was not until 8:35 a.m. that Kissinger called Alexander Haig, Nixon's chief of staff, who was with a vacationing Nixon in Key Biscayne, Florida. Kissinger told Haig to inform the president that war had begun.[11] Both he and Haig speculated on the role that the Soviet's might have played. Perhaps they had convinced the Egyptians that "a little stirring" was needed to encourage some diplomatic activity, Kissinger pondered. Perhaps "those maniacs have stirred a little too much."[12] Kissinger also dispatched an official memo to the White House Situation Room summarizing the actions that he had taken, asking that it be delivered to the president at 9:00 a.m.[13]

At 8:50 a.m., Kissinger spoke with National Security Council Deputy General Brent Scowcroft. Irate that he had not received word of the impending attacks until that morning, Kissinger barked, "Whoever kept these messages from me has a heavy responsibility." He added, "It is not often you can get a war started."[14] According to Marvin and Bernard Kalb, by 9:00 p.m. the prior day, Ray Cline had concluded that war would start the next day, if not sooner. They write, "Others at the State Department shared his sense of alarm, but somehow they couldn't communicate their acute apprehensions to the Kissinger cocoon at the Waldorf Towers. The

3. The Inadequacies of Diplomacy and Bureaucracy 69

two hundred and forty miles from Foggy Bottom to midtown Manhattan proved to be unbridgeable. No one wanted to take responsibility for disturbing the Secretary in New York on a Friday evening, after hours."[15] An aide to Kissinger later conceded:

> Maybe if we were in Washington, we would have gotten Cline's message. We would have picked up the proper vibrations. But after the Secretary's talk with Zayat, Sisco made plans to play golf on Saturday, and [State Department spokesman Robert] McCloskey made plans to spend the weekend in Connecticut. Everything was calm at the Waldorf. The Secretary was sure, as we all were, that there wouldn't be a war.[16]

At 8:50 a.m., Kissinger told Scowcroft to "put the fleet into position" but to tell the Department of Defense to "shut up about military moves or anything." Scowcroft told him there would be a meeting in just a few minutes of the Washington Special Actions Group (WSAG) to look at options.[17] Scowcroft chaired the meeting at 9:01 a.m. which was attended by James Schlesinger, now secretary of defense, chairman of the Joint Chiefs of Staff Admiral Thomas Moorer, Deputy Secretary of State Kenneth Rush, CIA Director William Colby, Deputy Assistant Secretary of State for the Near East Alfred Atherton, Deputy Assistant Secretary of Defense for International Security Affairs James Noyes, and several staff members. While the group would meet regularly throughout the war, Kissinger, either alone or in consultation with a distracted Nixon, would make most of the key decisions.

It was still unclear who had fired the first shots, and much of the discussion centered on speculation. Schlesinger felt that had the Arabs attacked first, it would have marked the first time in twenty years that the Israelis had not: "I just don't see any motive on the Egyptian-Syrian side," he said. Moorer opined that the Israelis attacked in order to "knock off" the Soviet equipment before it became operational. Atherton was the most prescient: "This is the last day in the year when they [the Israelis] would have started something." Besides, there were no signs of advance Israeli preparations.[18]

In fact, Sadat chose October 6 because it fell on a Saturday during the Yom Kippur festival in Israel, writes Sadat biographer, Raphael Israeli, a time when everyone would be fasting and praying and Israeli defenses would be lax. By mid-afternoon, those Israelis who had been fasting would be exhausted and the sun would be setting in the west, blinding Israeli defenders on the east side of the Suez Canal who would be facing the attacking Egyptians. Additionally, that October was the month of Ramadan, and the Israelis would be unlikely to believe that the Egyptians, who would be fasting, would attack. To ensure that they were battle-ready, Sadat secured special clerical permission for the soldiers to eat prior to launching the battle.[19]

In New York, Kissinger rapidly concluded that it was Egypt and Syria that had launched a surprise attack. At 9:20 a.m., he spoke with Dobrynin, who insisted that Zayat was blaming Israel. "You and I know that is baloney," he told Dobrynin. "How is it that the Syrians and Egyptians are starting at the same minute all along the front if it started with an Israeli naval attack?"[20] At 9:25 a.m., Kissinger spoke directly with Nixon for the first time, whereby he conveyed his belief to the president that the Arabs struck first. "Don't take sides," Nixon chided. "Nobody ever knows who starts the wars out there." Kissinger stated that there was likely to be a United Nations Security Council meeting that day to which Nixon responded, "We ought to take the initiative."

The two decided that Kissinger, on behalf of the president, would contact Brezhnev to seek a "joint approach," agreeing to take a neutral position regarding who started the war and favoring a ceasefire with a return to the status quo *ante bellum*.[21] The strategy, according to Kissinger, was to leverage the current policy of détente to "prevent the Soviet Union as emerging as the spokesman for the Arab side" and to buy time to allow the military situation to clarify what he believed would be a "rapid Israeli victory." The issue of whether or not the Soviets had any foreknowledge of the attacks was a question that loomed large in Kissinger's mind.[22]

According to Victor Israelyan, then a member of Soviet foreign minister Andrei Gromyko's senior staff, "The very fact that Nixon had appealed to Brezhnev was welcomed in the Kremlin." Israelyan continues:

> The Soviet leader was glad that the American President was so prompt in doing so. Brezhnev considered himself a founder of détente and was proud of his summits with President Nixon in 1972 and 1973. Witnesses recall that Brezhnev had tears of joy in his eyes when he was standing on the lawn of the White House in 1973. Listening to him on many occasions, I had the impression that he sincerely believed he could be a champion of Soviet-American détente and at the same time a supporter of anti-imperialist, anti–American forces and movements all over the world. The Soviet leader saw Nixon's message as an omen of Soviet-American cooperation during the crisis and an indication of U.S. interest in maintaining détente.[23]

Nixon had reasons to believe that Brezhnev might be willing to cooperate. In May 1972, both had signed the Anti-Ballistic Missile Treaty, the culmination of the first round of Strategic Arms Limitation Talks (SALT I), which had begun in November 1969, near the end of Nixon's first year in office. Additionally, trade talks were in the works and an Administration proposal to grant the Soviets Most Favored Nation status. A rapport and shared respect had developed between the two leaders. As Andrei Gromyko, then the Soviet foreign minister, writes:

> I remember Nixon's words to Brezhnev at the end of his first visit to Moscow, in May 1972: "According to American data, the U.S.A. and the U.S.S.R. have built up enough weapons to destroy each other many times over." To which Brezhnev replied: "We have come to the same conclusion." It was just this sort of openly expressed mutual understanding that informed the work preparing the provisional agreement on measures to limit strategic offensive weapons, or SALT I, which was completed when Nixon was in Moscow, when the treaty was signed.[24]

Kissinger opted for delay on the part of the United States with the intention of intervening to stop the war only after the Israelis had made significant gains. It was a strategy that played well with Kissinger's overarching objective in the Middle East, namely to eradicate Soviet influence in the region. The Arabs would soon see the futility of relying on Soviet arms and would turn to the U.S. to broker an overall settlement. Also, the contacts with Sadat, albeit indirect, and the expulsion of the Soviet advisors from Egypt, had convinced Kissinger that the Egyptian president held the key to a settlement, with America playing a dominant role, at the expense of Moscow, in what he hoped would be imminent peace negotiations.

At the beginning of the war, Moscow's strategy was, like that of Washington, to wait and see how the war progressed. As John Scherer writes, "If Egypt were successful, Moscow could share the credit. If it were not, Moscow could trade arms for increased political influence. The Russians had to convince Sadat they were indispensable to provide the arms for military victory or indispensable to exert the diplomatic pressure to obtain the ceasefire."[25] Convincing the Egyptians of American indispensability in obtaining a ceasefire and subsequent peace agreement was precisely Kissinger's Egyptian strategy as well.

However, as William Quandt astutely notes, the Soviet effort to obtain a ceasefire in the first few days of the crisis "seems best understood in terms of Soviet-Syrian relations and Moscow's desire not be become militarily involved." Quandt continues:

> A short war would minimize dangers. The Syrians, if successful, might recover some territory, as would the Egyptians. The shock of the war alone might stimulate the Americans to press the Israelis through diplomatic channels for further concessions after the war. The Egyptian plan for a long

war was more dangerous. It could lead to an Arab defeat, once the Israelis mobilized and recovered from their surprise. And it seemed designed to maximize the risks of superpower confrontation, which might suit Egypt's needs, but not necessarily Moscow's. Finally, Moscow had little reason to feel grateful towards Sadat, whereas Asad remained on friendly terms. When presented with the fact that war was imminent, the Russians seemed to have decided to throw their weight behind the Syrian concept of a short war rather than the more risky Egyptian strategy of a prolonged conflict.[26]

At 9:35 a.m., Kissinger called Dobrynin to propose a joint approach. "If you take the position that you will have to defend the Arabs, we will be forced into the position of defending what we believe—of making clear we believed the Arabs launched the attack, and we are then in a hell of a mess." Using as leverage the specter of a rupturing of détente, something the Soviets badly wanted, he added, "That will affect a lot of our relationships." He told Dobrynin that the U.S. would not proceed in the Security Council until there was a reply from Moscow, expressing his hope that there would be no unilateral action from Moscow. Dobrynin agreed to relay the message.[27]

During the day, Kissinger's executive assistant, Lawrence Eagleburger, had spoken to Israel's foreign minister, Abba Eban, who asked that Eagleburger pass on a message to Kissinger requesting that any Security Council action be delayed until Monday.[28] Israel wanted time to "recoup its position." Eban stated that Israel would accept no ceasefire as long as Syrian-Egyptian troops are "over the line." Noting that the military situation was "not unsatisfactory," Eban announced that Israel would accept a ceasefire in place, but only once they had reversed losses on the battlefield.[29]

At 12:45 p.m. Kissinger spoke with Haig who told him that he and the president would be returning to Washington. Kissinger advised against it. "I would urge you to keep any Walter Mitty tendencies under control," he said.[30] Nixon's priority was to announce his choice for a new vice president—on October 10, Vice President Spiro Agnew would resign and plead no contest to criminal charges of extortion, tax fraud, bribery and conspiracy—and concerns about Watergate weighed heavily on the president. Haig said of Nixon that "he knows if he is sitting here in the sun and there is a war going on he is in for terrible criticism." Kissinger iterated his desire that Nixon stay in Florida. "If he returns early it looks like a hysterical move ... if the Soviets took a position of having kicked us in the teeth that would be a signal that ... things are getting serious." He added, "I would hold him until the first thing in the morning." Haig agreed.[31] Haig wrote in his memoirs that Nixon, within an hour of learning about the crisis,

3. The Inadequacies of Diplomacy and Bureaucracy 73

announced that he wanted to go to Washington to take "personal command."[32]

Kissinger left New York for Washington at 2:30 p.m. By now, information was coming in from the battlefield. One hundred thousand Egyptian troops and 1,000 tanks engulfed Israeli forces on the east bank of the Suez Canal; 35,000 Syrian troops and 800 tanks had broken through Israeli lines in the Golan Heights.

While en route, Kissinger received a response from Moscow. The Soviet leadership had received news at the same time as the U.S. that military activity had begun, the message stated. "We are considering now, as you do, possible steps to be taken."[33] To Kissinger, this indicated that, like the U.S., the Soviets were stalling for time. At 3:50 p.m. now in Washington, Kissinger gave Dobrynin his response. "Anatol, I have your message," he said. "I can't say it is a model of solidity. It either means you are confused or you are cooperating with them [the Arabs]." Kissinger then upped the ante, warning that if the debate moved to the General Assembly, as had been requested by Egypt, as opposed to the Security Council, where the U.S. exercised a veto, the U.S. would consider it a "frivolous act."

In 1973, the United Nations General Assembly was not a friendly forum to either the United States or Israel. Established in 1945 with fifty-one members, by the early 1970's, it had gained another eighty members, 70 percent of which could be classified as "developing," "third world," or "non-aligned."[34] As the voice of the non-aligned nations grew, calling for a "new international economic order," the once dominant position of the United States diminished, and Americans became increasingly "critical and circumspect" of its efficacy.[35] Conservative political scientist Francis Fukuyama wrote that the United Nations of the early 1970s was "looked upon with great suspicion by the American people."[36] John Scali, U.S. Ambassador to the United Nations, best articulated the adversarial relationship in the U.N. in a widely reported speech to the General Assembly in February 1973, when he attacked the "tyranny of the majority" and criticized the existing practice of adopting "one-sided, unrealistic resolutions that cannot be implemented."[37] Three years later, B.K. Shrivastava wrote that American interest in the United Nations hit rock bottom during the Nixon-Kissinger years and that there were "no indications of a revival in American interest."[38]

The proliferation of bloc voting served to cement the wedge between developing nations and the West. In his memoirs, Kurt Waldheim, who was installed as secretary-general in September 1972, wrote that "overlapping coalitions" of non-aligned nations had "radically altered the entire character of the United Nations" with bloc politics tending to "dominate decision making."[39] As he departed as the United States ambassador to the United Nations in December 1972, George H. W. Bush told reporters that blind bloc voting posed the biggest threat to the United Nations. "The more moderate voices fear to speak out," he said, "because they feel they will appear less ... loyal to their group. So they keep their silence."[40] The Arab and African coalition stood as the largest obstacle to American designs—its nations voted as a bloc 77 percent of the time.[41]

On October 6, what Kissinger wanted was delay, as he was convinced that the Israelis would rapidly turn the tables on the battlefield. "We are certain it will turn out to be a military victory for the Israelis," he told Dobrynin. "Then everyone will come to us. If it turns nasty [in the United Nations], we will shut off communications for a while." Kissinger informed Dobrynin that the Administration would wait until 5:00 p.m. for a Soviet response.[42]

The Soviet reply came from Dobrynin at 5:45 p.m. which in Kissinger's view "amounted to another procrastination."[43] The Soviets had ostensibly not yet heard back from the Arabs. Dobrynin hedged, "We have a serious doubt about what kind of results could be achieved by a hasty convocation of the Security Council meeting right now." He went on to warn that such a meeting would only "lead to open polemics between yours and ours" and that the Soviets would "be forced to state our known position [that Israel is an aggressor illegally occupying Arab land] and open confrontation with you."[44] In Kissinger's estimation, "like everyone else, the Soviets were waiting on the outcome of the battle."[45]

Based on Israelyan's account of what was happening inside the Kremlin, Kissinger misread the Soviet delay. He writes:

> Although Brezhnev liked the idea of an urgent joint Soviet-American action in the Security Council aimed at stopping the war, he did not want to commit himself without consulting the Arabs. As [First Deputy Minister of Foreign Affairs, Vasilii] Kuznetsov later recalled, "some comrades," participants in the October 6 meeting, believed that such an action without formal Arab consent would contradict the principle of "proletarian internationalism." I asked Kuznetsov, "If we and the Americans just go ahead and get a cease-fire favorable to the Arabs, how could that seem to be a blow to proletarian internationalism?" Kuznetsov replied, "Can you imagine what would happen if some of the Arabs oppose our joint step with the Americans, and the Chinese consequently veto the resolution? Do you want the Chinese to become leaders of the national liberation, anti-imperialist forces?" That was it. For the first time during the October War, the "Chinese Syndrome" came up and influenced Soviet decision-making."[46]

3. The Inadequacies of Diplomacy and Bureaucracy

Early that evening, Kissinger chaired the second meeting of the WSAG during the war. The overriding question was how to "best take advantage of this crisis to reduce Soviet influence in the Middle East."[47] Kissinger was concerned that if the Arabs were humiliated, it would be difficult for the Soviets not to get drawn in, which could lead to a superpower confrontation. Additionally, they might decide to use the war as a pretext to reassert their influence in the region. Kissinger said, "This is a very critical period in our relations with the Soviets. If the Soviets get themselves into an anti–U.S. or an anti–Israel position, they can kiss Most Favored Nation status goodbye ... they have a big stake in this." The consensus was that "after two or three more days," Israel would "have the upper hand." Still, as a security precaution, it was decided to move the Sixth Fleet closer to the fighting.[48]

Kissinger hoped to establish a ceasefire and a return to the lines before the war. At 8:48 p.m. he spoke again with Zayat, to whom he floated such a proposal. Zayat, who was convinced that the Egyptians would make further progress, disagreed with Kissinger's assertions that Israel would soon be advancing. He called the idea "very strange," adding that Cairo would consider the idea of returning "madness." Kissinger responded that the Egyptian point had been made, and that "something positive could come out of this.... I just wanted you to know that I'm open for discussion." Zayat assured Kissinger that Egypt would not go to the General Assembly. The U.S. should make a proposal, Zayat suggested. "Now is your chance," he said, "to speak to both Israel and Egypt. Israel had lost its confidence while Egypt had regained it.[49]

Kissinger realized that he was walking a fine line. In order to establish the U.S. as the unchallenged peace broker in the region, he had to maintain the confidence of the Egyptians. Yet in order to persuade Israel to make concessions, it too would have to see the U.S. as a reliable partner. While American and Israeli interests would inevitably diverge, it would be crucial to stick by the Israelis, all the while minimizing Soviet involvement.

At 9:10 p.m. Kissinger met with a Chinese delegation headed by Ambassador Huang Chen and stressed that the basic strategic objective of the U.S. was to prevent the Soviets from gaining a dominant position in the Middle East. "Israel is a secondary, emotional problem having to do with domestic politics here," he told the ambassador. He stressed, "Our objective is always, when the Soviet Union appears, to demonstrate that whoever gets help from the Soviet Union cannot achieve his objective, whatever it is." Given Chinese support for the Arabs and the plight of the Palestinians, Kissinger defended U.S. support for the Israelis. "Our assumption is that as the talks develop, we will have to separate ourselves from the Israeli point of view to some extent," he said. "But in order to separate ourselves from Israel in diplomacy later, we have to be able to promise that in case of an attack we can give them some protection."[50]

By the end of the first day, American strategy was set. The U.S., which expected a quick Israeli victory, would maintain a low profile during the crisis. Kissinger would maintain close diplomatic contact with the Soviets, Egyptians, and Israelis. He would push for a return to the *status quo ante*, though such a proposition had virtually no likelihood of being accepted. Given that Israel had been attacked, it was a defensible position. Once Israel turned the tables, the United States would then acquiesce to a cease-fire in place.

On Sunday, October 7, Kissinger spoke with Haig at 9:35 a.m. There was still no word from the Soviets on how they would proceed and no country had yet called for a meeting of the Security Council. It seemed to Kissinger "intolerable" that the Security Council was doing nothing amidst all the fighting. Yet delay suited his purposes. The Israelis had taken a beating and were saying that they would need until Wednesday or Thursday to finish the job. Kissinger stressed to Haig that if the issue made it to the Security Council before the Israelis turned the tables, the U.S. would be in a difficult position. "The Israelis will never forgive us for a straight ceasefire [in place] and they'd never observe it anyway." It would make it seem that "we have turned against the Israelis," an action that would have "incalculable domestic consequences—and international ones."[51]

Kissinger wanted to ensure that the U.S. held the upper hand, vis-à-vis the Soviets, in future peace negotiation, and Israeli support was crucial. Also, he needed Israel's support for political reasons. Kissinger felt that by helping the Israelis, they would be more willing to use their influence to help the Administration obtain Most Favored Nation Status for the Soviets, a policy central to détente that was being stymied by Senators Henry Jackson (D–WA) and Charles Vanik (D–OH), who insisted that it should be linked to the Soviets allowing more Jewish emigration to Israel. Jackson, in league with budding neoconservatives, had become a thorn in the side of the Administration, touting that defending the rights of Jews who wanted to emigrate was to uphold a "traditional [American] commitment to individual liberty, a commitment that he claimed was "enshrined in the Universal Declaration of Human Rights which had been unanimously adopted by the United Nations" twenty-five years earlier. He had successfully garnered the support of American Jewish organizations and the AFL-CIO, which had a lot to lose with a Soviet trade agreement.[52]

3. The Inadequacies of Diplomacy and Bureaucracy   77

Additionally, in February 1973, Wilbur Mills (D–AR), Chairman of the House Ways and Means Committee, joined with 259 other House members to introduce legislation nearly identical to the measure being sponsored by Jackson and Vanik in the Senate.[53]

For Kissinger, interfering with Soviet domestic policies was anathema to his personal inclination to respect national sovereignty. More significantly, he was aware that exercising such pressure on the Soviet Union risked derailing détente, an absolute cornerstone of his and Nixon's geopolitical strategy. As notes Mario Del Pero, both viewed détente as accomplishing multiple geostrategic objectives including reducing the risk of a devastating nuclear conflict, preserving the U.S.–U.S.S.R. duopoly of power, and facilitating the evolution of the Soviet Union from a revolutionary power intent on destabilizing the global system into supporter of the status quo.[54]

Much to Kissinger's liking, the Soviet Union continued to stall, thereby giving the Israelis more time, despite assurances to him from Dobrynin that a message from Soviet Premier Leonid Brezhnev would be forthcoming in the next two hours. At 10:18 a.m., Kissinger spoke with Nixon, and expressed his concern that someone on the Arab side would likely submit a resolution for a ceasefire in place, which would put the U.S. "in a hell of a position in vetoing." Nixon presciently responded, "We don't want to be so pro–Israel that the oil states—the Arabs that are not involved in the fighting—will break ranks [with the U.S.]."

Kissinger and Nixon spoke again at 2:07 p.m. There was still no response from the Soviet Union; Kissinger suggested if they didn't hear from Dobrynin by 4:00 they should move forward and call a Security Council meeting. Nixon replied, "At least calling for a Council meeting shows some action.... We don't have to hear from Brezhnev. If we want to change our views, we can change our views." Kissinger agreed that doing nothing while war flared in the Middle East was unacceptable. "It's almost inexplicable how a war can go on for two days without the U.N. even meeting," he said.[55]

At 3:10 p.m. Kissinger spoke with Haig. "I am beginning to think those sons of bitches in Moscow are schnookering us," Kissinger complained. He recommended that the Administration move forward with a press statement calling for a Security Council meeting at 5:00 p.m. Haig agreed. In a foreshadowing of what would be a major confrontation with Defense Secretary Schlesinger, Kissinger complained that he was getting "frantic" appeals from Israel for Sidewinder missiles, but they were getting the "runaround" from the Defense Department. He worried that if the Arabs were to come out ahead with the help of Soviet weapons, they would be totally unmanageable. The president was in "full agreement" that Israeli needs should be met, Haig said.[56]

Dobrynin delivered a vague response from Brezhnev at 3:25 p.m. "You know as well as I do it doesn't say anything," Kissinger chided Dobrynin.[57] "Clearly, the Soviets wanted to let the war run its course a little longer or else they did not have as much influence with their Arab friends as we had thought," Kissinger wrote.[58] Dobrynin's memoirs support the latter hypothesis. "During the first days of the conflict, Moscow was under strong pressure from Cairo and Damascus to keep the whole thing out of the United Nations while they thought they were winning on the battlefield," he recalled. "Brezhnev initially agreed with them, although reluctantly, because we were against the war in general, and besides, we did not believe that the Arabs would finally win."[59]

At 4:40 p.m. Kissinger informed Dobrynin that the president had decided to announce in forty-five minutes that the U.S. was requesting a Security Council meeting. It was unavoidable, Kissinger assured. "I think it's useful—keep the same principle we discussed yesterday and we keep calm with each other," he offered. "If your Ambassador conducts himself the same way, we will get through the day." The U.S. would not table a resolution that evening, though the next day was a possibility, Kissinger told him.[60] Shortly afterwards, he informed Israeli foreign minister, Abba Eban, of the upcoming U.S. request for a Security Council meeting. The idea was to give the appearance of taking action, while at the same time using the Security Council meeting as a vehicle for delay. "We will count on your eloquence," Kissinger hinted, "and in this case [we] wouldn't mind if you sacrificed eloquence to length."[61]

Around this time, the Administration received its first direct contact from Cairo, in the form of a secret message addressed to Kissinger from Sadat's security advisor, Hafiz Ismail, informing him of Egypt's terms for ending the war. Its contents were no different from previous communiqués from Cairo—Egypt would not negotiate until Israel withdrew from all occupied territories. To Kissinger, however, what mattered most was not the content of the message but that it represented an overture from Egypt to the U.S. "Sadat was inviting us to participate in, if not take charge of, the peace process, despite the fact that at the U.N. we were advocating that he give up territory that he considered his own and that his armies had just captured." Significantly, Sadat stated that Egypt did "not intend to deepen the engagements or widen the confrontation."[62]

At 6:00 p.m. Kissinger convened a WSAG meeting. The CIA esti-

3. The Inadequacies of Diplomacy and Bureaucracy 79

mated that Israel would begin to reverse its losses the following day and would win the war by the end of the week. Kissinger summed up the U.S. strategy:

> Egypt doesn't want a confrontation with us at the U.N. and the Soviets don't want a confrontation with us. Period. Our general position will be a restoration of the ceasefire lines. The Arabs will scream that they are being deprived of their birthright, but by Thursday they will be on their knees begging us for a ceasefire. ... We're trying to get this over with a limited amount of damage to our relations with the Arabs and the Soviets. If we can also put some money in the bank with the Israelis to draw on in later negotiations, well and good.[63]

At 8:20 p.m. Kissinger spoke with Dinitz who confirmed the CIA's estimations. "By tomorrow noon, we will be at our full striking capacity; we need two to three good fighting days." His objective was military aid. Kissinger counseled, "My advice is to get what you can out of the country [U.S.] tonight." Dinitz wanted planes. "While the fighting is going on, it will be difficult," Kissinger told him.

Kissinger conferred with the president at 10:30 p.m. Both were skeptical that anything positive could be achieved at the next day's Security Council meeting, which had been set for 3:30 p.m. Both belligerents were confident in their own ability to gain the upper hand on the battlefield. "The U.S.," Kissinger said, "would not propose a resolution which will only be defeated." Nixon responded, "If the U.N. is going to fail, let it fail without us." He added, "The thing to do now is to get the war stopped. That would be [a] great achievement. One of the greatest achievements of all. People in this country would think ... really tough."[64]

The president greatly admired strength and toughness. Writes his biographer Richard Reeves: "He clung to the word and the idea of being 'tough.' He thought that was what had brought him to the edge of greatness. But that was what betrayed him. He could not open himself to other men and he could not open himself to greatness."[65] Importantly, Nixon felt toughness a necessary attribute when conducting U.S. foreign policy. He felt that perceptions of America's weakness represented the greatest obstacles to checking Communist forces in Vietnam. He gave hints of this in his first inaugural address: "To all those who would be tempted by weakness, let us leave no doubt that we will be as strong as we need to be for as long as we need to be."[66]

The Munich crisis a year earlier is rife with examples of Nixon's penchant for being tough. The president's knee jerk reaction upon hearing of the Israelis' deaths was to threaten to break diplomatic relations and cut off economic support to any countries harboring guerrillas. "I think we have to be awfully tough," he said. When Haig indicated that there might be some problems with the Chinese, the president responded, "Screw the Chinese on this one. Be very tough."[67] Though he eschewed personal confrontation, Nixon courted it in foreign affairs. Days after Munich, Nixon discussed making changes in his cabinet in his next term and Rogers was at the top of his list. The secretary wasn't "tough" enough, the president said.[68]

Nixon's prediction of the United Nation's inability to resolve the crisis was astute. The battle, for Israel, would go from bad to worse, and ultimately, it would be Nixon's orders for an aggressive airlift of military that would turn the tide. A memo issued at the end of the day by the State Department's Middle East Task Force reported that it had been a difficult day on the battlefield with "heavy casualties and losses of equipment" on both sides. In the Golan Heights, the Syrian air-defense system had exacted a heavy toll on Israel Skyhawk and Phantom planes. In Sinai, the Egyptians thwarted an Israeli attempt to break through their line with tanks.[69] As morning broke in Washington on October 8, it was evident that the Israelis would not achieve the rapid victory that was hoped for, and indeed, crucial to Kissinger's strategy. Without it, the hope that the Arabs would turn to the United States, realizing the futility of relying on Soviet arms, would be unattainable. The so-called radical Arab states would be emboldened. The moderate states might come to question the wisdom of allying themselves with the United States.

Despite the heavy Israeli aircraft losses, on October 8, the situation seemed far from bleak. A joint estimate by the CIA and State Department's Defense Intelligence Agency (DIA) predicted that Israel would turn the tide on the Golan Heights by the following night. On the Egyptian front, the report stated that "several more days of heavy fighting might follow as the Israelis work to destroy as much as possible of Egypt's army." Dinitz confirmed the optimistic assessment during his call with Kissinger. "Our military people think that a good possibility [is that] we will push the Syrians all the way across the ceasefire line and we are also moving out the Egyptian forces in the Sinai."[70]

However, such optimism was premature. The following day, news would arrive from Israel that conditions on the battlefield were deteriorating. More ominously, the Administration began to receive reports that the Soviet Union was beginning to pour arms into the region. Despite the desire of Kissinger—and Nixon—to counter with U.S. arms shipments to Israel, they were met with considerable resistance from the Department

3. The Inadequacies of Diplomacy and Bureaucracy   81

of Defense. The American response would be a slow one, and for Israel, a costly one.

Still, on October 8, Kissinger hoped to continue with his strategy of diplomatic delay. Once the Israelis reached the boundaries that existed before the war, he thought, the U.S. would accept a simple ceasefire. If the Israelis moved beyond those lines, the U.S. would return to its original position of restoring the *status quo ante*. "It was in our interest, or so it seemed, to keep everything as calm as possible," Kissinger wrote.[71] During his speech at the Security Council, U.S, Ambassador Scali stated that a ceasefire based on the *status quo ante* would be the "least damaging" solution, though he did not propose a vote.[72]

Late that morning, the prime minister of Iran sent Nixon a communiqué from Sadat. It stated, "Egypt has now been obliged to fight and to take casualties. It still wants peace, a lasting peace in the area." Kissinger, who saw a burgeoning relationship with Sadat as the key to a dominant U.S. role in the peace talks that would ultimately take place post-bellum, wrote back: "I would like to reiterate that the United States will do everything possible to assist the contending parties to bring the fighting to a halt." He added, "The United States, and I personally, will also actively participate in assisting the parties to reach a just resolution of the problems which have so plagued the Middle East.[73]

At 9:54 a.m., Dobrynin conveyed orally to Kissinger a message from Brezhnev to Nixon: "We have contacted the leaders of the Arab states on the question of the ceasefire. We hope to get a reply shortly. We feel that we should act in cooperation with you, being guided by the broad interests of maintaining peace and developing the Soviet-American relations."[74]

Kissinger spent much of the day politicking. It was imperative to garner the support of Congress and forestall any claims that the U.S. was not doing its best to help Israel. He conferred with Senators Mike Mansfield (D–MT) and Hugh Scott (R–PA), the majority and minority leaders, as well as Jacob Javits (R–NY) and Ted Kennedy (D–MA), urging them to support the Administration's policies, namely a call for a return to the status quo ante, and to refrain from ascribing blame for the outbreak of hostilities. That same day, much to Kissinger's satisfaction, a resolution of support was passed unanimously in the Senate.[75]

By evening, there was good news from the Soviets. At 5:40 p.m. Kissinger got word from Dobrynin that the Soviet Union would offer no resolution that would call for a ceasefire in place. "Our representative in the Security Council," Dobrynin said, "has instructions not to have any polemics with the American representative. Kissinger offered a promise to Moscow that there would be no U.S. resolution forthcoming."[76] He was pleased by conciliatory remarks that Brezhnev had made that day at a Moscow luncheon for visiting Japanese prime minister Kakuei Tanaka. The Soviet Union, Brezhnev said, supported "a fair and lasting peace ... and guaranteed security for *all* countries and peoples of the area which is so close to our frontiers."[77] As far as the General Assembly, Kissinger had arranged with its president, Leopoldo Benites, that only the parties directly involved would speak, and that the matter would be referred to the Security Council.[78]

Despite apparent progress, Kissinger issued an indirect warning to the Soviets, during an address at a Pacem In Terris (Peace on Earth) conference: "We shall resist aggressive foreign policies," he said. "Détente cannot survive irresponsibility in any area, including the Middle East."[79] Kissinger wrote in his memoirs that the warnings were "intended less as a threat than as an artist's flourish on a nearly completed canvas. By the end of the third day of the war, we went to bed expecting a repeat of the Six Day War of 1967."[80]

That evening, during the daily WSAG meeting, the CIA reported that the Israelis were continuing to make progress on both fronts and had virtually retaken the Golan Heights. "We seemed to have reached our goal," Kissinger wrote. Israel was expected to win a decisive victory within forty-eight hours. "Thus the focus was on how we could pick up the pieces," he wrote, "and prevent an explosion in the Arab world and a possible oil embargo."[81] Following the meeting, Kissinger met with the president. The challenge now, said Nixon, was the Israelis, who "when they finish clobbering the Egyptians and Syrians, which they will do, will be even more difficult to deal with than before."[82] For the moment, it appeared that Kissinger's strategy of diplomatic inactivity had paid off.

The Delayed Airlift

Events on October 9 would shatter any optimism on the part of Kissinger and the president. The situation on the battlefield took a downward turn, and it was becoming clear that Israel would not achieve the rapid victory that had been hoped for. It would be apparent that Israel needed arms, quickly, and in great supply. However, despite Kissinger's best efforts, it would be nearly a week until U.S. shipments arrived in any great number. While the Defense Department stalled, the president, with Watergate continuously on his mind, barked unheeded orders to bolster Israel. In the end, however, he proved that he was up to the challenge,

3. The Inadequacies of Diplomacy and Bureaucracy   83

when he issued an unequivocal directive for an all-out effort to bolster the badly ailing Israelis.

At 1:45 a.m., Dinitz phoned Kissinger at home to arrange a meeting for first thing that morning with Kissinger, himself, and the Israeli military attaché, Mordechai Gur. The situation had become more "difficult" and Dinitz wanted to discuss additional military supplies.[83] During their meeting, at 8:20 a.m., Dinitz and Gur advised Kissinger, Scowcroft and NSC staffer Peter Rodman that Israel's losses had been staggering. They had lost forty-nine airplanes and about five hundred tanks. Dinitz informed Kissinger that there were obstacles imposed by the Defense Department that impeded El Al planes from picking up supplies from American soil. Additionally, Israel needed planes and tanks, which the El Al planes were unable to carry. "It's important; it's urgent," pleaded Gur. He proposed that the U.S. Air Force deliver the tanks in civilian planes to Europe, which the Israelis could then take by ship. Kissinger replied, "You have to realize that to take planes from combat units will be in every newspaper in the world." He told Scowcroft to see what he could do, and to call CIA Director William Colby and "tell him to give them [the Israelis] every bit of intelligence we have."[84]

Following the meeting, Dinitz and Kissinger, per Dinitz' request, conferred alone. The situation was grim. Golda Meir wanted to come to the U.S. to personally plea to Nixon for more aid. Writes Kissinger, "I rejected the visit out of hand and without checking with Nixon." It would be a sign of panic, he felt, and would remove Israel's prime minister from the scene of a major war.[85] According to Walter Isaacson, Kissinger later mentioned to Herman Eilts, U.S. Ambassador to Egypt at the time, that at this meeting, Dinitz gave "intimations that if they didn't get military equipment, and quickly, they might go nuclear."[86]

A memo written to Kissinger by William Quandt summarized the political quandary that the U.S. now faced as a result of recent Israeli losses: "If we call for an immediate end to the fighting, we will irritate the Israelis, which may mean a loss of influence in future negotiations. If we do not manage to end the fighting soon, however, our relations with the Arabs and possibly even the Soviets could suffer."[87] In order to obtain a ceasefire in place, an agreement would have to be reached with the Israelis that would assure them of strong military and diplomatic support in the aftermath of the crisis. This, however, would make them more difficult in later negotiations toward an overall settlement. Kissinger writes in his memoirs: "It was clear that there would be no ceasefire unless Israel seemed to be gaining; Israel would have to pull itself together and overcome what was beginning to look like incoherence. To restore confidence, tangible evidence of American assistance was required."[88]

At 9:40 a.m., Kissinger convened a WSAG special session, attended by only its most senior members, which boded of a lack of support for any direct military support for Israel. CIA Director Colby felt that Israel was doing well and was trying to obtain the maximum aid possible as a symbol, "a sign of unrestricted support." Schlesinger's concern was that if the U.S. turned a losing battle around for Israel, it would be nearly impossible to obtain Arab support after the war. Kissinger disagreed. His assessment was that a defeat of Israel via Soviet arms would "skewer the political as well as the strategic equilibrium in the Middle East." Aiding Israel at this time was therefore in "America's strategic interest."[89]

That morning, there was disturbing news regarding the Soviets. One report informed Kissinger of an increase in the number of Soviet supply ships heading toward Syria and Egypt. Another stated that the Soviets had boosted the number of warships in the Mediterranean. A third declared that the Soviet chargé in Jordan had told King Hussein that the "Soviets fully support Arabs in conflict with Israel" and urged them to "enter the battle now."

In fact, the level of Soviet military involvement had escalated precipitously. According to press reports, the Soviet Union alerted approximately 300 transport aircraft, including An-22s, An-12s, IL-62s, IL-18s and TU-154s. A Soviet airlift from Hungary flew about 900 sorties; combined with the airlift, Moscow delivered an estimated 200,000 to 225,000 tons of military equipment during the course of the war. The Soviet Union launched a reconnaissance satellite sometime around October 10 to provide better intelligence on the Middle East. Additionally, at some time during the war, Moscow delivered an unspecified number of SCUD missiles to Egypt, thereby introducing the newest and most deadly type of technology to the region. In fact, the first use of SCUD missiles in the history of warfare occurred when Sadat launched three into Israel just minutes prior to a ceasefire going into effect, albeit with no significant outcome.[90]

At 8:15 a.m., Dinitz met with Kissinger in his White House office to plea for more planes and tanks—Israel had lost at least fifteen Phantoms and forty-five Skyhawks. Additionally, Dinitz said, electronic jamming equipment was needed to combat Egypt's SAM missiles. Kissinger agreed to handle the situation on an urgent basis. The two spoke again at 11:45 a.m. Kissinger complained about his difficult dealing with the Pentagon's bureaucracy.[91]

Kissinger called Dobrynin at 11:29 a.m. who claimed to know nothing

3. The Inadequacies of Diplomacy and Bureaucracy

of the Soviet chargé's remarks in Jordan.[92] At 12:32, he called Dobrynin back to tell him that a similar appeal by Brezhnev to Algerian president Houari Boumedienne had been made public. "I hope Moscow understands that if it turns out that you fooled us you are going to pay a heavy price in your relationship with us," he chided.[93]

At 4:45 p.m. Kissinger met with Nixon, who was "preoccupied with his domestic scandals"; the president had been working on the announcement of Agnew's resignation, which was to occur within twenty-four hours. "The Israelis must not be allowed to lose," Nixon declared. He told Kissinger to speed the delivery of consumable goods and aircraft to Israel, and to ensure the replacement of all Israeli aircraft and tank losses, which would free them from the need to maintain excessive reserve stocks during the war. The Administration would also supply Israel with electronic equipment, including jamming devices, and Israeli planes would be allowed to pick up missiles at the Oceana Naval Airs Station in Virginia Beach.[94]

At 6:10 p.m. Kissinger met with Dinitz, and informed him of the president's decision. Kissinger informed him that all consumables would be taken by El Al planes, but with the "El Al" painted out. Dinitz complained that he was getting resistance from the Defense Department. His people had spoken to General Sumner who said the U.S. would not accept Israeli planes even with the "El Al" gone. "Oh baloney," said Kissinger. "You will see a change." Fully cognizant of Israeli's influence in Congress, he added that it is "absolutely essential ... that senators and congressmen don't go around attacking the president."[95]

Kissinger called Dinitz back at 7:25 p.m. to inform him that Schlesinger had

Portrait of Alexander Haig, Nixon's chief of staff during the war.

remedied the situation, that there would be no more resistance with the planes. He also warned that it was becoming very difficult for the U.S. to resist a ceasefire in place proposal. "We can drag it out," Kissinger said, "but there is a limit to what can be done. We, of course, would not specifically introduce it, you have no worries on that score."[96] In other words, the Israelis needed to make progress on the battlefield.

When Kissinger awoke on Wednesday, October 10, there was "ominous news." The Soviets had begun an airlift to Syria. Though details were sketchy, about twenty transport aircraft were en route via Hungary and Yugoslavia.[97]

At 8:13 a.m., Dobrynin called Kissinger with an important message. After "difficult and prolonged" consultations with the leaders of Egypt and Syria, the Soviets would not oppose a Security Council resolution in favor of a ceasefire in place. The Soviet representative would abstain from voting. Kissinger asked for a few hours' time to consider the Soviet offer, adding, "You can say it's a constructive message."[98] However, such a ceasefire ran totally counter to Kissinger's strategy of allowing the Israelis to recoup their losses. Additionally, given current circumstances on the battlefield, the Israelis would refuse it. Kissinger wrote in his memoirs:

> Had we gone along with the Soviet plan and pressured Israel to agree, the war would have ended in a clear-cut victory for the Soviet-supplied Arab forces. The United States' position in the postwar diplomacy would have been severely impaired. The proposition that we alone among the superpowers could produce progress would have been exploded.... The probability of another war would have been high, since Israel would want to regain its supremacy; the Arabs would become convinced that they could break every negotiating deadlock with a new assault.[99]

Kissinger immediately called Dinitz and told him that everything depended on the Israelis pushing back to the prewar lines or beyond them as quickly as possible.[100] They spoke again at 10:45 a.m. to discuss the Soviet airlift. Dinitz complained that while the Arabs were receiving help, Israelis were spending their time "painting Jewish stars off Israeli planes." Then he updated Kissinger on the status of the battle. In the Golan Heights, the Syrians had been stopped, but Israel was sustaining heavy tank losses. In the Sinai, more than twenty thousand Egyptian troops and four hundred tanks had crossed the Suez Canal. Israel needed supplies immediately.[101]

As the Syrian front weakened, King Hussein was under pronounced Arab pressure to enter the war. At 11:20 a.m. Scowcroft called Dinitz to inform him that there were intelligence reports that Hussein had sent a limited Jordanian force into Syria. Scowcroft requested, on behalf of Kissinger, that Israel not respond with an attack against Jordan.[102]

3. The Inadequacies of Diplomacy and Bureaucracy 87

At 12:15 p.m. Kissinger spoke with U.N. Ambassador John Scali, who informed him that the Iranian ambassador to the U.N. had spoken with Zayat and advised him, "It seems to me you already have a victory. You should now be thinking of the next step." "We are open to a move towards peace and will study it," replied Zayat.[103] At 1:00 p.m. Kissinger writes that he received a message from Ismail, who made it clear that Cairo was "not yet ready to clinch its gains." However, the message indicated that Egypt was no longer insisting on the "*prior* withdrawal of Israeli troops to the pre–1967 boundary," a subtle shift that Kissinger saw as an indication that there might be room for negotiation.[104]

That morning, Schlesinger canceled a scheduled noontime meeting with Dinitz in which the shipment of military supplies to Israel was to be discussed. According to Marvin and Bernard Kalb, Assistant Secretary of Defense William Clements, a Texas oilman, had persuaded Schlesinger to delay his discussion with Dinitz until more information about American inventories could be established.[105]

At the same time, U.S. support of Israel in the crisis was leading to animosity from the more "moderate" oil producing Arab countries, and

Nixon with Egyptian President Anwar Sadat during Nixon's visit to Egypt in June 1974.

signs of a threat to U.S. oil interests were beginning to intensify. Deputy Secretary of State Kenneth Rush attended a meeting that day with top executives from Exxon and Gulf oil companies. B.R. Dorsey, Chairman of the Board of Gulf, reported that the Kuwait Minister of Oil and Finance had called an emergency meeting of the Arab oil ministers to discuss the role that oil might play in the Middle East conflict. According to a representative of the Kuwait Oil Company, the minister was sharply critical of the U.S position. His message was "Don't force us into something drastic; do not compel us to act prematurely against U.S. oil interests; the West must leave us alone and not intervene against the Arabs." James Lee, President of Gulf, stated that there was increased parliamentary and public pressure on the Kuwaiti government to take action, and the survival of the royal family was at stake. Lee was concerned that Kuwait might nationalize U.S. oil interests, which could lead to the Saudis doing the same. Kenneth Jamieson, Exxon Chairman of the Board, said that King Faisal had been "absolutely infuriated" by Kissinger's request to ask Syria and Egypt to pull back to the October 6 lines. He urged the U.S. to avoid any overt act or public statements that would aggravate the situation.[106]

That same afternoon, Vice President Spiro Agnew resigned, pleading no contest to charges of tax evasion in his home state of Maryland. Occurring just as domestic outcries against the Administration over Watergate were coming to a roar, the future of Nixon's presidency was becoming increasingly shaky. For Kissinger, the pressure could not have been higher to find a satisfactory solution to the Middle East crisis.

Additionally, the NSA and CIA began receiving reports stating that Soviet shipments into Damascus and Cairo were indeed "massive." Soviet Antonov–22s, the Russians' largest transport plane, were landing at regular intervals—it was estimated that each of these carried thirty-six hundred tons of military equipment.[107]

At 8:27 p.m. that evening, United Nations Secretary-General Kurt Waldheim called Kissinger to say that the Security Council meeting was "not satisfactory." Zayat had informed the nonaligned countries on the Security Council, Peru, Kenya and Guinea, "to avoid any resolution ... because they wanted to continue fighting." Waldheim added that the Israelis were not interested in a resolution either. He lamented, "More and more people ... are asking me 'what is the Secretary doing to stop the fighting.'"[108] "This suited us fine," wrote Kissinger. His aim at the time was "to slow down diplomacy without appearing obstructionist, to urge a speedup of [Israeli] military operations without seeming to intervene, and then to force a ceasefire."[109]

3. The Inadequacies of Diplomacy and Bureaucracy

Early in the morning, on Thursday, October 11, Kissinger met with Dinitz to discuss the military situation. During the night, Israel had swept across prewar lines into Syria and Defense Minister Moshe Dayan had told the press that the Israeli army was headed for Damascus. Yet the Soviets were continuing to pour military equipment into the region. Dinitz stressed the need to get the Pentagon to supply Israel with planes, tanks and equipment on an emergency basis.[110]

Domestic pressures to accelerate the resupply of Israel were swelling. The press was reporting that some Israeli officials and Senator Henry Jackson were accusing the U.S. of procrastinating in resupplying Israel, and that the Administrations desire for realizing détente was being exploited by the Soviets.[111] At 11:00 a.m., Kissinger met with the president, who was concerned. "I want you to lean very hard on the Israeli ambassador [and say] that I am very distressed about these stories.... I will not tolerate this, and if I hear any more of this, I will hold him responsible," said Nixon.[112] In his memoirs, Kissinger called this "one of the emptiest threats imaginable."[113]

Kissinger immediately called Shalev, reprimanded him, and warned that there were limits to how long he could maintain his policy of procrastinating on a ceasefire. He told Shalev, "We cannot ask the U.N. to slow down with this announcement." Referring to Dayan's comments, he added, "What in the hell am I now going to tell the Russians? This looks like the most extreme form of collusion and bad faith."[114]

Meanwhile, it had become evident that Israeli planes would be insufficient to deliver the necessary supplies and equipment to Israel, and the WSAG committee decided to charter flights with civilian airlines. However, when Kissinger spoke with Assistant Secretary of State Joseph Sisco, at 2:40 p.m. Sisco told him that he was having difficulties convincing the civilian carriers to cooperate. Sisco suggested that in order to have the carriers "get off their dime," the Department of Defense, in coordination with the Department of Transportation, should threaten to mobilize their aircraft in the name of a defense emergency. He bemoaned that the Defense Department was "dragging their feet."[115] Sisco then spoke with Schlesinger who promised to "nudge" the National Air Association.[116]

Kissinger spoke with Schlesinger about the need to accelerate arms to Israel. He urged the defense secretary to charter twenty American transport planes to fly emergency supplies into Israel. Schlesinger resisted. Even a limited airlift would infuriate the Arabs, making them likely to impose an oil embargo, he argued.[117]

Kissinger had been dodging Dobrynin all day—he still owed him a reply on the ceasefire option—but he wanted a response from the Israelis.

The Kenyans had called a meeting of the Security Council that evening. At 3:05 p.m. Kissinger and Dinitz talked. "I can delay the Security Council meeting through tonight," Kissinger offered. "But I can't avoid doing something with the Russians."[118] In order to buy time, Kissinger advised Sisco to tell Scali that "under no circumstances" was he to say anything in the Security Council.[119]

At 7:55 p.m. Scowcroft called Kissinger to tell him that 10 Downing Street was calling to speak with the president. "Can we tell them no?" Kissinger asked. "When I talked to the president he was loaded."[120] Kissinger took the call, from British prime minister Edward Heath at 8:00 p.m. who reported that Jordan's King Hussein was under pressure to move a brigade into Syria. He asked Kissinger if the U.S. might intervene with the Israelis to allow him to "do this as a minimum" and not attack.[121] "They [the Jordanians] will just stand there," Kissinger informed Dinitz at 8:10 p.m. "This is called, Dr. Kissinger, to fight war with all the conveniences," Dinitz quipped.[122]

The day closed with the Israelis breaching the main Syrian defensive line, though the situation remained static in the Sinai. Additionally, Hussein was under considerable pressure from both Syria and Iraq to move the brigade to the southern Syrian line, though he was hoping to stall it until the following evening.[123] The Kalb brothers state that during that night, Kissinger had decided that his only alternative was to open a massive airlift of arms to Israel. They write: "Russia had to be stopped—not only to save Israel, but in his mind, to spare the world from the possibility of a bigpower confrontation." Fundamental to his decision was the Soviet airlift, which drastically undermined Israel's ability to win a quick victory. "Just as he had misjudged prewar intelligence," the Kalbs add, "so too had he misjudged the will and capability of the Arabs and the duplicity of the Russians."[124]

On the morning of Friday, October 12, Kissinger spoke with Dinitz and pressed for a definitive response from Israel as to whether or not they planned to attack the Jordanian troops. Dinitz said he would get clarification.[125] Kissinger wrote, "Only in the Middle East is it conceivable that a belligerent would ask its adversary's approval for engaging in a war against it."[126]

Kissinger spoke with Schlesinger and told him, in the president's name, to charter twenty civilian transport planes. Schlesinger replied that the Pentagon had already attempted that, but it had failed. Kissinger told him to get the planes, and get them quickly.[127]

At 8:35 a.m., Kissinger briefed Nixon, who was preoccupied with the vice presidential situation. Kissinger told the president that he would be giving a press conference that day, the first during the crisis. Nixon responded, "I don't know anybody that's got a better idea as to what we're doing."[128] At 11:04 a.m., as Kissinger was en route to his press conference, Dinitz told him that Israeli forces were thirty kilometers from Damascus and that they were shelling the airport.[129] The Soviets responded by placing seven airborne divisions on alert.[130]

During the press conference, Kissinger, who was under domestic criticism for continuing to defend détente despite the Soviet airlift and Brezhnev's plea to the president of Algeria, spoke in carefully measured terms: "We ... do not consider that Soviet actions as of now constitute the irresponsibility that ... would threaten détente. When that point is reached, we will in this crisis, as we have in other crises, not hesitate to take a firm stand. But at this moment we are still attempting to moderate the conflict."[131] Kissinger warned that the situation did have the potential to get "out of hand." He added: "It is, of course, an extremely volatile situation. The Middle East may become in time what the Balkans were in Europe before 1914. That is to say, an area where local rivalries that have their own momentum will draw in the great nuclear powers into a confrontation that they do not necessarily seek or even necessarily start."[132]

By now, the press, and as a consequence, the nation, were becoming increasingly alarmed about the possibility of an oil embargo. A journalist asked Kissinger whether Arab threats to cut off oil supplies would impact the decision to resupply Israel. "We have made a very serious effort in this crisis to take seriously into account Arab concerns and Arab views," Kissinger replied. "On the other hand, we have to pursue what we consider to be the right course; we will take the consequences."[133]

At 6:00 p.m. Dinitz, accompanied by General Gur, had a tense meeting with Schlesinger and other Pentagon leaders. Dinitz discussed the massive Soviet airlift and lamented the "unbelievably slow response" of the Americans. Schlesinger stated that there would be no more than sixteen Phantom jets sent to Israel. The U.S., he warned, had to maintain a "low profile," so as not to antagonize the Arabs. Dinitz retorted:

> Mr. Secretary, in the recent period, we have undergone two crises in the Middle East. One, the Syrian and Jordanian crisis of 1970, and the other one, we are going through now. In 1970, your country needed something from us. Now we need something from you. I must humbly say that we acted differently at the time of that crisis than you do now.[134]

Things heated up with the Soviets that evening. At 7:00 p.m. the Soviet chief of mission, Yuli Vorontsov, requested an immediate meeting between Kissinger and Dobrynin; Dobrynin had an "urgent" message, said Vorontsov.[135] Kissinger, who was going to the White House for a ceremony where Nixon would announce the selection of his new vice president, said that he could talk with Dobrynin there. When they met, Dobrynin had two messages: the first assailing the "barbaric bombings" by Israel of peaceful population centers, and the second protesting an attack by Israeli torpedo boats on a Soviet merchant ship. "The Soviet Union," warned the message, "will of course take measures which it will deem necessary to defend its ships and other means of transportation." Kissinger threatened that "any Soviet military intervention—regardless of pretext—would be met by American force."[136] It was ironic, given that, that same day, Congress had passed the War Powers Act, which curtailed the president's ability to commit U.S. troops.

Immediately following the White House ceremony, when Nixon announced his choice of Gerald Ford for vice president, Kissinger found potentially good news awaiting him. Lord Cromer, the British Ambassador to the U.S., called to say that London would be willing to put forth a resolution in the Security Council for a ceasefire, provided that they had some assurances that it would pass.[137] Kissinger immediately contacted Dobrynin to gauge his reaction. Dobrynin, often cagey, told Kissinger he had "no right to say flatly that the Egyptians will accept it, but they [in Moscow] do say that if you put it forward on the assumption that the Egyptians will accept it, it would be a very good gamble."[138]

Kissinger conferred with Lord Cromer at 9:33 p.m. and reported Dobrynin's comments. "What you people have to assume," he told Cromer, "is that we wouldn't ask you to do this if we didn't think there was a reasonable possibility [that the Arabs would accept it]." He added, "My own judgment is that it is the right thing to do. I believe it is the way to peace or at least a good gamble on it and I think it would be a useful role [for London] to play.... The reason we have asked you is because we thought you were the most trustworthy of the members of the Security Council."[139]

At 11:20 p.m. while Kissinger was waiting for a response from London, Dinitz arrived at his White House office and stated Israel's willingness to accept a ceasefire in place. "I must tell you," hedged Dinitz, "our decision whether to start a new offensive or not depends on our power. We thought we would have by now in Israel the implements to do it—the bombs, the missiles, etc."[140] Kissinger asked exactly what the problem was. Dinitz complained that he had had a difficult meeting with Schlesinger and that he could not get a clear answer on arms supplies. The charters had been delayed by three days, he said, and Israel would run out of ammunition

3. The Inadequacies of Diplomacy and Bureaucracy

in two or three days.[141] He added that if a "massive American airlift" did not start immediately, it would be a signal that the U.S was reneging on its promises, and that "we will have to draw very serious conclusions from all this."[142]

Kissinger, note the Kalbs, not unaware of domestic considerations, understood that the Israelis might soon "go public," which would provoke an upsurge of pro–Israeli sentiment, and provoke another blow to a weakened administration. They quote an NSC insider: "The Congress was behind the Israelis. The press was behind them. And to judge from the polls, the public was behind them. If the Israelis had gone public at that time, it could have been the end of the Nixon Administration." A high State Department source told them:

> There were enough people in the country just looking for a breach of confidence in *foreign* affairs, above and beyond Watergate. We had always told the Israelis, "When the chips are down, we're with you." Well, the chips were down, and it looked as though we were not with them. They had taken a terrible beating from the Arabs. They were the victims of aggression. No doubt about that. They held their hand, because Kissinger told them not to strike first. After all that, we reneged. We didn't come through. That's all Jackson needed. If Dinitz had gone public with everything he knew, it could have toppled the Administration.[143]

Kissinger wrote that he immediately called Schlesinger. "I don't know what it is," he said. "It isn't my job. I just don't see—except for you, I don't know anyone over there who has any intention of making this happen," Kissinger chided. He added, "I just find it hard to believe that every company would refuse to charter unless somebody sort of told them in a half-assed way." Schlesinger responded with a solution: "We could take these ten or twelve C-130's that we are planning to give them, load them up and let them go all the way." "Well, let's do that," Kissinger said.[144]

The two spoke again at 12:49 a.m., and accusations flew on both sides. From Kissinger's perspective, the Israelis were blaming the Administration, which had been promising for days that supplies would arrive quickly. As of yet, they had not. "Every day it didn't happen," he complained. "If it had been moved, they would have been all right." Schlesinger was skeptical that the Israelis were short on ammunition; he claimed that the Israelis, specifically General Gur, were less than forthcoming about the supply available. "They simply cannot be that short of ammo," he told Kissinger. "It is impossible that they didn't know what their supply was—and suddenly they've run out of it." Kissinger replied, trying to be conciliatory, "Look, they have obviously screwed up every offensive they've conducted.

And they are not about to take responsibility themselves. I have no doubt whatever that they are blaming us for their own failures."[145]

There is ample evidence that the Pentagon deliberately delayed shipments to Israel. According to Peter Rodman, "Bill Clements was dragging his feet. Henry did not blame Schlesinger, but the Pentagon bureaucracy."[146] Joseph Sisco speaks of a tense meeting with Pentagon officials. "I went with Henry to the Pentagon," he recalls, "and got into a shout match with them, as did Henry. I said to him: 'We're not going to move these people. You have got to get on the telephone with the president.'"[147]

However, the Pentagon was not monolithic in its thinking. Though Schlesinger did show some resistance, and Clement was anything but empathetic toward Israel, Air Force Chief of Staff George Brown, and his head of intelligence, George Keegan, worked on their own authority to prepare for a military airlift in case it was ordered by the president. Admiral Elmo Zumwalt was favorable to the Israeli requests. Thomas Moorer, Chairman of the Joint Chiefs of Staff, was more conflicted. Though he favored from the start a military airlift to resupply Israel, he found the Israelis difficult and hoped they would not receive all the items on their wish list.[148]

Another school of thought is that it was unlikely that Schlesinger could have undermined Kissinger, who was at the apogee of his power. Said William Quandt, in a private interview, it was Kissinger who ordered Schlesinger not to resupply Israel:

> I remember Kissinger saying to Schlesinger in one of the meetings, "You are going to have to bear the responsibility for whatever delay there is because I have to deal with the Israelis on the diplomatic front. Nixon and I cannot be viewed as the problem; right now is not the time" ... It wasn't Schlesinger, he was doing what he was told: "get ready to do it but don't do it!," and so he had to take the fall.[149]

In his book *Decades of Darkness*, Quandt warns against any accounts of U.S. policy during the war that emphasize bureaucratic or personality factors. He writes that the "problem with these perspectives is that they do not account for the fact that individuals from widely different backgrounds agreed on each of the major decisions." Quandt continues:

> Whatever their subsequent relationship, Kissinger and Schlesinger did not argue over basic policy in the October War. Whatever their personal feelings toward Israel, Deputy Secretary Clements and Air Force General Brown helped organize a remarkably efficient airlift to Israel once the orders were given. Bureaucratic politics was barely in evidence, so tight was Kissinger's control over the policy-making machinery.[150]

3. The Inadequacies of Diplomacy and Bureaucracy

Others concur that the reported differences between Kissinger and the Department of Defense have been overplayed, that in fact, differences were deliberately exaggerated by the Administration to placate the Israelis. For instance, Edward Sheehan claims that "Nixon told the Pentagon to 'play tough,' to appear to impede major deliveries to Israel until such time as he and Kissinger determined otherwise. Neither Nixon nor Kissinger intended to be rushed by the Israelis, and both of them coveted the credit amongst American Jews should later circumstances constrain them to unleash an airlift."[151]

One of the most scathing critiques of Kissinger's conduct during the war is that of Italian historian Mario Del Pero, who accuses him of being at the "zenith" of his "unscrupulousness" at that time. According to Del Pero, Kissinger "worked to delay the airlift ... in the hope of trading U.S. military aid for help from the Israeli government and the American Jewish community in stopping [the] Jackson-Vanik [amendment]." He accuses Kissinger of contacting Dinitz "to ask him to intercede" with Jackson to withdraw the bill, which was under discussion in Congress.[152]

Haig describes the relationship between Kissinger and Schlesinger as a "bitter rivalry," writing that the two men "disagreed about nearly everything." According to Haig:

> Schlesinger had his own policy priorities. It soon became evident that he feared that U.S. intervention on the scale mandated by the president would alienate the Arab nations and might lead to an oil embargo against the West. He found reasons to delay shipments to Israel, citing the military and diplomatic dangers of a massive airlift by U.S. military aircraft and the legal difficulties in using civilian aircraft to transport arms into a war zone.... Kissinger repeatedly complained to me about what he described as "Schlesinger's sabotage."[153]

Speaking later of events, Schlesinger offered his own explanation:

> Here is where we stood: The Israelis were increasingly desperate. They were running short of some supplies and were beginning to economize on consumption rates. We at DOD were under conflicting pressures. First, we were now being urged to get substantial supplies to Israel quickly—or, it was hinted not too obliquely, the DOD would be at fault if Israel were defeated. Second, we were not supposed to show the U.S. hand. The DOD or the Department of Transportation (not the White House) was supposed to find aircraft to be chartered. Such charters were largely unavailable though it was a prevalent, if unrealistic, belief at the Department of State that airlines could readily be persuaded to allow their aircraft to be chartered.
>
> Under those circumstances, I decided that the constraint was simply irreconcilable with the demand. In early evening on Friday, I called the

White House with this essential message: There is simply no halfway house. If the United States wanted supplies to be delivered to Israel in time, it would have to be the MAC (Military Airlift Command) aircraft all the way into Israel.[154]

By the end of the night, Kissinger and Schlesinger, after checking with Haig, had developed a tentative three-point plan. The Pentagon would load ten C-130 aircraft with ammunition and fly them to Israel. Supplies would be shipped to the Azores where they would be picked up by Israeli aircraft. Finally, the Administration would continue to press for charters.[155]

An option was for the U.S. to send directly jumbo C-5A jets into Israel. However, the possibility of an Arab oil embargo could not be ignored. It would require a beleaguered president to ultimately break the bureaucratic deadlock. The sequence of events on Saturday, October 13, is somewhat unclear. What is clear, however, is that at some point during the morning, the president unambiguously ordered a military airlift of supplies to Israel. It was to mark a major turning point in the war.

Kissinger spoke with Haig that morning, at 9:35 a.m. Haig had conferred with Schlesinger. "Jim admitted to me he investigated this thing and his people did drag their feet," Haig told Kissinger. "He's goddamned upset about it." Haig added that Schlesinger had said that he thought the Israelis had a plan to draw the U.S. into the war. He told Kissinger that he reprimanded Schlesinger: "These are judgments for Henry and the president to make and you have to do what the president wants done." Kissinger blamed Schlesinger for the Israelis "slackening off," adding that the delay got "the whole diplomacy thing screwed up."[156]

Kissinger's attention turned to the ceasefire resolution. He had not yet heard back from the British. At 9:37 a.m., Kissinger phoned Dobrynin and floated the idea that if things fell apart, perhaps they should ask the Australians. He also informed him that he had just received word that the Egyptians were planning an airborne landing in the Sinai. "We all have to realize that if anything looks like trickery, we will have to—it will affect things," Kissinger threatened.[157]

Immediately after, Kissinger conferred with the British foreign minister, Sir Alec Douglas-Home. The British were getting cold feet about the ceasefire proposal and were beginning to have doubts that Sadat would agree to it. "All you have is Dobrynin's word that the Russians believe Sadat would agree, and our information is that they could not agree to this," Douglas-Home told Kissinger. Kissinger informed him of the warning he had made to Dobrynin. "My impression is if they [the Soviets] have tricked us on this ... they will pay the price of our entire relationship. They have

3. The Inadequacies of Diplomacy and Bureaucracy

all to lose." Douglas-Home agreed to bring it up again with Prime Minister Edward Heath, but he worried that British credibility would be "completely lost" if they were to propose a ceasefire only to have it rejected.[158]

By then, the Defense Department had located three C-5A jet transports that were capable of flying sixty to eighty tons of supplies directly into Israel. Kissinger spoke with Nixon who wanted to proceed. "Do it now!" he ordered.[159] According to Kalb and Kalb, at 10:30 a.m., Nixon summoned Kissinger, Schlesinger, Moorer, Haig and Colby to an emergency meeting at the White House. The authors write:

> They heard the president ask one key question: Why had there been a delay in implementing his previous orders about supplies for Israel? Schlesinger tried to explain his difficulty in chartering civilian transport planes. "To hell with the charters," Nixon exploded, according to one eyewitness. "Get the supplies there with American military planes! Forget the Azores! Get moving! I want no further delays."[160]

At 10:45, Kissinger convened a WSAG meeting. He began by threatening, "The president said if there are any further delays in carrying out orders, we want the resignation of the officials involved." He then turned to Schlesinger. "Our thinking is that the bureaucracy is dragging its feet on the grounds that we are going in on the Israeli side." Schlesinger countered, "We weren't asked to get in until Thursday night. The Israelis never told us they had shortages." Kissinger tried to be reconciliatory: "I am sure the history books will show Israel was defeated by poor planning and lousy tactics. But right now, I have the diplomacy going and I can't make it work unless the Arabs are sweating."

The conversation switched to a discussion of the mechanics of the airlift. "Let's fly in some U.S. planes," Kissinger told the group. "Let's get the charter going. I want the Arabs to think the Israelis may go wild when they get equipment." Schlesinger responded that they were using the U.S base in Torrejon, Spain, which could not be employed for a large-scale operation without the permission of the Spanish. Clements, apparently impressed by the president's unambiguous orders, suggested a "massive airlift." "No, we will lose all our Arab friends," replied Kissinger. "Let the C-5's go in until we can get a charter going," he added.[161]

At 12:32 p.m. Kissinger phoned Dinitz to inform him that he would send three C-5As transports that day through the U.S. base in Portugal; in addition, he would send at least three C-141s already in the Azores to Israel. He added that the number of Phantoms had been increased to fourteen, and that they would arrive in Israel on Monday night. He then confronted Dinitz:

> I just again have been called by [Senator Henry] Jackson, threatened with a congressional investigation, being told this is a lousy example of crisis management and he is going to demand an overall review of the national security system. I must say this—if I get one more threatening call by anybody, I am going out of the supply business. And with all my friendship, I am not going to stand for it.[162]

That afternoon, the situation on the diplomatic front collapsed. At 1:40 p.m. Dobrynin called Kissinger with the news that Moscow had rejected the Australian option.[163] At 3:35 p.m. Douglas-Home informed Kissinger that London would not move forward with the proposal for a resolution, saying that Sadat had let it be known that he would not support it. "The Russians would, in our view, have no chance whatever of looking on Sadat and forcing him to do so," he stated.[164]

During a conversation with Dobrynin at 4:00 p.m. Kissinger accused the Soviets of having "tricked" the U.S. into believing that Sadat would accept a ceasefire. "It looks as if you want this war to continue and let us go through three days of meetings with the Israelis and British in the meantime." Still, that afternoon, there was good news regarding the airlift. Nixon had transmitted a harsh message that morning to Portugal, and bowing to the pressure, the Portuguese agreed to allow the U.S. to use its bases in the Azores to fly equipment to Israel. At 4:05 p.m. Kissinger informed Scowcroft and told him to commence the flights, adding, "I think those bastards [the Soviets] understand only brutality. If they want to play, we will play."[165]

Kissinger spoke with Dobrynin at 4:25 p.m. and let it be known that the U.S would be flying planes into Israel. "We are prepared to stop our aerial supplies when you are," he told Dobrynin.[166] He then announced to Cromer that the president was taking the British decision not to propose a Security Council resolution "extremely ill." Kissinger added, "When we look over the crises of the last three years, we just don't seem to be able to get together." Kissinger informed Cromer that the U.S. was starting an airlift into Israel. "There will probably be a confrontation," he said, adding, "The one consolation ... the West has—we will all go down together; at least we are doing it with the worst possible grace." Cromer asked what the U.S. posture would be when the "Arabs start screaming oil at you." "Defiance," Kissinger confidently replied. "We have no choice."[167]

Dobrynin called Kissinger at 7:55 p.m. with an oral message from Brezhnev. The Arabs, he said, were objecting to a Security Council resolution that dealt only with a ceasefire. They insisted it be tied to withdrawals of Israeli troops from Arab territories that were occupied in 1967.

3. The Inadequacies of Diplomacy and Bureaucracy   99

Kissinger retorted, "We have worked for three days on the assumption you are now canceling," referring to the proposed joint abstention by the superpowers to the resolution that the British were to have proposed. "Where does this leave us?" Kissinger asked, adding, "Nowhere ... now we are right back to where we were last Monday."

Dobrynin attempted to justify the Soviet position. "For two days our positions [were] very close, we were prepared to abstain ... then the Arabs changed their position." "In the meantime," Kissinger barked, "you sent in 140 airplanes. May be why the Arabs are so tough now." He added, "Tonight Egypt is launching an attack in the Sinai. Tomorrow, when some American airplanes reach Israel, the Arabs are going to start yelling. We will not under any circumstances let détente be used for unilateral advantage." Kissinger was furious. He continued:

> Until this afternoon, I believed [we] had [a] possibility of pressing for a settlement, pressing for a ceasefire. [The U.S. and Soviets] are obviously on [a] collision course. What do you think we can say to the people on Monday? ... You don't think we will accept a military setback in the Middle East. You can't believe it. ... Until this minute not one American plane has landed in Israel. Not one! My whole strategy has been based on reliance on you. I can tell you, in addition to whatever else is achieved, my own credibility ... is not exactly high at this moment.

Circumstances had changed, Dobrynin responded. "Why do we have to deal with you [on matters] that depend on Sadat?" Kissinger asked rhetorically. "Why not deal with Sadat directly?" Dobrynin coldly replied, "It's up to you and the president to decide. But there could be disastrous results."[168]

As the day opened, on Sunday, October 14, Egypt had launched a new thrust into the Sinai Peninsula. To Kissinger, it seemed there were two possibilities: either the Israelis were drawing them out of range of their belt of anti-aircraft SAMs or else the Egyptians were really in trouble. The Israelis had stopped their advance toward Damascus.

He met with Nixon that morning, at 9:04 a.m. Speaking of the airlift, the president stated, "It's got to be the works." He continued: "We are going to get blamed just as much for three planes as for 300. [I'm] not going to let the Russians come in there with a free hand." The president wanted it to be clear in future public statements that the U.S. was not "fueling the war." Rather, it should be positioned that "we are sending supplies, but only for the purpose of maintaining the balance so that we can create the conditions that will lead to an equitable settlement."

Nixon returned to a theme that was always in the back of his mind during his second term: the idea of imposing a comprehensive settlement on the Arabs and Israelis. "What ought to happen is that even though the Israelis will squeal like stuck pigs ... we ought to say that Brezhnev and Nixon will settle this damn thing," he told Kissinger. "That ought to be done."[169] It was wishful thinking and a strategy completely at odds with that of Kissinger's gradualist approach. Yet ordering the airlift was a bold and decisive move, and a maneuver that ultimately ended the delay caused by the bureaucratic infighting. As Asaf Siniver notes, "Nixon's rare act of leadership ... also transformed the dynamics of the WSAG discussions. Whereas during the first week of the war, the approach to the crisis was rather hesitant, once an unequivocal presidential directive had been issued, discussions turned more purposeful and emphasis shifted from deliberation to implementation."[170]

Kissinger's special assistant, Peter Rodman, affirmed that Nixon's taking a strong hand was evidence that Nixon had "not entirely lost his touch."[171] However, ordering the airlift would prove to be his last instance of decisiveness during the war. As the war progressed, Watergate intensified, and the president would become increasingly distracted and preoccupied with preventing the unraveling of his Administration. However, his decision to aggressively and unabashedly support Israel would have enduring consequences. For the Israelis, it immediately turned the war in their favor. For the United States, it would catalyze an Arab oil embargo. For Kissinger, it marked the end of bureaucratic intransigence during the crisis. For the duration of the war, he would be calling the shots.

Yet Nixon can hardly be absolved from blame. Obsessed with Watergate, the scandal involving Agnew, and his need to find a new vice president, Nixon allowed Kissinger the leeway to stall, at a time when a diplomatic solution might have prevented the war from escalating. As the war escalated, and Soviet involvement became clear, Nixon might have more decidedly preempted the bureaucratic battles that prevented a rapid American military response. Given the domestic embroilment in which he found himself, for Nixon, the October war could not have begun at a more inopportune time. As the war continued to rage, Nixon's problems would only get worse.

CHAPTER 4

The Tide Turns

Despite Nixon's decision to accelerate the airlift to a full throttle, he was plagued by critiques that he was doing either not enough, or too much, to aid the Israelis. In Washington, most notable among his critics was Senator Henry Jackson, who was the figurehead of an emerging cadre of Cold War hawks who would later be dubbed as "neo-conservatives." Jackson and other hard-liners accused Nixon of being overeager for détente, and therefore of being soft on the Soviets as manifested by the delayed supply to Israel. This bothered Nixon, who was eager for the military to take action. At the same time, public opinion was inflamed by well-founded claims in the press of an impending oil embargo. Americans increasingly saw Israel as the victim of increasing Arab cupidity fueled by the world's growing dependence on Arab oil.

Across the Atlantic, Europeans were incensed by what they saw as a unilateral decision by the president to supply Israel, which placed their own countries at risk of an oil embargo. Negotiations with Moscow continued to deteriorate during this time. Still, by the end of the week, there were indications that the American airlift had borne fruit, and Kissinger received an urgent invitation from Brezhnev to fly to Moscow.

As the specter of an Israel defeat dissolved, Kissinger's attention shifted to postwar issues. Most challenging was the question of how to assure U.S. dominance and minimize Soviet influence at the negotiating table, and ultimately, in the region. Moreover, it was clear that for any diplomatic progress to be made, Israel would need to show flexibility on the terms of Proposition 242 and its vague demands that it withdraw from occupied territory, which the Israelis were vehemently opposed to doing. Both Kissinger and Nixon felt that a strong Israeli showing on the battlefield would demonstrate to the Arabs the futility of reliance on Soviet backing. However, the more powerful Israel became, the more intransigent it would be in negotiations.

On Sunday, October 14, at 9:04 a.m. Kissinger and Nixon spoke. Kissinger began by briefing the president on the military situation. The Israelis had claimed that they had knocked out 150 Egyptian tanks and only lost fifteen of their own. Additionally, they were making gains toward the Suez Canal. Nixon responded, "The main thing is who wins this damn battle—it isn't the territory, you know—that is what we must remember about World War I and II—you can give up gobs of territory, the question is, do you beat the enemy. Now if the Israelis let them—I think they ought to let them in there and kill them."[1]

Kissinger stated his strategy.

> Should the Israelis clobber the Egyptians that will turn out to be a pretty good position. Then we move to a simple ceasefire. The Egyptians may have been ready to accept that before the Israelis got into Syria. Now the Egyptians are demanding a return to 67 borders; now that's absolutely out of the question, short of a huge defeat as a result of the war.... So now what we are trying to do is, I've talked to Dobrynin about that last night after you and I talked, is to see whether we can find a formula that links the ceasefire to the peace settlement.[2]

Nixon's concerns turned to Israel intransigence. "We've got to squeeze the Israelis when this is over and the Russians have got to know it," the president insisted. "We've got to squeeze them goddamn hard. And that's the way it is going to be done." Kissinger then clarified his diplomatic objectives. "I think what we need now," he told Nixon, "if we can find a resolution that doesn't flatly say the 67 borders, but leaves it open—something that invokes the Security Council Resolution 242 that speaks of withdrawals, and that's something everybody has already agreed to once." Nixon agreed and stressed that the airlift needed to be "the works." "What I mean," he told Kissinger, "is we are going to get blamed just as much for three planes as for 300... [I'm] not going to let the Russians come in there for—with a free hand.... This is a deadly course, I know, but what I meant is, Henry, I have no patience with [the] view that we send in a couple of planes."[3]

Kissinger chaired a last minute WSAG meeting at 9:16 a.m. Schlesinger announced that six C-5s and 22 C-141s would be ready to fly that evening, which would enable the U.S. to fly in fifty tons an hour—1,600 tons were en route already. The Soviets airlift had been about 3,000 tons. Moorer offered that the U.S. could step things up even more. Yet Kissinger stuck to his strategy. The Israelis needed to win, but not in the stunning fashion of 1967, which had left Egypt humiliated and alienated, and Israel doggedly refusing to enter into any negotiations over the territory it had acquired. Rather, ever with his eye on Cold War geopolitics, Kissinger's goal was to extricate the Soviets from any subsequent peace negotiations. A battered, but victorious Israel would best fit his plan. "Ideally, he said, "Israel would win without exorbitant costs and quickly. But we don't want Israel totally intractable."

The discussion turned to the possibility of an Arab oil embargo. Kissinger mistakenly downplayed its urgency. "An oil cutoff was not mentioned in any of the conversations I have had in the last three weeks," he said, discounting the American public's growing concern. "All I have received are hysterical calls from oil companies," he added. Regarding diplomacy, Kissinger stated that the objective was now to link a call for a ceasefire to a vague reaffirmation of Resolution 242. "The Egyptians must know that they [the Israelis] cannot go back to the 1967 borders," he said.

At 11:10 a.m., Kissinger met with Nixon, who was exuberant that the resupply was going at full force. "If we are going to do it, don't spare the horses," Nixon rejoiced. He wanted to send a message to Brezhnev. "Everything I am sending goes in your name," Kissinger assured him. Nixon approved, and said he'd like to send a new message to Brezhnev saying: "Now look here. The peace of not only this area but the whole future relationship is at stake here and we are prepared to stop if you are and we are prepared." He told Kissinger to make it "conciliatory but very tough," expressing that with "great reluctance ... we are prepared to give tit for tat."[4]

By noon, U.S. transport planes were arriving in Israel every fifteen minutes. At 12:36 p.m. Kissinger spoke with Dobrynin. "We are prepared to stop the airlift immediately after a ceasefire if you are prepared to stop your airlift," Kissinger stated. "But if not, we can increase it considerably.... We are not going at our maximum capacity or anywhere near."[5]

Kissinger spent much of the day advising allies of the Administration's intentions. At the top of his mind was Saudi Arabia, not only due to its paramount importance as an oil supplier, but because of its pivotal role as a U.S. ally in the Cold War. It was considered a "moderate" Arab nation, and a vital asset in executing the tenets of the Nixon Doctrine. The Saudis regarded as unacceptable the occupation by Israel of Arab territory and the imposed plight of the Palestinian refugees, and tensions between Saudi Arabia and the United States had been steadily mounting since 1967.

Kissinger needed to reassure King Faisal, to whom he sent two messages, the first ostensibly from the president and the other from himself. The first message stated, "We share with Your Majesty a strong desire to avoid prolongation of the fighting and especially to keep the conflict from spreading to involve countries which are not now combatants." He added, "We too are concerned that the Soviet Union not be given an opportunity to reassert its influence in this area."[6] His own message explained the airlift. "We had no alternative but to begin our own airlift," he wrote. "It is extremely important to note that it was only after the Soviet supply effort had reached massive proportions that ours began."[7]

Ever mindful of the unilateral role that he hoped the U.S. would play in the post-war negotiations, Kissinger also sent a message to Ismail for Sadat:

> The U.S. wishes to inform the Egyptian side that it is prepared to cease its own airlift resupply efforts immediately after a ceasefire is reached. The United States wishes to emphasize again that it recognizes the unacceptability to the Egyptian side of the conditions which existed prior to the outbreak of recent hostilities. The U.S. side will make a major effort as soon as hostilities are terminated to assist in bringing a just and lasting peace to the Middle East. It continues to hope that the channel to Egypt established with so much difficulty will be maintained even under the pressure of events. The U.S. will do all it can in this sense.[8]

By Monday, October 15, the airlift was "proceeding in stunning fashion," wrote Kissinger, carrying an average of 1,000 tons per day, matching in one day, "what the Soviet Union had put into all the Arab countries combined in all of the previous four days."[9] The Middle East Task Force reported that, the prior night, the Egyptians launched a major armored attack in the Sinai, which, according to Israeli military sources, backfired and resulted in the destruction of 280 Egyptian tanks. An Israeli spokesman stated that the Israeli air force initiated attacks on Egyptian and Syrian airfields, enemy missile batteries, fuel depots and armored divisions.

However, the report also contained some worrisome news. The oil companies and embassy officials believed that King Faisal "will feel he will have to take 'some' retaliatory action if the U.S. makes an announcement concerning U.S. military resupply of Israel."[10] Despite Kissinger's prior dismissals, the possibility of a Saudi oil embargo loomed densely over the horizon. It was a troublesome possibility, not only for its potential impact on the U.S. economy, but also because its effects would be devastating to America's allies, specifically Western Europe and Japan, which had no alternative supply of petroleum. Ironically, there were also press reports about a resolution from Senator Jackson calling on the Administration to accelerate its effort to supply Israel.[11]

At 9:08 a.m., Kissinger spoke with Schlesinger and informed him that the Soviets had contacted him around three o'clock in the morning with a proposal to go back to the ceasefire line of Saturday. "We ought to think very carefully about supplying [Israel] ammos for the destruction of Damascus," warned Schlesinger. During a WSAG meeting at 10:08 a.m., Moorer gave an estimate of the military situation. Ship losses had been six to one in Israel's favor, aircraft three to one, and tank losses two to one. The conversation turned to oil. Moorer stated that the Europeans and Japan "expected the U.S. to carry the burden." Kissinger threatened: "There is a limit beyond which they can't push us without losing their NATO relationship ... they can't afford to go into open opposition to us." Kissinger summed up his plan. "Our strategy is to convince the Arabs and the Soviets that they will be pushed against the wall and that time is on our side. What the Israelis want is less important." He added, "The only way we can wind this up is if the Soviets see we won't quit and won't panic; if the Europeans see that they are pushed between losing their NATO relationship and lining up with us."[12] At a State Department meeting at 3:15 p.m. Kissinger said, "The conditions that existed between 1967 and 1973 cannot be permitted to be repeated. But for us to have an influence ... we must be perceived by the Israelis to be the source of their survival, by the Arabs as strong enough to be a major factor, and yet open-minded enough not [to] have gone beyond what was imposed on us."[13]

Kissinger sent a backchannel message to Ismail, in which he blamed the American resupply on the Egyptian refusal to accept the ceasefire proposal and the Soviet airlift. The message stated:

> The United States wishes to emphasize again that it recognizes the unacceptability to the Egyptian side of the conditions which existed prior to the outbreak of recent hostilities. The U.S. side will make a major effort as soon as hostilities are terminated to assist in bringing a just and lasting peace to the Middle East. It continues to hope that the channel to Egypt established with so much difficulty will be maintained even under the pressure of events.[14]

Tuesday, October 16 was, for Kissinger, a good day. It was announced that he had been awarded the Nobel Peace Prize with Le Duc Tho for negotiating an end to the Vietnam War.[15] In the Middle East, Israeli armored forces had crossed to the western bank of the Suez Canal. Additionally, news arrived that Soviet Chairman of the Council of Ministers Kosygin was en route to Cairo, clearly in an attempt to persuade the Egyptians to stop fighting.

The situation in Europe, by contrast, was far from ideal. Relations between the European nations and the U.S. were straining, ironically so, as Nixon had declared 1973 to be the "Year of Europe." NATO Secretary General Joseph Luns had accused the U.S. of being overzealous about rapprochement with the Soviets, warning that the Americans were being lulled into a false sense of security. Donald Rumsfeld, the U.S. permanent representative to NATO, admonished representatives that the U.S. "did not take kindly" to suggestions that Washington was foolishly drawn into détente, and it did not "welcome" such pronouncements. Rumsfeld called for "allied unity and support" of U.S. actions to prevent the Soviet airlift from "tipping the military balance."[16] An additional source of tension between the U.S. and Europe was the threat that the American airlift to Israel represented to Europe's oil supply. That day, the Saudi deputy foreign minister called in the ambassadors of European countries to urge them to "use their influence to change America's policy in the Middle East," and warned them that "the Saudis must react by decreasing oil production" which would "hurt the EC countries first."[17] Writes Kissinger biographer Alistair Horne:

> With her own domestic production, coupled with supplies from Western Hemisphere countries like Venezuela, the United States itself could—for the foreseeable future—shrug off the Arab measures. But to Europe, the pain was immediate, the long-term threat incalculable. Combined, the Middle East oil cuts dramatically upset the world oil market. Europe, which felt itself to be a mere bystander in the Yom Kippur War, was outraged at the apparent insouciance with which the United States had embroiled the European countries in this calamity.[18]

Yet as Ragaei el Mallakh has noted, there was hesitation among Administration officials to link the supply of Arab oil with the Arab-Israeli problem and American foreign policy. In March 1973, Joseph Sisco was insisting that the mutual economic interest between Arab petroleum countries and the United States would not be "jeopardized" by the Arab-Israeli dispute. The president's first energy message in April made no connection to tensions in the Middle East and the oil supply. It was not until September, responding to Saudi demands for a more evenhanded American approach in the Middle East, that Nixon linked U.S. oil requirements to foreign policy. Writes el Mallakh, "Indeed, the October War scuttled the long-cherished U.S. government hopes that talk of a cutoff was bruited only by the so-called radical Arab states—that oil and politics did not mix."[19]

During the WSAG meeting at 10:08 a.m., Kissinger was less concerned with oil and more anxious for faster results on the battlefield. "Are the Israelis really trying?" he asked rhetorically. Colby stated that they were claiming the shortage of equipment as a reason for not being more active. "And this is our fault, of course," Kissinger responded sarcastically. "I used to think the Vietnamese were the most obnoxious to deal with." Kissinger mocked Sadat's recent call for a peace conference involving all parties. "With Palestinian participation and representatives from all the other Arab countries, that would be a happy forum for us, not to mention the Israelis," he said. Referring to a trip to Cairo by Soviet premier Alexei Kosygin, Kissinger griped, "When you read the Egyptian public demands and compare them with what is obtainable, someone has to bring them back to reality." He complained about the anti–Soviet tone of stories appearing in the press. "We must keep this whole thing low key," he warned, adding, "If we can finish this off without a confrontation with the Soviets and without ripping our relations with the Arabs, we will have earned our money." The group decided that the airlift of equipment to Israel should exceed that of the Soviets by 25 percent. "It should look to the Soviets unambiguously that we are putting in more than they," Kissinger stated. The group agreed that the president should go to Congress to ask for funds for military assistance to Israel and Cambodia. "I'll tell Dinitz to turn loose his Senators. I'll tell him it's a package deal. If we can't get something for the others, we will drag our feet on Israel."[20]

That day, Kissinger sent a backchannel message to Ismail, responding to an invitation for him to visit Egypt once hostilities ended. "Dr. Kissinger greatly appreciates the thoughtful invitation of the Egyptian side to visit Egypt. Once a ceasefire has been achieved, he would be glad to give that invitation the most serious and sympathetic consideration as part of a serious effort to bring a lasting peace to the Middle East." However, it also contained a warning: "The Egyptian side has an important decision to make. To insist on its maximum program means continuation of the war and the possible jeopardy of all that has been achieved. The outcome will then be decided by military measures." Kissinger added, "Circumstances for a U.S. diplomatic effort would not be propitious."[21]

Kissinger spoke with Nixon at the end of the day. Nixon, referring to a recent call by Senator Mike Mansfield for a Mideast conference at the United Nations, asked, "What in heaven would be decided?" "Mr. President," replied Kissinger, "it would kill us. It would be the Israelis and us against six other nations. Insane." He added, "Last week was too easy, done too much with mirrors—better solution this week, when we have shown our muscle." Nixon responded, "Well, the Israelis ought to be awfully grateful after this."[22]

Also on October 16, in response to the American decision to resupply Israel, the eleven members of the Organization of Arab Petroleum Exporting Countries (OAPEC) agreed to cut production by five percent, and to continue reducing it by an additional five percent until Israel withdrew from all the occupied territories and the "legal rights" of Palestinians were restored. Separately, the six Persian Gulf members of the Organization of Petroleum Exporting Countries (OPEC) increased the price of oil by 70 percent, from $3.01 to $5.12 a barrel. Several countries including Libya, Kuwait and Saudi Arabia threatened a total embargo against the United States. Said the Kuwaiti Minister of Oil and Finance, Abdul Rahman al–Atiqi, the intention of the initial reduction was to continue toward a "complete embargo on oil to the United States" and to demonstrate that the Arab oil producers were "front line fighters" in the war against Israel.[23]

Kissinger maintained in his memoirs that the "true impact of the embargo was psychological," adding that it was "the fear that it might be extended—that Arab production might shut down further—that triggered a wave of panic buying by Europe and Japan, which constricted supplies and drove up prices even more."[24] That point of view was shared at the time by the Central Intelligence Agency which prepared a paper on October 19, declaring that the effect of the oil embargo on the United States "would be relatively small, and after the first month, the brunt of the cutback would fall on Europe and Japan." The paper concluded: "It is perhaps fortunate that this particular crisis occurred now rather than a few years hence," since by then it was predicted that the U.S. would be importing five million barrels per day of Arab oil.[25]

The analyses of both Kissinger and the CIA were correct that American reliance on oil imports from Arab countries was relatively insubstantial. Prior to the war, in 1973, U.S. oil needs had been met by 63 percent domestic production, 9 percent Arab imports and 28 percent non–Arab imports. In contrast, Western European needs were met by only 3 percent domestic production, 69 percent Arab imports and 29 percent non–Arab imports. Without any domestic sources, Japan's oil needs were met by 43 percent Arab imports and 57 percent non–Arab imports.[26] Clearly, Europe and Japan had a lot more to lose in the case of an oil embargo. By the war's end, the Arab oil embargo plunged Europe into economic disarray and political confusion.[27]

Kissinger met again with Nixon at 8:44 a.m. on Wednesday, October 17. He briefed Nixon on the military situation: "We are not slowing anything down just because he [Kosygin] is there [in Cairo]. We are pouring in arms at a rate about 30 percent greater than they do." Referring to

Cairo's demand that Israel withdraw to the 1967 border, Kissinger counseled:

> Well, I think it is unattainable, Mr. President, and in my conversations I have always fudged it and said that is an issue that should be addressed within the context of the Security Council Resolution 242 ... The major point to make to these people is to separate the ceasefire from the post-ceasefire. And the argument that I found very effective is—they want America to engage itself in the diplomacy afterwards—that you promised to do. But that means also now that the war has to be brought to an end under conditions which enable us to be in touch with all of the parties.[28]

At 9:42 a.m., Dobrynin called Kissinger to officially inform him that Kosygin was in Cairo. He added that he was sending a message from Brezhnev to the president, which had some "general" information but that was presented in an "interesting" way.[29] The letter, which was hand delivered at 10:30 a.m., stated:

> Whatever is the outcome of the present hostilities—and it is difficult to foretell it—one thing remains clear: there will be no stable peace in the Middle East unless Israel withdraws from the occupied Arab lands. This is the crust of the matter—and we are deeply convinced in it.... The opinion is being formed that the U.S. supports only one policy of Israel, the policy of expansion and annexation of foreign lands. You may disagree with that. But we would like to let you know our appraisal if both we and you want to look into the future. We, on our part, have been doing and will do everything in order not to allow such a turn. We would like to hope that the American side would act in the same way.[30]

At 11:10 a.m., Nixon and Kissinger met with a delegation of foreign ministers from Saudi Arabia, Morocco, Kuwait, and Algeria. While cordial, the ministers did not hesitate to voice their dissatisfaction with the airlift and the United States' overt support of Israel. The Saudi foreign minister Saqqaf expressed the Arab concerns:

> Israel is now being helped by the United States by force. Israel is not being threatened by the Arabs with annihilation. Your help to Israel is seen as hostile to the Arab world. We want no more than a return to the 1967 borders and respect for the rights of refugees to return to their lands or be compensated for what they have lost. This would be enough to guarantee the stability and integrity of Israel.

Nixon, who despite the travails of Watergate retained his diplomatic spark, countered that the airlift was in direct response to the Soviet military intervention. He lectured:

You say a settlement must include Israeli withdrawal from the 1967 borders. I could say, sure, we accept that, but there is no use making commitments we can't deliver on. We don't want any more broken hopes. What has happened in this tragic war, and some good usually comes of tragedy, is that the military-security situation in the Middle East has changed. This means that now conditions have been created where we can use our influence to get negotiations off dead center in moving toward a permanent, just and equitable peace such as you want.

My decision will not be affected by U.S. political considerations—ever! My decisions will be affected by my knowledge of the area and my commitment to the independence and integrity of all the states there.... I will work for a ceasefire, not in order to trick you into stopping at the ceasefire lines, but to use it as a basis to go on from there for a settlement on the basis of Resolution 242. I make this commitment to you.... We will use restraint, and we hope you will.

Nixon added, "I want to say to you that my friend, Dr. Kissinger, is a refugee from the Nazis and he is Jewish. But I assure you that he will not be moved by domestic pressures in this country." Foreign Minister Sabah of Kuwait responded, "We are happy to have Secretary Kissinger as a colleague. I want you to know that we are not anti–Jewish. We are all Semites together."[31]

Kissinger spoke with Nixon at 1:40 p.m. and told him, in his characteristically obsequious manner when dealing with the president, "I wanted to let you know, these Arabs are floating on air. They say you are a great man and that you spoke to them with a sincerity they knew you would." Nixon responded, "This meeting with the Arabs just about killed the damn press people. They expected all hell to blow up." Kissinger replied, "Well, [I] trotted out the poor foreign ministers." "At a time when we are supplying Israel," Nixon added. The president again brought up Senator Mansfield's suggestion to hold a United Nations conference. "Really something," Nixon called it. Kissinger chimed in, "[They] never support what we are doing."[32]

The WSAG met at 3:05 p.m. that day. Clements asked how Kissinger proposed to break the "logjam" in the Security Council, now that the British option had fizzled. Kissinger responded that the U.S. wanted it that way. "The worst thing," he said, "would be for some eager beaver to start moving in the Security Council until the pieces are in place." Sisco added, "If someone makes a move before everyone is prepared, we will get a Security Council resolution demanding withdrawal to the 1967 lines which we would have to veto." Kissinger then announced that he wanted a sealift to Israel, which the president supported. "We'll be much better off if we have things on ships and on their way when there is a ceasefire," he said. "Otherwise we will have to fight over every goddamned ship." Articulating his strategy, he said:

> The president has said it and I have said it. We are now in a war of attrition. Without our airlift, Israel would be dead now. We have a dual problem with Israel: we have to keep the stuff going to them for the sake of our reliability, but we must have the option to turn it off after a ceasefire if we want to. We will pay less with the Arabs for anything that is already at sea. I want to see ships popping out of harbors. Clements is the greatest expert I know at procrastination and he's also the greatest expert on speeding things up.

The subject then moved to oil. Kissinger was skeptical of an embargo. "We don't expect a cut-off now in the light of the discussions with the Arab foreign ministers this morning," he stated confidently. "Did you see the Saudi Foreign Minister come out like a good little boy and say they had had very fruitful talks with us?" Said Charles DiBona, Assistant to the President for Energy Policy, who, along with Governor John Love, had just presented a proposed emergency energy program, "The European markets are in complete disarray.... We have to be particularly careful about what we say, and have to watch very carefully this winter, even if there is no cut off." Added Governor Love, "If we get by without this extreme emergency, we will still have problems. In the Mediterranean there has already been a cutback by about 12 percent in the amount of crude available. We'll feel it in the fleet—we'll have to seek alternative sources for our ships there." Kissinger responded, "We must see to it that the Europeans can never again behave as they are behaving now." Referring to the energy program, Kissinger added, "The Arabs have to know that blackmail is a losing game."[33]

At the end of the WSAG meeting, Kissinger, who had left to see the president, returned and announced that Nixon wished to see them. Nixon, preoccupied with politics but engaged in the crisis, thanked them for their efforts and articulated his strategy for the sealift:

> I know the sealift is controversial but we must be credible. I want it to go forward. Our diplomacy will probably work before it gets there, but we must get the message to Israel and to the Soviet Union. We can't get so much to them that they will be arrogant but we can't be in the position where Israel puts pressure on Congress for us to do more.
>
> There is still lots of danger. There are lots of units in that area. The Soviets have got to choose: Will they risk our whole relationship in order to test us in the Middle East? They have got to know we won't be pushed around in our support of any nation anywhere. The second point is that we have to do enough to have a bargaining position to bring Israel kicking and screaming to the table.[34]

At 5:20 p.m. Kissinger received a call from Dinitz. He had a message from Dayan saying that he had returned from the front and "liked it very much." Dinitz added that he had talked to Meir on the telephone. "She said people are crying in Israel. She went to the airport and saw American guys coming with the planes and said it was one of the most exciting sights of her life." Dinitz stated flatly that Israel "will not accept a specific reference to the 67 borders." Kissinger assured him that "neither would the U.S."[35]

Nixon's cabinet met at 3:09 p.m. Thursday, October 18. Secretary of the Treasury George Shultz had just returned from a meeting with the Soviet leadership, whose members were concerned about Senators Jackson and Vanik's crusade to tie granting the Soviets Most Favored Nation status to reforms in Jewish emigration, a move which the Administration viewed as jeopardizing détente. In what ultimately became the Jackson-Vanik Amendment, it was a response to what were termed the Soviet Union's "diploma taxes," fees of up to $30,000—the value of a state subsidized higher education—which were levied on Jews in order to emigrate.[36] It was signed into law on January 3, 1975, by President Gerald Ford following a unanimous Congressional vote and was ultimately scrapped by President Barack Obama in 2012.[37]

"Brezhnev and Kosygin were genuinely puzzled about things going on in the United States," Schultz said. "They seemed genuinely sincere about détente. Brezhnev asked me: 'Is the problem really about Jewish emigration, or does the United States want to go back to the Cold War?' They seemed to be saying that if this is the way people think Jews will get out of the Soviet Union, they are mistaken." Nixon responded:

> The significant thing is that Brezhnev has staked his leadership on better relations with the United States. He needs us for European détente, for trade, and to keep the United States from tilting toward the Chinese. This puts the Middle East into perspective—what will they do. Last May—in May of '72—they didn't chuck us for the mining of Haiphong. Of course they must support their clients, but the question is whether they will do it at the jeopardy to all the other fish they have to fry.

The president added that before the war, Israel felt it had no incentive to negotiate. However, the situation had changed. The Israelis were battered as a result of the struggle and would be forced to reappraise the situation. Kissinger concurred, stating that Israel could not just enhance its position by military means. It had to negotiate. He elaborated on the global ramifications of the war, vis-à-vis the Soviet Union, and the need to avoid a superpower confrontation:

At the president's very first Cabinet meeting, he said that the greatest danger in the Middle East would be that local powers would draw the super powers in, as happened in World War I. We have resisted letting the local clients dictate the pace of events. Both the U.S. and the Soviet Union have friends to support. The test is whether we can support them and still retain our balance with each other.

We could have grandstanded. A Security Council resolution would just have lined people up and brought acrimony. We are trying to get a consensus before we move. When you ask whether the Soviet Union is snookering us, you have to ask what we haven't done which we would otherwise have done. In practice we have been extremely tough—in massing a great airlift, with no bases except for the Azores from the Portuguese—whom we have kicked around.

Kissinger emphasized that he had dealt moderately with the Soviets, and that the Administration's overall goal was to foster a settlement of the Arab–Israeli problem:

We have told the Soviet Union this is a test of détente but we have not thrown down the gauntlet. We have our communication lines out to the Arabs. The president met with them yesterday. We are trying to use diplomacy as a bridge to a decent settlement. We will make our case to the public after the diplomacy has concluded. What you should know is we are trying to conclude in a way to lead to a settlement; we responded to the challenge of the Soviet airlift. Soviet behavior is ambiguous. We are not trying to confront them; we believe they will be working something out.

Nixon made clear that any potential settlement could not ignore, as the Israelis hoped, a reference to U.N. Resolution 242. "The Soviet Union has a problem with the Arabs," he said. "They have done well and don't want to negotiate except on terms Israel can never buy. We are working on a ceasefire with a connection to 242." Kissinger chimed in: "242 is not a new proposal. It is very dangerous to speculate about any particular formula. The major problem now is to get the parties into a negotiation with a formula so vague that each party can save face."

Still, the immediate goal was to keep the Soviets out of Egypt, while at the same time avoiding a superpower confrontation. Said Nixon, "The key point is to try to keep the Soviet Union from sending in their own personnel. Do we want to push the Soviet Union—this is what I hear from the "new hawks"—so far that they do this and confront us with a terrible choice?" Kissinger added: "We are taking tough action but speaking softly. We should not escalate until we see how the diplomacy can work out. We are being very quiet and we have put in massive material, with only a modest reaction from the Arabs."[38]

Kissinger received a call from Dobrynin that evening at 8:45 p.m. that suggested a major shift in the Soviets' attitude. Dobrynin had a message from Brezhnev to Nixon containing the specifics of a formulation that might be included in a joint Soviet-American draft resolution to the Security Council. Dobrynin read the three key points over the telephone:

1. A call to both sides to immediately cease fire and end all military action on the positions where the troops actually are.
2. A demand to start immediately after the ceasefire a phased withdrawal of the Israeli troops from the occupied Arab territories to the line in accordance with Resolution 242, with completion of this withdrawal in the shortest period of time.
3. A decision to start immediately and concurrently with the ceasefire appropriate consultations aimed at establishing a just and honorable peace in the Middle East.

Kissinger asked, "Appropriate consultations with whom?" Dobrynin responded it should be the participants who were immediately involved in the conflict, the Soviet Union and the United States.[39]

At 9:35 p.m. Kissinger met with Nixon and informed him of the message. "They are moving in our direction but are not quite there yet," Kissinger said, adding, "I have the impression the Israelis may be doing well in the tank battle." "That will move the Russians," Nixon replied. "Well, we shouldn't count our chickens but I think you have pulled it off again," Kissinger told the president. He added, "It will take us another 48 to 72 hours."

Kissinger told Nixon he was sending a vague response in the president's name to Brezhnev to say that the president was "holding things together here" and that a "constructive outcome is highly desirable." The president advised Kissinger to "Just assure him we are prepared to follow through," adding, "We don't want them to think we'll get in cement."[40] The message, which was delivered to the Soviet Embassy at 10:30 p.m. Washington time, praised the proposal as a "statesmanlike act" and "provided the basis for a reasonable solution to the fighting, while at the same time giving the greatest possibility for negotiations to follow. The message continued:

> We share the General Secretary's view that what is going on in the Middle East is a "test of the determination of both our powers to strictly adhere to the course they took in their relations and in international affairs." For our part, we want to continue to build on the important understandings that have been achieved between us as a result of the two meets at the Summit. The crisis can and must lead to cementing the relationship between us.
>
> The situation in the Middle East is indeed complex, as the General Secretary indicates. We each have special relationships with various states in the area and both of us are in a position to influence the situation. We say this

particularly mindful of the fact that, provided we are able to achieve a cease-fire that brings with it the beginning of a process towards a fundamental settlement, there will exist new opportunities for bringing about a durable and just peace.

A new situation will have developed in the area, not based on the supremacy of one party over the other. We expect this new reality to erase the humiliation which the Arabs felt over the defeat of 1967. It will also bring about a more reasonable attitude on the part of the parties and offer hope that more than a respite between two wars can be achieved.

The message promised that "in the days ahead we will be doing a good deal of thinking" about the matter, and concluded, "We expect that once this conflict has been brought to an end, the need for a durable settlement will have become more firmly rooted, with both sides."[41]

At 10:45 p.m. Kissinger spoke with Scowcroft regarding the Soviet proposal. "Points one and three are highly acceptable," he said. Point two was not, he said, as the call for a withdrawal to 242 would be unacceptable to the Israelis. Kissinger added that the Israelis were "as obnoxious as the Vietnamese." Kissinger also commented on the military situation. The Israelis were going across with more tanks, which he feared would "turn into a turkey shoot" when the Egyptians lost the protection of the SAM belt. "They won't be able to get supplies. They'll die of starvation." Scowcroft responded, "The Israelis are very smart and audacious and willing to take chances and back them strongly."

Kissinger offered his prediction of what the consequences of the Egyptian rout would be:

It is going to turn into a nightmare. I wonder if and when I should go to China. The Russians suggested negotiations be conducted between them and us and not have any other UN members, together with the Arabs and Israelis. You can imagine what [P.R.C. Premier] Chou En Lai is going to say to this. Of course, the Europeans will go right up the wall.

Kissinger added, "I think this is the end of Sadat," and gave Scowcroft his analysis of the situation. "When all is said and done, it is a Soviet defeat. The same reasons why we could not accept an Israeli defeat will operate against them and ... that should make them [the Arabs] realize they should get on our side." He added, "In the nutty Arab world I am sort of a mythical figure. The Arabs think I'm a magician."[42]

That day, a message was sent from Dinitz to Kissinger stating Meir's concern that "any mention of 242 in connection with the ceasefire would be interpreted by the Egyptians and the Arabs as a reference to the '67 lines." It continued, "The battle is not over yet and the Soviets are already trying to dictate to Israel political moves designed not only to save their client states but also to reward them. We will not be party to such a move."[43]

On Friday, October 19, the WSAG met at 10:04 a.m. Governor Love and Charles Dibona, assistants to the president for energy policy, reported that moves by the Arab oil producing countries to curtail the oil supply had been "relatively moderate," but acknowledged that the use of oil as a "pressure point" might increase. CIA Director Colby warned: "The immediate impact of the cutback will not be very large. But the longer term impact will be greater and will place a greater degree of power in Arab hands down over the years." Colby stressed that the situation was already worse for the Europeans. "European consumption is 15 million barrels a day, 11 million of which comes from the Arabs," he injected. "That's 72 percent. They have already chewed into that by the 2 million barrel a day cut."

Chairman of the Joint Chiefs of Staff Admiral Moorer gave an update on the military situation, which was becoming increasingly bleak for the Egyptians. The Israelis had just put a bridge across the Suez Canal, which they were crossing in great numbers. "The Egyptians can't get coordinated," he reported. "They're letting the Israelis nibble them off piecemeal.... The Israelis are bombing hell out of the bridges. The Egyptians' main problem is indecision." Kissinger concluded, "We may have a massacre." Regarding diplomacy, Kissinger said he expected to hear something from the Soviet Union within a day, now that Kosygin had returned from his trip to Egypt. "We had one intelligence report," he said, "saying that the Soviets were putting the Egyptians under great pressure for a ceasefire. Their minds are beginning to work." He boasted, "I think this crisis is the best run one we've had since we came here. The next 96 hours will tell the tale."[44]

At 11:04 a.m., news from the Soviets arrived. Dobrynin called Kissinger and read the contents of a message from Brezhnev to the president suggesting that Kissinger come "in an urgent manner to Moscow to conduct appropriate negotiations with him as with your authorized personal representative. It would be good if he could come tomorrow." The tone of the message was at once urgent and conciliatory:

> The events in the Middle East become more and more dangerous. Our two powers, as we have agreed, must do the utmost in order to keep the events from going beyond the limits, when they could take even [a] more dangerous turn. If they develop along this way there is a danger that harm could be done even to the immediate relations between the Soviet Union and the United States.[45]

The reason for the meeting, said Dobrynin, was so that Kissinger could meet with Brezhnev, Alexei Kosygin, Chairman of the Council of Ministers, and Andrei Gromyko, Minister of Foreign Affairs; they could all speak freely, rather than sending telegrams back and forth. Kissinger responded, "Anatol, when the Soviet Government makes such a proposal on the basis of urgency it is not a matter we take lightly."[46]

According to Victor Israelyan, the suggestion to invite Kissinger to Moscow was made by Dobrynin, but it was not acted upon without lengthy discussion. The question most troubling to the Soviets was what if Kissinger chose to turn down the invitation. However, there were some, including Israelyan, Vasilii Kuznetsov, and Andrei Gromyko, who felt that it was Kissinger who sold the idea to Dobrynin. "He might be fishing for an invitation," Israelyan offered. "This man is a self-promoter, Vasilii," Kuznetsov opined. Gromyko agreed, positing that Kissinger had engineered the invitation in order to raise his own political standing. Nevertheless, writes Israelyan, Dobrynin's suggestion that Kissinger be invited was welcomed at the Kremlin.[47]

Kissinger wrote in his memoirs, "The invitation solved most of our strategic problems. It would keep the issue out of the United Nations until we had shaped an acceptable outcome. It would discourage Soviet bluster while I was in transit and negotiating. It would gain at least another seventy-two hours for military pressures to build."[48]

Nixon and Kissinger met at 11:34 a.m. Immediately after, Kissinger called Dobrynin to tell him that he would go, but asked why it was that Gromyko was not coming to Washington. Dobrynin explained Moscow's thinking:

> This is really the idea—not to send a telegram telling what was said by Sadat [during his meeting in Cairo with Gromyko] or what was said back and forth. They would like you for one day to come there and them I am sure [Premier Alexei] Kosygin will brief everybody. This is my impression why they are asking this one; because he is fresh to speak [about] what he was thinking and they could [all three: Brezhnev, Kosygin and Gromkyo] discuss with you.[49]

Kissinger and Dobrynin spoke again at 1:35 p.m. Kissinger requested that both parties say publicly that the invitation to conduct "urgent consultations" came at the request of the Soviet government. "You understand," Kissinger said, "[this] will present us with enormous domestic difficulties." It was agreed that an announcement would be made at 2:00 a.m., with Kissinger (and Dobrynin) having departed an hour earlier.[50]

Kissinger wrote that the visit "could not have taken place at a more complicated time from the point of view of our domestic situation."[51] Nixon was negotiating the release of the Watergate tapes. His refusal led to the resignation of Attorney General Elliot Richardson and Deputy Attorney General and Acting FBI Director William Ruckelshaus, and the firing of Special Prosecutor Archibald Cox on October 20. Two days later, the House of Representatives started impeachment proceedings against Nixon.

At 3:20 p.m. Kissinger spoke with Haig, who told him the president wanted to announce the trip that evening at the same time that he would announce that he was sending a desist order to Cox. Kissinger strongly objected, calling it a "disaster." He said, "My honest opinion is that it is a cheap stunt. It looks as if he is using foreign policy to cover a domestic thing." He added, "It will forever after be said he did this to cover Watergate. I really would plead with you." Kissinger suggested they call some newsmen "in the middle of the night." It would still be a "big thing," he said, "but not the same as having the president going on TV and announcing it."[52] The two spoke again at 3:35 p.m. Haig informed Kissinger that the president agreed to not make the two announcements simultaneously, but that he wanted the news of Kissinger's trip to come from the White House, as opposed to the State Department, that night, before the midnight press deadline to file a news report. "It is no joy to be in Moscow under these conditions, as it is," Kissinger said. "Anything the president says makes it tougher."[53]

That afternoon, in a special message to Congress, Nixon asked for $2.2 billion in emergency aid for Israel. The request marked a turning point. For the first time, the Administration was proposing to give, rather than sell, arms to Israel. In his message, the president stated: "The United States is making every effort to bring this conflict to a very swift and honorable conclusion, measured in days not weeks. But prudent planning also requires us to prepare for a longer struggle."[54]

Kissinger spoke with Dinitz at 7:09 p.m. and told him the importance of helping the president "look good" in front of the nation and ensure that he "is not accused of having sold anyone out," in the likely event that the ceasefire were linked to the implementation of Resolution 242. "You will need him very much in the diplomacy that follows," Kissinger said.[55]

At 7:17 p.m. Kissinger met with Schlesinger, Colby, Moorer, and Scowcroft, and advised them of his strategy. The trip would delay things for a few days, he said, allowing additional time for the airlift to proceed while offering the Soviets a "face-saver." He added:

> I will work for a simple ceasefire, with maybe a call for negotiations. The trouble is Israel doesn't want anything, but I may have to include a reference to 242. Everyone knows in the Middle East that if they want a peace they have to go through us. Three times they [the Arabs] tried through the Soviet

Union, and three times they failed.... Keep the aircraft going to Israel so Israel will be grateful and can't say we screwed them in their hour of triumph.[56]

Kissinger wrote in his memoirs:

We had achieved our fundamental objectives: We had created the conditions for a diplomatic breakthrough. We had vindicated the security of our friends. We had prevented a victory of Soviet arms. We had maintained a relationship with key Arab countries and laid the basis for a dominant role in postwar diplomacy. And we had done all this in the midst of the gravest Constitutional domestic crisis of a century.[57]

As Kissinger prepared to embark on his trip to the Soviet Union, he felt confident and secure in the conviction that he had played his cards right. The Israelis were making significant military advances, a direct result of the airlift. The Soviets were cooperating. The Saudis, despite threats, had yet to impose an embargo. It was difficult to anticipate that within a week, the entire situation would unravel, and the United States and Soviet Union would be headed toward a major confrontation.

CHAPTER 5

Negotiating a Ceasefire

The results of Kissinger's visit to Moscow, and of his subsequent visit to Israel, have been oft debated because of their questionable efficacy and the dubious shadow they cast on Kissinger's character. Within two days of arriving in Moscow, Kissinger and Brezhnev came to agree on terms of what would be Resolution 338 of the United Nations Security Council, which called for an immediate ceasefire to the war. However, Kissinger deliberately subordinated the wishes of Nixon, who wanted an overall settlement in the Middle East, imposed by the Soviet Union and United States. Significantly, the ceasefire broke down just as quickly as it began, when Israel resumed its military initiative and nearly devastated the Egyptian Third Army, the pride of the Egyptian forces. There is much to suggest that the Israelis were bolstered by signals from Kissinger, who in essence gave them a "green light" during his visit, indicating that a slippage on the terms of the ceasefire would be acceptable to the United States. Given the ensuing direct confrontation between the superpowers, a direct result of Israeli ceasefire breaches, Kissinger's meeting with the Israelis, the content of which was largely unknown to Nixon, had deleterious consequences.

Mr. Kissinger Goes to Moscow

On Saturday morning, October 20, Kissinger left with Dobrynin for Moscow at 2:00 a.m. He was certain that Kosygin had straightened Sadat out during his visit to Egypt. The Soviets wanted a peaceful resolution, and Egypt was no longer in a position to disagree. The United States had saved

5. Negotiating a Ceasefire

Israel from a potentially devastating military situation. Their dependence on the U.S. would be patently clear to them. Though any steps toward a settlement would have to include a reference to Proposition 242, its wording was sufficiently vague to assure Israeli compliance. Kissinger had every reason to be confident.

On the surface, the visit would be a success. The Soviets were indeed anxious to broker a ceasefire, and agreement would be quickly reached regarding the specific wording of a United Nations resolution. Yet there were spots in Kissinger's apparently flawless maneuvering. For instance, a ceasefire fell far short of Nixon's expectations, which were for Kissinger to formulate a more comprehensive solution to the problem in the Middle East. However, this strategy ran counter to that of Kissinger's objective of extricating the Soviets from the peace process. Additionally, Kissinger dismissed Nixon's hope for a wider settlement as a political ploy devised by the president to elevate himself from the quagmire of Watergate. The result was a ceasefire resolution which Kissinger neglected to present to the Israelis prior to its adoption by the United Nations Security Council. Israel, enraged, had little desire to observe the ceasefire's terms.

En route to Moscow, Kissinger sent a telegram to Scowcroft which stressed the importance to the negotiations of continuing the American airlift. Kissinger wrote:

> The negotiations I am about to undertake will be tough, and I will need to have some bargaining chips to give up should the occasion warrant. We can use it to get the Soviets to stop the airlift. Thus I want you to be extremely careful that Defense does not now begin cutting back on our effort.... If the Israelis cannot pull it off and bog down I will need all the bargaining leverage I can muster.[1]

He followed up with a second telegram to Scowcroft stating that he concluded, after speaking with Dobrynin, that the Soviet aims were indeed a joint U.S.-Soviet Security Council resolution and peace negotiations.[2]

While Kissinger was in-flight, Nixon sent a message to Brezhnev which Kissinger would later claim nearly sabotaged the negotiations. The message from Nixon stated, "Dr. Kissinger speaks with my full authority and that the commitments that he may make in the course of your discussions have my complete support."[3] Kissinger, who was unaware of the contents of the letter to Brezhnev until after he returned from his first session with the Soviets, was outraged. He intended to use ostensive consultations with Nixon as a ploy to stall and buy more time. He dispatched a message to Scowcroft saying, "I was shocked at the tone of the instructions, the poor judgment of the Brezhnev letter, and the failure to let me know in advance that a press statement would be issued." He added:

> The letter to Brezhnev has already been used against me; the General Secretary refused to accept it when I told him I would have to refer any scheme back to Washington for consideration, citing the fact that I already had full powers granted me by the president. As a result, my position is almost insoluble. If I carry out the letter of the president's instructions, it will totally wreck what little bargaining leverage I still have.... I want you to know that I consider the tone and substance of his instructions to me to be unacceptable.[4]

Nixon sent Kissinger a telegram with an even more shocking message than the one he had sent to Brezhnev. More than just seeking a ceasefire, Nixon wanted Kissinger and Brezhnev to work out the details of a total peace settlement, which directly contradicted Kissinger's strategy. Nixon wrote:

> I believe that, beyond a doubt, we are now facing the best opportunity we have had in 15 years to build a lasting peace in the Middle East. I am convinced that history will hold us responsible if we let this opportunity slip by.
>
> It is therefore even in Israel's best interests for us to use whatever pressures may be required in order to gain acceptance of a settlement which is reasonable and which we can ask the Soviets to press on the Arabs.
>
> I now consider a permanent Middle East settlement to be the most important final goal to which we must devote ourselves. U.S. political considerations will have absolutely no, repeat, no influence whatever on our decisions in this regard. I want you to know that I am prepared to pressure the Israelis to the extent required, regardless of the domestic political consequences.
>
> Please convey to Brezhnev: Tell him that this is an area, as distinguished from MFN [Most Favored Nation status] where I can deliver on commitments without the requirement for Congressional approval. Point out to him that if he and I together can be reasonable and achieve a Middle East settlement it will be without question one of the brightest stars in which we hope will be a galaxy for peace stemming from the Nixon-Brezhnev relationship.
>
> Tell him that each of us has very difficult clients and that we must therefore keep our commitments in as general terms as possible. Assure him, however, that our reluctance to be specific is not the result of any intention to avoid reaching settlement but that it is based on our conviction that this is the only way he and I will be able to get our clients in line and thereby achieve a settlement. ... The Israelis and Arabs will never be able to approach this subject by themselves in a rational manner. That is why Nixon and Brezhnev, looking at the problem more dispassionately, must step in, determine the proper course of action to a just settlement, and then bring the necessary pressure on our respective friends for a settlement which will at last bring peace to this troubled area.[5]

Kissinger recalled: "I was horrified. The letter meant that I would be deprived of any capacity to stall. Moreover, it implied that the Soviets and we would impose an overall Mideast settlement on the parties and that I was empowered to discuss that subject as well—a concession totally contrary to our strategy until now, which sought to separate the ceasefire from a political settlement." He added, "Undoubtedly, Nixon's eager involvement reflected a desire to be identified with something more elevating than the interminable and sordid legal disputes over the Watergate tapes."[6]

Kissinger's reaction is a clear indication of the extent that Watergate had cemented his dubiousness and skepticism about Nixon's ability to manage foreign affairs. Despite having received a clear and unambiguous directive from the president to broker an overall peace settlement, a position which Nixon had consistently embraced, Kissinger saw Nixon as acting from purely political motives. As a result, he remained dogged in his determination to limit Soviet involvement, and obstinate in his objective to limit negotiations to a simple ceasefire.

That evening, there was more disturbing news from Washington. In response to the U.S. airlift, Saudi Arabia had announced an oil embargo against the United States, a blow that was to shock the U.S. economy and that of its allies for months, and sour relations with the Arab world for years to come.[7]

Kissinger met with Brezhnev on October 20 at 9:15 p.m. Also in attendance were Foreign Minister Gromyko, Dobrynin, Brezhnev's aide Andrei Aleandrov, and the head of the Foreign Ministry's U.S. Department, Georgii Kornienko. Kissinger was accompanied by Joseph Sisco, Assistant Secretary of State, Helmut Sonnenfeldt, the senior staff member for the National Security Council, Alfred Atherton, Sisco's deputy, and Winston Lord, of the State Department.[8] Although Kissinger did not want to start the talks immediately upon his arrival—his policy was never to begin difficult negotiations while recovering from a change in time zones—Brezhnev invited him to the Kremlin and initiated a general exchange on U.S.-Soviet relations and a more specific dialog about the crisis in the Middle East. According to Israelyan, Brezhnev told the Politburo the next morning during its meeting that "Kissinger did not want to start negotiations immediately upon his arrival, but I insisted on it."[9]

As the meeting commenced, Kissinger asserted, "If we want to come to some understandings, I will still want to check them with the president." He added, "There are many forces in the U.S. right now that are attempting to exploit the current crisis to destroy a policy they have always opposed, namely rapprochement between the United States and the Soviet Union.

Therefore, if we should succeed in this trip to develop a joint agreement that would bring an end to the war on reasonable terms, it will be the best counterargument to these people who have claimed that we can no longer cooperate." Brezhnev responded that "[agreement] will bring an end to all allegations about the two superpowers wanting to dictate their will to others.... If we can bring an end to the gunfire, we can also bring an end to these slanderous allegations."

Kissinger recapped the three principles of Brezhnev's letter to Nixon, and said that it was basically acceptable. Regarding the second point, and its demand that Israel would withdraw its troops from the occupied Arab territories in accordance with Resolution 242, which Kissinger knew would be unacceptable to the Israelis, he said, "We can accept it in principle; the rest of it is expressed with perhaps unnecessary precision and refers to matters like 'to the line of Security Council Resolution 242.' As you know, the resolution does not establish a line, but a general principle. It contains an idea, Mr. General Secretary, and if we work on it in a spirit that you and I have expressed, we should be able to find a formulation that is mutually acceptable." He added, "It is my impression that Israel, at this moment, would reject a reference to Security Council Resolution 242. I must simply point this out for your information."

Brezhnev said, "Realistically, if our two countries could come to a conclusion, then we would be believed by all parties. If the U.S. and the Soviet Union could find an acceptable form to provide the necessary guarantees, if that were done, it would be believed by the Arab world, the Israelis and the entire world. I am convinced—because our guarantees are not taken lightly."[10]

It was not until after his meeting with the Soviets, at 3:00 a.m., that Kissinger spoke with Haig. "Will you get off my back?" Haig snapped. "I have troubles of my own." Kissinger asked, "What troubles can you possibly have in Washington on a Saturday night?" Haig replied, "The president has just fired Cox, Richardson and Ruckelshaus have resigned and all hell has broken loose."[11]

It was to become known as the "Saturday Night Massacre." Watergate Special Prosecutor Archibald Cox had refused to accept summaries of the Watergate tapes that had been prepared by Senator John Stennis. Cox wanted the tapes themselves, and he rejected Nixon's proposal that, in exchange for them, he renounce the right to subpoena further documents. That day, Nixon ordered Attorney General Elliot Richardson to fire Cox. Richardson refused, and resigned in protest. Nixon then ordered Deputy Attorney General William Ruckelshaus to fire Cox. He also refused and resigned. This series of events marked the beginning of the end of the Nixon Administration. Of his conversation with Haig, Kissinger wrote in his memoirs, "That is how I learned what troubles one can have in Washington on a Saturday night."[12]

The following day, October 21, Scowcroft responded to Kissinger's message, revealing the chokehold that Watergate had on the president's thinking. He wrote:

> You must understand that the president was demonstrating his leadership in the crisis. All the actions which took place were designed to illustrate that he was personally in charge.... The tape issue and the Richardson-Ruckelshaus-Cox affair is now dominating the news and activities here. Initial media reaction has appeared quite negative. The development of this domestic crisis gave additional impetus to efforts Saturday to show that the president's ability to govern was unaffected by Watergate related turmoil.... I was not surprised by your reaction to the message of instructions but, as you have frequently said, you need to know the president's mood and what he is thinking. That message of instructions conveyed far better than any description I could have given his mood of the moment.... Believe me, we are doing our best.[13]

On Sunday, October 21, Kissinger met again with Brezhnev and the Soviet leadership from noon until 4:00 p.m. Prior to the meeting, Kissinger received "skimpy" and ambiguous intelligence reports from Washington regarding the fighting in the Middle East. In fact, Israeli troops continued to advance on Damascus and were continuing to flank Egyptian troops west of the Suez Canal. He would later surmise that the Soviets were better informed. "For when we met Sunday noon in Brezhnev's Politburo office," he wrote, "we found the Soviet team so eager to settle that there was really no negotiation in the strict sense."[14]

Kissinger was indeed correct to assume that the Soviets were ready for a ceasefire. During the Politburo meeting that morning, Brezhnev had received word from Vladimir Vinogradov, the Soviet ambassador in Cairo, that Sadat was ready to stop the fighting. According to Israelyan's transcript of Brezhnev's account:

> I had hardly fallen asleep after I returned from the Kremlin when, at 4:00 a.m., I was awakened by Vinogradov's call. He said: "I have just been invited by Sadat, who after saying he was sorry to call at such a late hour informed me that he had returned from the command post, where his commanders reported on the situation at the front. Sadat asked me to tell Leonid Ilyich [Brezhnev] that while at the front he had decided to ask the Soviet comrades to take all possible measures to arrange an immediate ceasefire." What are the conditions?" Vinogradov asked. Sadat replied that the troops should stay

in the positions they occupied at that time; he did not mind the Israeli troops staying on the western bank of the Canal. Sadat also wanted the Soviet Union to make efforts to arrange disengagement of the troops. He expressed his desire that the Soviet Union sponsor a ceasefire motion at the Security Council. After the ceasefire, a peace conference could be held, in which the Soviet Union, the United States, and perhaps some other great power would participate.[15]

Kissinger also received encouraging news from Washington regarding Sadat's willingness to stop the fighting. A message from Ismail arrived indicating that the Egyptians might be willing to separate a ceasefire from an overall settlement. Cairo would, Ismail wrote, content itself with the convening of a peace conference and a "guarantee" by the United States and Soviet Union of the ceasefire and a speedy withdrawal of Israelis. According to Kissinger, "We were in no position to give such a guarantee, much less in conjunction with the Soviets. On the other hand, I did not consider Ismail's message Egypt's the last word on the subject either."[16]

The meeting began with Brezhnev alleging that Kissinger had accepted the three-point plan, which was not the case, particularly the second point and its references to Resolution 242. The conversation quickly moved to developing the specific wording of a ceasefire resolution. Significantly, Kissinger was determined to act in direct contradiction to Nixon's instructions. The last thing he wanted was a comprehensive peace settlement involving the Soviets. Firstly, the Israelis would never accept it. Secondly, the entire basis of his strategy was to assure U.S. dominance of, and Soviet exclusion from, a Middle East peace plan. He suggested to Brezhnev: "We try to reach agreement. We can then decide on tactics. In principle, if we reach agreement, then we should submit it soon after to the Security Council to bring about an end to hostilities."

Kissinger addressed point three of the Brezhnev proposal, which sought "a decision to start immediately and concurrently with the ceasefire appropriate consultations aimed at establishing a just and honorable peace in the Middle East." He proposed a rewording: "Call upon parties concerned to start immediately and concurrently with a cease fire appropriate negotiations under *appropriate auspices* aimed at achieving paragraph two above and aimed at establishing a just and durable peace in the Middle East."

Brezhnev wanted that he and Kissinger be clear, at least between themselves, that "appropriate auspices" meant the United States and the Soviet Union, though the resolution should not be written that way. "You and I here will agree that negotiations will be conducted under our joint auspices, and prior to adoption of this resolution, you will in confidence tell the Israelis and we the Arabs, that negotiations will be conducted under our auspices, and we will naturally be loyal to the word each of us gives each other. If you could agree to that, we will proceed, although this would not be an easy thing to achieve." Kissinger, who wanted to minimize Soviet involvement to the extent possible, proposed saying "'between the parties under appropriate auspices.'"

The two then turned to questions of timing. Kissinger wanted to give the Israelis as much time as possible to advance on the battlefield. The Soviets, in contrast, wanted the fighting to end quickly. Brezhnev proposed that the ceasefire should take place in "five hours, or three hours, or immediately" after the resolution was passed. Kissinger proposed twenty-four hours. Continuing to try to buy time, Kissinger proposed that the Security Council receive the request for a meeting at 4:00 p.m. New York time, calling for a meeting at 9:00 p.m. Gromyko stated, "What it takes is really 30 minutes to get it together."

In his memoirs, Gromyko makes little attempt to conceal his lack of enthusiasm for Kissinger, whom he characterizes as having "one particular quality of which he says nothing in his memoirs—his extraordinary ability to switch positions." He writes:

> For almost the entire period of his tenure as secretary of state, Kissinger practiced the technique of applying pressure on the Soviet Union wherever possible, whether in Asia, Africa, the Middle East or anywhere else, as a way of forcing us to make concessions. Clearly this was a straight transfer to international affairs of the sort of wheeling and dealing that goes on throughout American domestic politics, and for as long as Washington employed this approach nothing useful could be achieved in talks with us. It was only when realism triumphed and the U.S.A. learned to take account of the interests of both sides that things improved.[17]

Again, Brezhnev brought up the issue of "auspices." The continuing discussion reflected the contradictory objectives held by each. Brezhnev wanted to maximize Soviet involvement; Kissinger wanted Soviet involvement in the peace negotiations to be as little as possible. To clarify, Brezhnev said, "if we say 'auspices,' it means we should be parties in the negotiation, not just postmen. If we say 'auspices,' it means that a representative from your side and from our side takes part in whatever negotiations are held." Kissinger said they should participate "not in every detail, but in the opening phase and at critical points throughout," adding, "I must tell you honestly the Israelis will violently object to Soviet participation."

After further discussion, Kissinger stated that he needed to get in touch with the president. "The president could overrule me," he warned. "It could happen, but I tell you as a friend, it won't happen." It was agreed that each side would notify its U.N. ambassadors immediately, and that Kissinger and Gromyko would work together to draft their instructions."[18] Garthoff astutely observes, "American policy was being made almost exclusively by Kissinger. Except for Nixon's interjection on October 13 to press ahead on the airlift to Israel, and his attempt on October 20, foiled by Kissinger, to work out a comprehensive peace settlement in collaboration with the Soviet leaders, Nixon had been swamped by Watergate and other problems."[19]

Kissinger and his team drafted a letter, on behalf of the president, to Meir, which outlined the terms of the proposed resolution. It was to be immediately cabled to Scowcroft in Washington and immediately handed to Dinitz. The letter stated:

> We believe this is a major achievement for you and for us and supportive of the brave fighting of your forces. It would leave your forces right where they are: there is absolutely no mention whatsoever of the word "withdrawal" in the resolution. For the first time, we have achieved the agreement of the Soviet Union to a resolution that calls for direct negotiation without conditions of qualifications between the parties under appropriate auspices.
>
> At the same time, we and the Soviets have agreed privately to make our joint auspices available to you and to the Arabs to facilitate this process, if this is agreeable to the parties. We do not know whether this proposal will be accepted by the other side [the Arabs] because among other things it is a far distance indeed from the five-point Sadat program announced the other day.[20]

Kissinger and his team drafted a message to U.N. Ambassador Scali in New York, stressing the need for time. "Your joint instruction says we would like the resolution adopted by midnight if possible," he wrote. "You should proceed at a deliberate pace in the Security Council. I do not mean delaying the matter or appearing to delay the matter. We agreed with the Soviets to midnight as a target for adoption of the resolution because of the stress Soviets put on speed. We do not have the same interest in such speed."[21] Additionally, Kissinger sent a telegram to Scowcroft telling him to "urgently call in Dinitz" and tell him, "We would understand if Israelis felt they required some additional time for military dispositions before ceasefire takes effect. We still want to shoot for target of twelve hours' time span between Security Council decision and beginning of ceasefire but could accept Israeli's taking slightly longer."[22]

At 6:30 p.m. Kissinger met with the Soviet ambassadors from Great Britain, France and Australia to inform them of the resolution. He wanted

5. Negotiating a Ceasefire

to make sure that American allies did not pose any obstacles. "Now I obviously cannot tell your Governments what to do," he said. "But anyone who is interested in a quick end to the fighting would presumably desist from trying to make amendments to this Resolution."[23] Kissinger, content that all immediate business had been successfully been dispatched, settled in for a one hour nap.

Kissinger awoke at 8:00 p.m. and found to his "horror" that, due to either a communications glitch, or perhaps Soviet jamming, as he surmises in his memoirs, the messages had not been sent. According to Kissinger, at least four hours were lost. Lawrence Eagleburger later described his reaction in a letter he sent to Kissinger:

> I recall sitting at a desk in a fairly large room in the villa, yelling over the phone at the communications people in the Embassy.... There were some twenty to thirty people in the room, all talking, with Joe Sisco (never a quiet fellow) taking the lead.
>
> Unbeknownst to me, you walked in at that moment and obviously heard what I was saying (I still haven't figured out how). There was a bellow along the lines of: "What, the cables aren't out yet!?!" I looked up, to find you standing in the middle of the room with smoke issuing from nose, eyes, and ears, and *no one* else (with an exception I'll mention in a minute) in sight. All twenty or thirty people—no doubt led by Sisco—had exited with a speed and facility that would have put Houdini to shame. The single exception was Winston Lord, who was sort of huddled in a corner, but—God bless him—prepared to hang around for the pyrotechnics and to clean up the blood (mine) when it was all over.[24]

What Kissinger did not know was just how close the Israelis were to surrounding the Egyptian Third Army. A report prepared by the State Department that evening stated, "If the Israelis manage to cut the Cairo-Suez route and continue to block the Cairo-Ismailia road, DIA estimates the Egyptian forces on the east bank would have only three to five days' supply remaining."[25]

Meanwhile, the oil embargo was underway. The Saudi Arabian Oil Company (Aramco) had ceased to load any oil tankers with U.S. destinations. The State Department estimated that if Saudi Arabia were to implement a ban on indirect shipment to the U.S. through Caribbean refineries, the immediate loss to the U.S. could be one million barrels per day. Losses were already at one million barrels daily as a result of cuts from other Arab countries.[26]

On Monday, October 22, at 8:45 a.m., Kissinger met with Gromyko. The two initialed a private agreement that stated that "under appropriate auspices" was intended to mean "the active participation of the United

States and the Soviet Union at the beginning and thereafter in the course of negotiations when key issues of a settlement are dealt with." Additionally, both agreed that the United States and the Soviet Union "will both use their maximum influence with the parties to the conflict to ensure that all POW's will be released within no later than 72 hours following the ceasefire," a subject that was of paramount importance to the Israelis.

Kissinger, who was going from Moscow to Israel, told Gromyko that he had set two conditions on the Israelis regarding his visit: "They had to accept the resolution and there had to be substantial compliance with the resolution." They had accepted both conditions, he said.[27] This could not have been further from the truth. Israel had not been consulted by Kissinger while he was in Moscow. According to Israeli journalist Matti Golan, Golda Meir was "shocked and furious" when, at 10:00 p.m. Israeli time, Ambassador Keating delivered to her the terms for the ceasefire—which Kissinger had already signed. Golan writes:

> The reports of [Israeli Minister of Foreign Affairs Abba] Eban and Dinitz had given her a firm basis for believing that the Moscow talks would end inconclusively. The last thing she expected, particularly after Kissinger's reassurances to Eban and Dinitz, was that he would put his own signature on an agreement without even consulting her. Mrs. Meir never said flatly that Kissinger had betrayed Israel, but this idea was obviously uppermost in her thoughts. At no time, however, did she suggest rejection of the agreement.
>
> As if to pour salt on her wounds, at a few minutes past midnight she received an urgent phone call from the British ambassador. She took the call during the cabinet meeting. The ambassador told her that a very urgent telegram from Sir Alec Douglas-Home had just arrived in which the British foreign minister implored the prime minister to consent to the Moscow agreement. Mrs. Meir said, "Thanks," making it sound more like a curse, and slammed down the receiver. She and the other ministers now realized that not only did Kissinger not consult her, but he informed her of the agreement after he told the British foreign minister—a conclusion simply reached by simply allowing for the time necessary for the British to route the message to Israel.[28]

Minutes before the ceasefire went into effect, an alarming event occurred, though its consequences were to be more symbolic than consequential. For the first time in history, SCUD missiles were fired, by the Egyptians at Israeli targets, an ironic development given that the expectation on both sides was that the war was drawing to a close. There are different accounts of the incident.

In Israelyan's account, there was escalating frustration among the

Egyptian leadership and the Soviet military advisors in Cairo that the most dangerous and advanced weapons on Egyptian soil had not been used. Vinogradov, the Egyptian ambassador tried to reach Gromyko, who was unavailable; instead he contacted Andrei Grechko, the minister of defense. "Go the hell ahead and fire it," was Grechko's order. Writes Israelyan: "When he learned of Grecko's order, Gromyko was outraged and strictly prohibited Vinogradov from carrying out the order. 'I am sorry, Andrei Andreyevich [Gromyko], I can't help it. The missiles have already been fired,'" Vinogradov replied.[29]

In contrast, Sadat writes in his version: "On October 22, just before the ceasefire came into effect, I went to the Operations Room and ordered two ground-to-ground rockets fired at Deversoir. I wanted Israel to learn that such a weapon was indeed in our hands and that we could use it at a later stage of the war; even though Israel had in fact realized from the moment the war broke out that we meant and did what we said."[30]

The "Green Light" in Jerusalem

Kissinger's visit to Israel, though amicable and productive by all appearances, set the stage for potential disaster. Already apprehensive about his meeting, where he knew he would be chastised for his inclusion of Proposition 242 in the U.N. ceasefire resolution, Kissinger went to great lengths to ingratiate himself with the Israelis. However, in so doing, he left the Israelis with the solid impression that he would turn a blind eye to any Israeli infractions of the ceasefire agreement, at least until he returned to Washington. The Israelis, never prone to decline an opportunity when presented with one, came dangerously close to devastating the Egyptian Third Army. The Soviet reaction, and the American counter-reaction, brought the two superpowers within arm's reach of a major confrontation. Kissinger's "green light" would prove to be a gaffe that he would long regret.

When Kissinger left for Israel, at 10:00 a.m. on October 22, Security Council Resolution 338 had been unanimously passed 14–0 about nine hours earlier. He arrived at 1:00 p.m. local time, and Abba Eban, the Israeli foreign minister, met him at the airport. In his memoirs, Eban wrote: "He seemed apprehensive when I told him that Golda was waiting for him. It sounded like a summons to see a stern headmistress."[31] Leonard Garment, the occasional U.S. envoy to Israel, was somewhat more generous in his summation of the only major international leader that Kissinger would refer to by using her first name: "[She] radiated a warm intelligence that reminded American Jews of their nurturing, nagging mothers. (Just ask Henry Kissinger.)"[32]

In her biography, *Golda*, Elinor Burkett writes that Meir and Kissinger were "oil and water." She continues:

> She never had much patience with intellectuals and she worried, too that that the American secretary of state was a bit of a self-hating Jew. While he'd been raised in an observant home, Kissinger had been sworn into office on a Saturday, thus forcing his Orthodox parents to walk to the White House, and used Nixon's personal copy of the King James version of the Bible rather than the Old Testament published in his hometown in Germany that his parents had brought with them.... "There's no greater expert on American policy than Kissinger," she once reported after he's issued yet another treatise on how Israel should conduct itself. "But on Israeli policy, I have my PhD."[33]

Kissinger met with Meir at 1:35 p.m. According to Meir's biographer, Elinor Burkett, the reception was even chillier than expected. "Why didn't you contact us during negotiations?" she scolded. When Kissinger responded that the Soviets had jammed his communications equipment, she retorted, "How did you stay in touch with your president, then?" Kissinger mentioned the verbal promise by Brezhnev that prisoners would be exchanged after the ceasefire. "What else did you agree to that's not written down?" she badgered.[34]

Kissinger offered Meir his reassurances, by painting the reference to the resolution as a diplomatic victory:

> During the summit, one method we used to avoid agreement was to refer to 242, and we succeeded. So in the president's mind, getting a reference to 242 is a success.
>
> He has been under tremendous pressure from the Arabs and from the oil people for a return to the 1967 borders. So, to refuse a reference to 242 would have been absolutely impossible in those conditions. And the reference to 242 gives you reference to secure and recognized borders. I want to tell you there are no side understandings on 242.

Kissinger told Meir, in another indication that he was willing to grant the Israelis some leeway, "If I were you—I'm not advising you—I would not begin negotiations until it [a ceasefire] happens. You'd be entitled to do nothing." Meir expressed her gratitude. "Without you," she told Kissinger, "I don't know where we would have been. I went to the airfield the other day and I watched the planes come in. It was more than I could ever have dreamed." She added, "We would have been in a better position [for a ceasefire] in a few days." Kissinger asked if she had received his message which stated, "If you needed a few hours at the other end...," Meir said it was "garbled." In a move he would later regret, Kissinger clarified his position. "You won't get violent protests from Washington if something happens during the night, while I'm flying. Nothing can happen in Washington until noon tomorrow," he said. "If they don't stop, we won't," she responded. Kissinger added, "Even if they do..."[35]

Writing later of when he learned that the Israeli troops had continued to advance after the ceasefire had gone into effect, Kissinger conceded: "I ... had a sinking feeling that I might have emboldened them." Israeli accounts are more explicit. According to Garthoff, one anonymous source told him that Kissinger had said with a wink, "In Vietnam, the ceasefire didn't go into effect at the exact time that was agreed upon."[36]

During a luncheon with Israeli leaders, Kissinger discussed the military situation and ceasefire. Of the Arabs, Dayan said, "They kept fighting ... they were determined, fanatic. It was a sort of jihad." Regarding negotiations, Kissinger said, "Once we get talks started, we're not going to float an American plan. That's not my plan or my method. I've been telling this to every Arab minister. They ask me, 'Will you use your influence with Israel?' And I say, 'There is nothing to use our influence about.'" He added, "The beginning of the process will be an historic event, even if it totally stalemates—which I expect, frankly." He clarified that U.N. involvement would be minimal, stating contemptuously, "We don't think Jarring or Waldheim is "appropriate auspices."[37]

At 4:15 p.m. Kissinger attended a military briefing by the Israeli army and air force chiefs of staff and the director of military intelligence. Army Chief of Staff General David Elazar said, "We didn't manage to finish the Third Army. We think it is possible to do it in two, maybe three days. We're in a very good advance, toward the Suez Canal. The idea was to encircle the Third Army and destroy and capture its forces."

Kissinger said nothing to dissuade Elazar or stress that the destruction of the Third Army would be unacceptable to the U.S. For this, he has been sharply criticized. In his memoirs, he attempts to explain his silence:

> There were grumbles about how Egypt's Third Army might have been fully encircled and destroyed in another three days of fighting. But these were the same leaders whose repeated predictions—"we need three more days"—had consistently been proved overoptimistic. Besides, there was no scenario by which Israel could have been given three more days without risking a superpower crisis and destroying the American position in the Arab world. Their tone was wistful, rather than recriminatory; more a nostalgia for the glories of 1967 than a reflection of the reality of the hour. The Third Army ... did not loom large in the discussions.[38]

Isaacson writes, "With Israeli leaders chafing to complete the encirclement of the Third Army, Kissinger made a bad mistake ... that he later claimed that he had in mind a few hours, not days."[39] According to Lebow and Stein, "Some participants in the meetings allege that Kissinger quietly encouraged Israel to violate the cease-fire and continue its offensive, at least for several hours. Others insist that Kissinger was singularly focused on the importance of Israel obeying the ceasefire."[40] Joseph Sisco, for instance, said of the meetings, "We took a tough line, a very tough line. The environment was very hostile. Golda Meir was furious. We took a very firm line."[41]

In an interview with Lebow and Stein, Kissinger denied that he encouraged Israel to violate the ceasefire:

> I did not encourage the Israelis. I did not want to see the Third Army destroyed. I thought they were emotionally exhausted and did not need a big sales pitch for a cease-fire. After all, they had gotten the direct negotiations that they had always wanted. I didn't press them because I didn't think that they needed to be pressed. I did not encourage the Israelis with more than minor adjustments. It is quite possible that the commanders in the field ran away with Golda.[42]

Nonetheless, he inadvertently created false expectations in Israel. This was in part, Kissinger claims, because he possessed limited military intelligence. As he relates in an interview with Lebow and Stein:

> Their [Israel's] major offensive was in the north. They told me that their armies were advancing in the north. I told them that they could horse around in the north for a few hours but that was it. I tried to stop them but I couldn't figure out where their armies were. We were looking toward the north. We were not looking in the south. Our satellites were fixed. We couldn't move them around. We were looking north. We didn't know where the Israeli army was."[43]

Lebow and Stein conclude that Kissinger "underestimated the difficulty of persuading Israel to accept an immediate cease fire and did not warn explicitly against a contingency that he thought was unlikely." They criticize Kissinger for paying too little attention to the mechanics of the ceasefire. The authors write, "Because the technical details of the ceasefire got only desultory attention, some Israelis at the meeting concluded that Kissinger was not overly concerned with its implementation on schedule."[44]

In their analysis, Kissinger's failure to warn explicitly against further military action was in some part due to" his personal conflict about the message he brought to Tel Aviv." He had promised Israel that he would consult with them before coming to any ceasefire agreement. In an interview with Kissinger, he acknowledged feeling guilty about the delay in communications from Moscow. Lebow and Stein also interviewed Peter Rodman, who confirmed that Kissinger felt "very guilty" about the communications failure because it shortened the preparation time he could give the Israelis. They add, "Yet Henry was stuck because Nixon undercut him by delegating authority to him and denying him the time to delay. Uneasy and guilty about the shortened warning time he had provided, Kissinger misled Israel's leaders about the impact of 'minor' violations of the ceasefire."[45]

The ceasefire went into effect at 1:12 p.m. (7:12 p.m. Cairo time), twenty minutes after the scheduled time. At 4:08 p.m. it began to unravel. The IDF announced that the Egyptians had opened fire on Israeli forces at a number of locations. Though Israeli and Egyptian reports from the battlefield varied, the Israelis boasted that their forces held a bridgehead on the west bank 32 kilometers deep and 40 kilometers wide, astride both the Cairo-Ismailia and the Cairo-Suez city roads, leaving Cairo in an exposed position.

In the meantime, unknown to Kissinger, Watergate frenzy had detonated. He received a cable from Haig:

> Unfortunately, you will be returning to an environment of major national crisis which has resulted from the firing of Cox and the resulting resignation of Richardson and Ruckelshaus. Because the situation is at a state of white heat, the ramifications of the accomplishments in Moscow have been somewhat eclipsed and their true significance underplayed. For this reason, it is essential that you participate fully in maintaining the national perspective and that a major effort be made to refocus national attention on the president's role in the Middle East settlement. An impeachment stampede could well develop in the Congress tomorrow although we are confident that cooler heads will prevail if the president's assets are properly applied.[46]

That evening, on a stop at Heathrow Airport on his way to brief Sir Alec Douglas-Home, Kissinger learned that impeachment proceedings were indeed beginning.[47]

Diplomatically, the situation was far from perfect. Israel did not agree to a ceasefire on the Syrian front; Syria had not yet agreed to accept the Security Council resolution. Iraq and Libya had outright rejected it. And the Executive Committee of the PLO has announced that the Fedayeen would continue to fight against Israel.[48]

Barry Blechman and Douglas Hart astutely argue that what Kissinger said to Meir in their meeting is much less important than the consequences. Kissinger left Israel believing that the end of the war was near and that with diplomacy any difficulties could be diffused. The Israelis were left with the understanding that they had some time to carry out their military objectives. And the Soviets, they write, "thought that Kissinger had taken them to the cleaners." They continue:

> This feeling of betrayal seems to have been central in determining Moscow's subsequent behavior. Kissinger himself apparently empathized. Upon learning that Israel had completed surrounding the Third Army after the cease-fire deadline, he is reported to have exclaimed, "My God, the Russians will think I double-crossed them. And in their shoes, who wouldn't?"[49]

Whether his motives were guilt over his delayed communication to Meir, a personal aspiration to see the Israelis maximize the impact of its final blow to Egypt, or a desire to score points with Israel that might be useful when he would later attempt to extract concessions from them, he would come to regret that he had handed them a green light to continue their advance. In the next two days, Israel would demonstrate an audacious resolution to continue its persecution of the Egyptian Third Army. The result was the one thing that the United States and Soviet Union most feared—a superpower showdown.

CHAPTER 6

The Failure to Avoid a Superpower Confrontation

During the next two days, what had been a regional conflict indirectly involving the two superpowers exploded into a direct confrontation between the United States and the Soviet Union. When Brezhnev suggested that the Soviet Union, in response to Sadat's pleas for assistance, might unilaterally send troops into Egypt, Kissinger and the WSAG ordered that U.S. forces be placed on DEFCON III, an alert entailing nuclear readiness. Numerous scholars—as well as the contemporary press—have argued that this was a drastic and dangerous overreaction that unnecessarily raised the stakes and brought the world within arm's reach of a global catastrophe.[1] Significantly, the decision was made in the absence of direct presidential authority. Nixon was largely, if not completely, absent from the WSAG deliberations that resulted in the DEFCON decision. Although the end result was an apparent, though arguable success, ultimately resulting in an end of overt hostilities, Kissinger may have exceeded his authority in bringing to bear needless force to counter what was likely to have been nothing more than a Soviet bluff to send troops to the Middle East. His actions demonstrate the most grave of Kissinger's miscalculations during the crisis, a direct result of his Cold War reductionism and willingness to employ brinkmanship in order to accomplish regional geostrategic objectives. That such a decision was undertaken in the absence of presidential authority makes it all the more egregious.

Israel Breaks the Ceasefire

Kissinger arrived in Washington on Tuesday, October 23, at 3:00 a.m. While en route, he felt confident that his trip had been an outstanding success. The negotiations with the Soviets could not have gone more smoothly. It had been just a little over two weeks since the war began, and he felt the self-assurance of a job well done. Kissinger had no idea that in the next two days, the entire situation would unravel. It would call into question Nixon's ability to govern, raise issues about the broad extent of Kissinger's authority, and jeopardize U.S.–Soviet relations and the very survival of détente. The next forty-eight hours would bring the United States and the Soviet Union close to the possibility of nuclear war.

After a few hours' sleep, Kissinger arrived at his office and found two messages, each with disturbing news. The first message was from Ismail, informing him that Israeli forces had broken the ceasefire, and were in the process of occupying new positions in Egypt. Egypt was taking "all necessary measures to ensure its security."[2] The second message was from the U.S. ambassador to Israel, Keating, who summarized a meeting he had had with Meir. She had noted that there was "considerable opposition to the government's action" regarding approval of the ceasefire. Keating related to Meir a conversation he had with the British Ambassador, who was concerned that there were "some major differences" between the U.S. and Israel over the resolution. "Perfidious Albion," she replied.

Keating expressed to Meir that there "would be some who might view with some skepticism information from GOI [Government of Israel] sources and who would wonder whether or not the Israelis might not be acting in violation of the ceasefire in order to achieve certain military objectives." Meir rebutted: "Israeli military commanders 'pleaded' for two or three days more time in the South in order to finish off the Egyptians." However, she said, "the Cabinet said a flat no and the orders went out that the ceasefire must be respected scrupulously." Israel, however, had "ordered its troops to continue fighting until unless the Egyptians stop." Keating was troubled. Reading between the lines, he expressed to Kissinger his concern that "the Israelis are going to shoot back, and if Egyptian attacks continue, I would not be at all surprised if the Israelis were to launch an attack designed to wipe out the Egyptian Third Army." He added, "If things reach this point, I'm not sure what kind of a ceasefire will be left to build upon."[3]

Kissinger shared Keating's skepticism. He remembered:

> The previous day's military briefing in Tel Aviv did not suggest a substantial Egyptian offensive potential; nor did the first part of Golda's remarks to

Keating imply that Israel commanders would be meticulous about the ceasefire...

I had indicated that I would understand if there was a few hours' "slippage" in the ceasefire deadline while I was flying home, to compensate for the four hours lost through the communications breakdown in Moscow. But this new fighting was continuing far beyond the brief additional margin I had implied. We were by now nearly twenty hours beyond the deadline. Nor did the Israelis claim—then or ever—that they had any sanction for their efforts save self-defense.[4]

U.N. Secretary-General Waldheim called Kissinger at 9:30 a.m. to report that the Egyptians were formally complaining of Israeli ceasefire violations and asking for a Security Council Meeting. U.S. intelligence confirmed Israeli military activity. A State Department report stated, "Israel pushed enormous quantities of equipment across the Canal during the night ... and succeeded in considerably strengthening its position on the West Bank." It also reported Egyptian troops were bitter at Sadat's decision to conclude a ceasefire.[5]

There were other ominous developments. The Egyptian state publication, *Al Ahram*, was claiming that "when Sadat received the U.S.—Soviet draft and accepted the ceasefire, it was based on 'full Israeli withdrawal from all occupied lands' and safeguarding of legitimate Palestinian rights." This was not the case. Firstly, the Israelis never would have agreed to it. Secondly, the wording of Proposition 242 was sufficiently ambiguous to offer them plenty of wiggle room. In Israel, the Likud opposition issued a declaration stating that the implementation of the Security Council resolution "will not lead to peace but will endanger Israel's security," and that a vote may be taken in the Knesset on Meir's decision to accept the ceasefire resolution."[6] If the ceasefire was still in place, it was tenuous.

Yuli Vorontsov, Minister Counselor of the Soviet Embassy, delivered to Kissinger a message from Brezhnev, at 9:30 a.m., stating that Sadat had officially informed the Soviets that Israel was in violation of the Security Council resolution. This, he claimed, was confirmed by Moscow's "own reliable information." The message reflected Brezhnev's outrage. He wrote, "This is absolutely unacceptable," adding, "All this looks like as a flagrant deceit on the part of the Israelis. We will express the confidence that the United States will use all the possibilities they have and its authority to bring the Israelis in order." Brezhnev suggested that the Soviet Union and United States "urgently submit to the Security Council a draft of appropriate resolutions" confirming Resolution 338 and demand "that the forces of the sides should be withdrawn to the position where they were at the moment of the adoption of the decision on ceasefire." He proposed that the U.S. and Soviet Union jointly request Waldheim to dispatch UN observers to supervise the observation of the ceasefire.[7]

Kissinger suggested to Vorontsov that they delay the start of the Security Council meeting until 2:00 p.m. and proposed that they delete any references to withdrawal to the ceasefire line, as it would lead to endless debate. Vorontsov responded sarcastically that obviously the Israelis had made gains or Kissinger would not have raised the issue. Kissinger said he would instruct John Scali, U.S. Ambassador to the U.N., to agree to Brezhnev's request.[8]

Kissinger realized that the situation was becoming graver. He saw that his entire strategy might completely unstitch. If Israel continued its assault, and the U.S. did nothing, his chances of emerging as an impartial peace broker would be seriously reduced. He writes in his memoirs:

> We were in a serious predicament. The urgency of Brezhnev's appeal suggested that the plight of the Egyptian Third Army was far more serious than our own intelligence had yet discovered or the Israelis had told us. If the United States held still while the Egyptian army was being destroyed after an American-sponsored ceasefire and a Secretary of State's visit to Israel, not even the most moderate Arab could cooperate with us any longer."[9]

Kissinger spoke with Dinitz at 11:04 a.m., who said that Meir wanted him to assure Kissinger "personally, confidentially and sincerely that none of the actions taken on the Egyptian front were initiated by us." Though Kissinger was doubtful, he did not express any misgivings to Dinitz. Rather, he informed Dinitz of the Soviet proposal, and told him that the U.S. would not accept a call for a withdrawal to the lines at the time the ceasefire went into effect; however, it would accept it with the stipulation of the ceasefire lines removed.[10] Kissinger wrote, "With all my affection for Golda, I thought she was imposing on my credulity with her definition of 'initiate,'" adding, "It was not plausible that the Egyptian Third Army should launch attacks after a ceasefire that had saved it from being overwhelmed; and that it should then immediately ask everyone within reach for yet another ceasefire, shooting all the time at passive Israelis who were only defending themselves while advancing."

Meir called Kissinger a few minutes later to repeat her assurances. Kissinger suggested that Israel pull back a few hundred yards from wherever it was and "call it the old ceasefire line." He asked, "How can anyone ever know where a line is or was in the desert?" Meir replied, "They will know where our present line is, all right." Kissinger later wrote, "Now I

6. The Failure to Avoid a Superpower Confrontation 141

understood. Israel had cut the last supply route to the city of Suez. The Egyptian Third Army on the east bank of the Canal was totally cut off. A crisis was upon us."[11]

At 11:25 a.m. Kissinger called Vorontsov to tell him that he had met with the president, and that Nixon wanted to delay the Security Council proposal. Whether or not he actually spoke to Nixon is questionable, as Kissinger had by now adopted the regular practice of speaking in the president's name. More precisely, as was evident in Moscow, Kissinger was not averse to taking a stance that ran directly counter to that of Nixon, to whom he frequently referred as "my drunken friend," as well as "this deeply tortured man," "paranoid," "flawed," "very strange," and "weird."[12] Vorontsov quipped, "Oh, that doesn't mean that the Israelis will take some more 50 miles of territory." Kissinger advised Vorontsov that the U.S. "definitely cannot accept" the phrase that both sides would withdraw to the position where they were at the adoption of the decision on the ceasefire." The U.S. would only consider a return to "where they were at the moment the ceasefire went into effect."[13]

Dinitz called Kissinger at noon, saying that the Israelis had objections about returning to the "original place," saying that he had intelligence that the Egyptians had opened an attack that inflicted considerable damage. Kissinger, who was growing frustrated with Israel protestations, asked what difference it made. "It makes only a difference in the sense that it would allow the Russians and the Egyptians to demand withdrawal of our forces on some of the positions that they are right now as a result of the Egyptian violation," Dinitz replied. Kissinger responded that the U.S. could abstain from a resolution saying that the parties would withdraw to their positions "at the time of the decision," but that they couldn't veto one that stated a withdrawal to the lines when the Resolution went into effect. "The easy way to settle it is to go back to the line," Kissinger urged, though he deemed it to be "indeterminable."[14] Of the conversation, Kissinger recalled, "Its essence was that Israeli forces would not withdraw from the positions they now held."[15]

Moscow continued to pressure Washington to, in turn, put pressure on the Israelis to observe the ceasefire. At 12:36 p.m. Brezhnev sent an urgent message to Nixon over the hotline stating, "Israel had flagrantly violated the Security Council decision." It went on: "We in Moscow are shocked that the understanding which was reached only two days ago has in fact been ruptured by this action by the Israeli leaders. Why this treachery was allowed by Israel is more obvious to you." The solution, Brezhnev wrote, was "in forcing Israel to immediately obey the Security Council decision." He added: "Too much is at stake, not only as concerns the situation in the Middle East, but in our relations as well."[16]

Kissinger was relieved that Brezhnev's message concentrated "simply on stopping the fighting," ignoring the question of "whether Israel should withdraw and to what line."[17] At 1:10 p.m. a reply went out "under Nixon's name" via the hotline:

> I want to assure you that we assume full responsibility to bring about a complete end of hostilities on the part of Israel. Our own information would indicate that the responsibility for the violation of the ceasefire belongs to the Egyptian aide, but this is not the time to debate that particular issue. We have insisted with Israel that they take immediate steps to cease hostilities, and I urge that you take similar measures with respect to the Egyptian side. You and I have achieved an historic settlement over this past weekend and we will not permit it to be destroyed.[18]

Twenty-five minutes later, Kissinger called Vorontsov to convey the U.S. decision to support a joint U.S-Soviet resolution for a ceasefire and for a return to the positions occupied when the ceasefire became effective. Kissinger said rather than fighting, it would be "better to argue about where the line is." He expected that to be a long debate. "Let them argue but just not fight," replied Vorontsov, who agreed to convey the message to Moscow.[19] Vorontsov called back almost immediately later to say that Moscow had accepted the proposal.[20]

Yet Moscow was not satisfied. At 2:26 p.m. Brezhnev took what Kissinger calls "the unheard-of step" of sending another message to the president, stating that the "Egyptian side is ready to cease fire immediately if the Israeli armed forces will cease fire." He requested that the president "categorically notify the Israeli government of this" as well as that the Security Council be convened "most urgently."[21]

Meanwhile, protestations from Israel mounted. That afternoon, the Administration received a scorching message from Golda Meir, stating: "It is impossible for Israel to accept that time and again it must face Russian and Egyptian ultimatums which will subsequently be assented to by the United States." She informed the Administration that Israel would not comply "or even talk about" the proposed resolution.[22] Kissinger concludes in his memoirs that Israel "seemed determined to end the war with a humiliation for Egypt."[23] Yet at no point did he confront Meir and warn that the continuation of Israeli aggression on the battlefield would be unacceptable to the United States. Such a strong message, given Israeli dependence on the U.S., would not have gone unheeded. Just as he emboldened the Israelis by allowing them some leeway in their observance of the ceasefire, his

6. The Failure to Avoid a Superpower Confrontation 143

reticence might very well have been interpreted by Meir as a "green light," to continue its aggression.

At 3:15 p.m. Sadat sent an urgent backchannel message to Nixon, formally requesting that the United States intervene, "even if that necessitates the use of forces, in order to guarantee the full implementation of the ceasefire resolution in accordance with the joint U.S.–U.S.S.R. agreement." Significantly, it was the first direct message from Sadat—the United States and Egypt had not had diplomatic relations for six years. The message continued: "We were asked to comply with the ceasefire resolution with the full understanding of the effectiveness of the joint guarantees. I hope that this intervention would be immediate and direct because Israel is taking advantage of the ceasefire to change completely the situation on the military front."[24]

Kissinger responded that evening, again on behalf of Nixon, dispelling the idea that there had been a guarantee: "Let me be equally frank, so that there will be no misunderstanding between us. All we guaranteed—no matter what you may have been told from other sources—was to engage fully and constructively in promoting a political process designed to make possible a political settlement." He added that the Administration was making "urgent representations" to Israel that it comply with Security Council Resolution 338, and recommending that Egypt do the same.[25]

At 8:30 p.m. there emerged the appearance of a respite. Dinitz called Kissinger to relay the message that Meir gave her "solemn pledge" that if the Egyptians did not shoot, the Israelis would not shoot either.[26] That evening, the Security Council passed Resolution 339 which called for the return of both sides back to the position they held when the ceasefire came into effect, and included a request from the United Nations secretary-general to undertake measures toward the placement of observers to supervise the ceasefire. Later that evening, Syria announced its formal acceptance of the ceasefire.

On Wednesday, October 24, the United States was to use the threat of nuclear readiness as a political weapon in its dealings with the Soviet Union for the first time since the Cuban Missile Crisis.[27] Kissinger arrived in his office at 8:00 a.m. to receive a message from Ismail informing him that "the Israelis have resumed their attacks" and that Sadat would be communicating with Nixon urgently to seek "effective measures to oblige Israel to observe the ceasefire."[28] An hour and a half later, Kissinger reached Dinitz by phone, who claimed that "the ceasefire went into effect and then the Egyptian Third Army tried to make efforts to break out of the siege.... A big battle has developed over which we are just blocking the Third Army from getting out of the siege." Kissinger replied, "Look, Mr. Ambassador, we have strong support for you, but we cannot make Brezhnev look like a goddamn fool in front of his own colleagues." Dinitz suggested that the U.S. military attaché in Tel Aviv be dispatched to the area to observe the situation.[29] In a conversation a few minutes later, Kissinger warned him, "If you wind up tonight having captured 20,000 Egyptians you won't be able to tell us that they started the fighting."[30]

Kissinger called Dobrynin at 9:45 a.m. and said, "Anatol, the madmen in the Middle East seem to be at it again." He explained that the Israelis claimed that they were being attacked, and that the Administration had sent a message to them demanding that the fighting be stopped. "This time the Egyptians may have started it," he said, "but we are not sure. We have no basis for judgment." Kissinger added, "One thing that Moscow is to understand [is that] we are not playing any games here. We made an agreement and it's now going to be enforced."[31]

Kissinger's next step was to attempt to reassure Sadat. He sent a backchannel message in Nixon's name at 10:17 a.m. stating, "We have just been informed by the Israeli prime minister that strict instructions have been issued to Israeli armed forces to stay in defensive positions and not to fire unless they are fired upon." He informed Sadat that U.S. military attachés were being sent into the area to ensure the orders were carried out.[32]

The crisis escalated. At 10:19 a.m., Dobrynin called Kissinger with a message to Nixon from Brezhnev. "Mr. President," read its notably formal salutation, "We have precise information that the Israeli troops are attacking now with tanks and military ships on Egyptian forces on the western part of the Suez Canal." Brezhnev's message continued:

> We are sure that you have responsibility to make clear to Israel that the troops should immediately stop their actions of provocation. We would like to hope that you and we would be loyal to our words which were given to each other and to the agreement we have reached with you. We would very much appreciate your message about the steps which are taken by you in order to insure that Israel will obey the second Security Council decision.[33]

Kissinger promised a response within several hours and asked Dobrynin to transmit a message to Brezhnev that the spirit of the weekend continued, and "we are not in a game of escorting five mile advantages which mean nothing to you or us."[34]

Following the phone conversation, at 10:21 a.m., Kissinger convened a meeting of the WSAG. Still optimistic, he told the group:

6. The Failure to Avoid a Superpower Confrontation 145

> I think we have come out in the catbird seat. Everyone has come to us since we are the only ones who can deliver. I think this will be true in the diplomacy, too.... We have made some real gains in the last few weeks, since everyone has learned that the U.S. is the essential ingredient. Israel has learned that they can't fight a war without an open American supply line—they can't stockpile enough to do it. That is the lesson they have learned. Their casualties are enormous.
>
> The Arabs may despise us, or hate us, or loathe us, but they have learned that if they want a settlement, they have to come to us. No one else can deliver. Three times they have relied on Russian equipment, and three times they have lost it. So, strategically, we have a very good hand if we know how to play it. All the Arabs have approached us, from the most radical to the most conservative.
>
> Our strategy is to hold these cards and to get a settlement. We cannot tolerate continuation of the status quo. On the other hand, we want to keep the supplies going in until we have a concrete proposal to put before the Israelis. It would be premature to start nit-picking them now, although we were brutal today with the Israelis in stopping the military activity...
>
> I'd like to arrange a meeting between [Vietnam's] Thieu and Golda and Duc and Dayan. They deserve each other.[35]

Given the severity with which events were unfolding, Kissinger's self-confidence is striking. In continuing to supply the Israelis while they continued to devastate the Egyptian Third Army, he was taking a big gamble that the Arabs would trust the U.S in future negotiations. Remarkably, Kissinger, throughout the course of events, significantly underplays the potentially crippling effect of Arab ire, as would become manifest in the oil crisis of 1973 and 1974, which had a serious, though debated effect on the American economy. Importantly, when viewed in retrospect, Kissinger seems heedless to the great blow that unrelenting U.S. support would wield to American standing in the Middle East for decades, by setting the stage for an antipathy that would be nurtured by years of uncritical U.S. support despite Israel's systematic violations of United Nations resolutions.

The group agreed that a team of U.S. military observers from the Defense Attaché's office in Tel Aviv would be sent to the East bank of the Suez Canal as ground observers and that the resupply sealift to Israel would be accelerated. Once underway, the airlift would be terminated. It was decided to send a U.S. team to Israel to determine the extent of damage, and to conduct an air reconnaissance mission over Egypt to take photographs. Kissinger boasted, "I think this is the best-run crisis we have ever had."[36]

Kissinger sent another backchannel message to Sadat, at 1:05 p.m.

stating that the U.S. had informed Israel that further offensive operations would lead to "severe deterioration" of relations and that the president had personally intervened with Meir. Additionally, he relayed that the U.S. had "formal assurances" from Israel that troops had not advanced since the beginning of the ceasefire at 7:00 a.m., that U.S. military attachés and U.N. observers had been invited to the front, and that Israelis were trying "to absorb fire without answer." At the same time, he issued a warning, informing Sadat that the Israelis were in possession of a message from the Egyptian Ministry of War which called on the forces to continue fighting, promised air support, and said that 250 tanks were being sent to break Israeli forces on the West Bank. Kissinger requested Egypt to "scrupulously observe the ceasefire agreement."[37]

Though he was confident that Israel had initiated hostilities, the post-war negotiations were constantly on his mind. He was walking a delicate line. On the one hand, it was imperative to maintain a key U.S. role in the peace process and to convince the Egyptians that he had done everything possible to restrain the Israelis. At the same, Israeli cooperation would also be a must. The Israelis needed to be shown that the United States came to them in their hour of need. He spoke with Schlesinger, Moorer, Colby and Scowcroft. "Our problem," complained Schlesinger, "is we don't know what to do. Should we replace [equipment] as the president said, or fill their wish list?" Kissinger replied, "It must be geared to two things. What they lost and what the Soviet Union is doing. Whatever we put in, Israel will not go to war again without opening a supply line to us." Schlesinger responded that the U.S was "deep into inventories." "I want a bulge now, over the next three weeks, and then a level thing that we can space out," Kissinger said. He added, "By December we will turn on them, but up to then, we don't want to have the Jewish community on us for not being generous now."[38]

As Bruno Pierri has noted, as the Israeli Army pursued the Egyptian Third Army, "there was a conflict of interests between Washington and Jerusalem regarding the ultimate purpose of the war." He continues:

> Though Israeli leaders had declared themselves in favor of a negotiated settlement, now that victory was in their hands they did not want to stop the troops until the Egyptian Army was encircled and possibly destroyed. The danger for American strategy was that Israel might do what the Soviets were not able to do, that is to deny Washington the chance to shape the region on the basis of an Israeli-Egyptian settlement.[39]

Brezhnev sent a message to Nixon, which arrived at 1:15 p.m. stating that the Soviets had "hard information" that Israeli forces were "fiercely

6. The Failure to Avoid a Superpower Confrontation 147

attacking" Egyptian troops and ships off the West Bank with "obvious intention to capture this port in gross violation" of the new ceasefire. "I wish to say it frankly, Mr. President, that we are confident that you have possibilities to influence Israel with the aim of putting an end to such a provocative behavior of Tel Aviv." He added, "We would like to hope that we both will be true to our word and to the understanding we have reached." He wanted to know what steps the Administration was taking to ensure Israel's "strict and immediate compliance with the decisions of the Security Council of this October 22 and 23."[40]

Kissinger called Dinitz and informed him of Brezhnev's message. "I have just talked to Israel about five minutes ago and they told me all is quiet," Dinitz said. Kissinger informed him of the U.S. strategy which was to support "the strongest call for an observance of the ceasefire" and to oppose the introduction of American and Soviet forces. He asked for "as much assurance as you can that you are not taking any military action." Dinitz promised to speak to Meir.[41] Meir writes in her memoirs that when Dinitz called, "I decided to pick up the phone and talk to Kissinger, rather than send yet another letter. I said, 'You can say anything you want about us and do anything you want, but we are not liars. The allegations are not true.'"[42]

A conversation at 4:25 p.m. between Schlesinger and Kissinger reveals that the U.S. still did not know if Dinitz' assurances were valid. Kissinger asked, "Is there any way we can find out if it's quiet for ourselves? The Israelis tell us it is, the Soviets are telling us it isn't."[43]

Ray Cline sent a message to Kissinger that afternoon with an appraisal of the situation. "Even if the major combatants stop shooting, this ceasefire appears much more precarious than its predecessors." He continued, "Israeli violations of the October 23 ceasefire—and possibly the October 24 ceasefire—appear to have reflected an effort definitively to isolate the Egyptians' southern salient [on the East Bank]." Cline added, "Apparently, Israel halted its victory drive only out of deference to Washington and has no real interest in letting Cairo get off 'so lightly.' With his army on the ropes, Sadat seems to have grasped at the ceasefire as a chance for his forces to catch their breath to reorganize, and to integrate the material delivered by the Soviet resupply effort, so that he will be in better shape for the next round."[44]

The situation changed dramatically at 7:05 p.m. Dobrynin told Kissinger that Soviet ambassador to the U.N. Malik had been instructed to support a Security Council resolution calling for the dispatch of American and Soviet troops if someone else introduced it. It was a proposal that Washington would never agree to.

At that point, Nixon called and interrupted the discussion. According to Kissinger, he was "as agitated and emotional as I had ever heard him." The president raved about his possible impeachment. "They are doing it because of their desire to kill the president," Nixon said. "And they may succeed. I may physically die." Nixon added:

> What they care about is destruction. It brings me sometimes to feel like saying the hell with it. I would like to see them run this country and see what they do.... The real tragedy is, if I move out, everything we have done will crumble. The Russians will look for other customers, the Chinese will lose confidence, the Europeans will—They just don't realize they are throwing everything out the window. I don't know what in the name of God...[45]

Kissinger wrote, "We were heading into what could have become the gravest foreign policy crisis of the Nixon presidency—because it involved a direct confrontation of the superpowers—with a president overwhelmed by his persecution."[46]

Kissinger spoke with Dobrynin at 7:15 p.m. Dobrynin informed him that Malik was instructed to vote in favor of a resolution to send troops—including Soviet troops—in order to enforce the ceasefire. "We will vote against it," Kissinger replied.[47] He called Scali at 7:25 p.m. instructing him to veto any such resolution, including any condemnation of Israel.[48] Immediately afterward, Kissinger called Dobrynin to urge him to not push matters "to an extreme," as the U.S. would veto any calls for sending military forces. Dobrynin replied that Moscow had "become so angry they want troops." He accused Kissinger of allowing the Israelis "to do what they wanted." Kissinger replied, "If you want confrontation we will have to have one. It would be a pity."[49]

At 7:35 p.m. Kissinger called Dinitz and assured him that Washington would veto any condemnation of Israel and the introduction of any foreign military presence.[50] Shortly thereafter, Kissinger spoke with Haig. Referring to the Soviets, he said, "We may have to take them on."

Kissinger spoke with Dobrynin again and urged him "to avoid the confrontation" between the U.S. and the U.N., and stressed that Washington's information was that there was no fighting going on. Dobrynin asked Kissinger to check the situation, after which he would send a telegram to Moscow.[51] They spoke again at 8:25 p.m. and Dobrynin informed Kissinger that Zayat, in a speech to the Security Council, had requested that the U.S. and Soviet Union send their forces. "I would still urge you to show great restraint," Kissinger said, adding, "It would be that from the closest cooperation we turn to a very dangerous course."[52]

According to Victor Israelyan, the issue of whether or not to send

Soviet troops to Egypt generated "heated discussion" in the Kremlin. He writes:

> A response to Sadat's suggestion was needed, one-way or another—that was the general opinion. But should the Soviet Union send troops to the Middle East together with the Americans or unilaterally? Here there were different opinions. Some were proponents of a joint action. Others were very reluctant to send troops, whether jointly or separately. But it was obvious to everyone that carrying out a complicated military operation in the final stage of the war was very risky and almost impossible.
>
> I remember [Soviet Chief of Staff Viktor] Kulikov at one point saying that by the time joint Soviet-American forces, or only Soviet forces, were ready for full-scale action, Cairo would have fallen and the war would be over. Nevertheless, something had to be done to prevent an unconditional surrender by Sadat, especially on the eve of the great political performance, the World Congress of Peace Forces.[53]

Scali and Kissinger spoke at 8:52 p.m. Scali informed him that Malik, in his speech, had "stopped short" of attacking the U.S. "He did call for everybody to break diplomatic relations and support sanctions against Israel. He noted that you had been to Tel Aviv and had great responsibility. He believes that the U.S. is in a position to force Israel to do what it wants it to do." Scali confirmed that Zayat had indeed formally requested the introduction of troops. Kissinger ordered Scali to give a speech opposing such a course.[54]

Kissinger decided to be explicit with Sadat that it was against Egypt's interest for the superpowers to send in troops. He sent an urgent message, in Nixon's name, informing Sadat that "it would be impossible to assemble sufficient outside military power to represent an effective counterweight to the indigenous forces now engaged in combat in the Middle East." The message stated: "Should the two great nuclear powers be called upon to provide forces, it would introduce an extremely dangerous potential for direct great power rivalry in the area." Kissinger added that the U.S. position was that only U.N. observer personnel should be sent to the region.[55]

Kissinger Goes to the Brink

At 9:32 p.m. Haig told Kissinger that the president had retired for the night. Kissinger writes that he and Haig "agreed we might be heading for the most explosive crisis of an unquiet tenure."[56] His intuition was dead on. Almost immediately, he received an urgent call from Dobrynin who had an ominous letter from Brezhnev to Nixon. Dobrynin proceeded to read over the telephone. It stated:

> The facts ... testify that Israel continues drastically to ignore the ceasefire decision of the Security Council. Thus, it is brazenly challenging both the Soviet Union and the United States since it is our agreement with you which constitutes the basis of the Security Council decision. In short, Israel simply embarked on the road to defeat.
>
> It continues to seize new territory. As you know, the Israeli forces have already fought their way into Suez. It is impossible to allow such to continue. Let us together, the Soviet Union and the United States, urgently dispatch to Egypt Soviet and American military contingents, with their mission the implementation of the decision of the Security Council ... concerning the cessation of fire and of all military activities and also of the understanding with you on the guarantee of the implementation of the decisions of the Security Council.

Dobrynin then lowered the boom:

> It is necessary to adhere without delay. I will say it straight that if you find it impossible to act jointly with us in this matter, we should be faced with the necessity urgently to consider the question of *taking appropriate steps unilaterally*. We cannot allow arbitrariness on the part of Israel.[57]

Kissinger writes that this was "one of the most serious challenges to an American president by a Soviet leader."[58] He immediately spoke with Haig. "I think we have to go to the mat on this one," Kissinger stated. Haig opined that Soviets were "playing chicken," adding, "They're not going to put in forces at the end of the war. I don't believe that." Kissinger asked Haig if he should wake the president. "No," Haig curtly replied.[59]

Kissinger wrote, "I knew what that meant. Haig thought the president too distraught to participate in the preliminary discussion. It was a daunting responsibility to assume. From my own conversation with Nixon earlier in the evening, I was convinced Haig was right."[60] Kissinger called a WSAG meeting to convene at the State Department at 10:30 p.m.

Kissinger spoke with Dinitz at 10:00 p.m. and informed him of the Brezhnev letter. "If the Soviets have decided to go in," Kissinger said, "I just think we turned the wheel yesterday one screw too much." He added, "We have to offer them something, which puts them totally in the wrong—I want to know if you can agree to return to the position you occupied before it all started." Dinitz replied, "How can this be done! I can inform the Prime Minister if you want me to, but I will tell you in advance..." Kissinger angrily cut him off. "I don't have time for this!" He added, "You have to check. They said either we will do it jointly with them or they will put in forces unilaterally." Kissinger was insistent. How should the U.S. reply as far as Israel was concerned? Dinitz agreed to speak with Meir.[61]

6. The Failure to Avoid a Superpower Confrontation 151

Kissinger then called Dobrynin and warned, "We are assembling our people to consider the letter. I just wanted you to know if any unilateral action is taken before we have had a chance to reply, that will be very serious." Dobrynin briskly replied, "Yes, all right." Kissinger threatened, "This is a matter of great concern. Don't you pressure us. I want to repeat again, don't pressure us." Dobrynin obliquely replied, "All right."

Kissinger wrote:

> In a subtle way, this conversation added to the impact of Brezhnev's threatening letter. It would have been easy for Dobrynin to say that the Soviets would in no case act until they heard from us. He might have indicated in the hundred ways available to a seasoned professional that we were overreacting, that the threat of unilateral action was a figure of speech, the normal recourse of a sovereign country that feels pushed against the wall.
>
> Instead, Dobrynin permitted the impression to stand that a crisis was indeed impending, and that nothing had changed to defer the possibility of a unilateral Soviet military move in the Middle East. That awareness dominated the deliberations that our government was about to start.[62]

However, Kissinger was reading too much between the lines. He interpreted Dobrynin's silence as threatening, when, in fact Dobrynin saw himself as merely a message bearer. In his memoirs, Israelyan recalls that he later asked Dobrynin to explain Kissinger's comments in his memoirs. Israelyan writes:

> Dobrynin stated that when delivering Brezhnev's message to Kissinger he had been guided by strict instructions to relay the message to the White House and to report back to Moscow that the instructions had been carried out. Because he had not been asked to comment on the message, and because he understood the seriousness and importance of the issue, he did not soften the message, nor did he do anything to create the impression that the crisis was inevitable.[63]

At 10:20 p.m. Kissinger spoke with Haig, who asked him if he had conferred with the president. Kissinger had not. "He would just start charging around—until we have it analyzed," Kissinger said. Kissinger was convinced that the Soviets were looking to exploit Watergate. "I don't think they would take on a functioning President," he opined to Haig. Haig asked if the upcoming WSAG meeting would be held at the White House. Kissinger replied that it would be at the State Department. "He has to be part of everything you are doing," Haig warned. Kissinger asked again if he should awaken the president. Haig evaded the question. "I wish you would hold it at the White House." Kissinger agreed.

The WSAG "meeting of principals," as it was called in State Department records, has generated much historical controversy, due to the gravity of the impending situation and the absence of both the president and a vice president (Gerald Ford had not yet been confirmed by the Senate). Kissinger notes that the White House later described it as a National Security Council meeting, claiming that it was "in effect the statutory membership of the National Security Council" minus the president and vice president.[64] Cline called it a "curious little rump NSC meeting," to which Colby was invited to "give a semblance of regularity to decision making."[65]

What Nixon knew about the contents of the meeting remains a matter of debate. Schlesinger and Scowcroft came to doubt that Haig had consulted with the president or that he had gotten Nixon's approval for the actions that were taken.[66] So did Admiral Elmo Zumwalt, then Chief of Naval Operations and a member of the Joint Chief of Staff. He recounts in his memoirs: "After the Joint Chiefs of Staff meeting adjourned, I came upon Bill Clements alone and communicated my suspicion to him. Bill said, 'I wondered the same thing and so I asked Jim [James Schlesinger] if the president was in on this. Jim said he was not.'"[67] Additionally, Helmut Sonnenfeldt, a senior member of the NSC staff, stated that Nixon did not participate in the discussion and "approved the recommendations early in the morning of the following day."[68]

The Kalb brothers observe that it is "curious" that Kissinger never saw the president that night. They write: "Nixon, who struck a number of his close advisers as 'remote,' remained in his living quarters, upstairs, while his advisers conferred downstairs. Kissinger talked with the Chief Executive only once—on the phone. All other messages were relayed through Haig. The last one, at about 2:00 a.m., set the stage for a 7:30 a.m. meeting with the president and Haig."[69]

Others have speculated that Nixon was intoxicated, a hypothesis that is not altogether without merit, given Nixon's ranting with Kissinger and Haig's evasiveness with Kissinger. Ray Cline, for instance, stated, "I've heard that President Nixon was upstairs drunk that night. I don't know that that's a fact, but it is clear and we didn't know it at the time how far Nixon was out of things in those days." In Cline's view, the WSAG meeting was a "kind of shell game, a superficial exercise," in that Kissinger "knew what he wanted to do all along." Cline feels that the others were summoned just to give the decision to go on alert the semblance of official action.[70]

On the other hand, Peter Rodman writes that the "truth about the Situation Room meeting is less dramatic than it has been portrayed." He writes: "For one thing, Nixon had emphasized to Haig, before he retired, that he wanted a strong response to the Soviets, including alert measures.

6. The Failure to Avoid a Superpower Confrontation

In addition, the record suggests that Haig left the Situation Room gathering at various stages of the evening to get Nixon's blessing of what was being discussed."[71]

Rodman's position is one that Haig takes in his memoirs. He writes that the president was tired, due to the pressures of Watergate, and "as usual, he preferred to let others set the options while he made his decision in solitude." Haig claims, "With a wave of his hand, he said, "You know what I want, Al; you handle the meeting."[72] Nixon's memoirs support this. He writes:

> When Haig informed me about this message, I said that he and Kissinger should have a meeting at the White House to formulate plans for a firm reaction to what amounted to a scarcely veiled threat of unilateral Soviet intervention. Words were not making our point—we needed action, even the shock of a nuclear alert.[73]

This account is substantially at odds with Nixon's account of the incident two days later in a televised news conference. In what he described as "the most difficult crisis we've had since the Cuban confrontation of 1962," Nixon assured the nation that he had been in charge. "When I received that information, I ordered shortly after midnight on Thursday morning an alert for all American forces around the world." He added, "Even in this week, when many thought the president was shell-shocked, unable to act, the president acted decisively in the interest of the country.... I have a quality which is—I guess I must have inherited it from my Midwestern mother and father—which is that the tougher it gets, the cooler I get."[74]

Though it is unlikely that the level of Nixon's involvement in the decision making process on that night will ever come to light, whatever Nixon actually did tell Haig, given his state of agitation, could hardly have provided the direction that the WSAG group needed to ensure that its decisions were in line with the president's desires. The meeting, chaired by Kissinger, included Colby, Schlesinger, Moorer, Scowcroft, Haig and Admiral Jonathan Howe, military assistant to the NSC. Minutes remain classified. However, in his memorandum for the record, written on October 26, Moorer describes the discussion that took place. After reviewing the events over the prior two days, Kissinger asked the question: "Why did the Soviets suddenly reverse themselves and without any warning all day, then 'bang,' we receive the Brezhnev threat?" He then advanced three possibilities:

1. The Soviets had this in mind all along, beginning with the time when the Egyptians collapsed, about October 13, and went through the charade of

inviting Kissinger to Moscow with the intention of seizing on any opportunity offered by the Israelis in violation of the ceasefire.
2. The Soviets did not have this action in mind, but the inevitable defeat of their client gradually sunk in and caused them to change course.
3. The Soviets felt they had been tricked by the Israelis, who, when viewed from Moscow, were guilty of gross violations of the ceasefire agreement.

Kissinger's conclusion, supported by his memoirs, was that the first option was dubious, and that the Soviet motivation would have to be either the second or third option, or both.[75]

During the meeting, Moorer pointed out that there were three military indicators that might possibly lead to the conclusion that the action was premeditated. First, seven airborne Soviet divisions had been placed on alert. Second, the Soviets had halted the airlift, which freed up the planes for lifting troops to Cairo. Finally, the Russians had begun an intensive sealift to Egypt, which could be delivering weapons to be used by the troops.

Additionally, there is evidence that there was a nuclear element to Soviet activity. The U.S. had been tracking a Soviet ship carrying radioactive material since it entered the Mediterranean on October 22. According to Blechman and Hart, "Our interviewees confirmed that the U.S intelligence community was quite positive that there was nuclear material aboard the ship, even though the reason for the activity could not be defined."[76]

Moorer stated that since the U.S. had only access to the one European airfield at Lajes, "the Middle East is the worst place in the world for the U.S. to get engaged in a war with the Soviets." He writes, "We kept coming back to the $64 question: 'If the Soviets put in 10,000 troops into Egypt, what would we do?'"[77] In Moorer's account, the general consensus at the meeting was that the Soviet threat was serious and calculating. Haig appeared "convinced that the Soviets were going to move at daylight." Schlesinger thought "the Soviets were using this to put pressure on the U.S. or to develop an excuse to move in their own forces in the Middle East."

Kissinger insisted the Soviets were taking advantage of the president's weakened political position because of Watergate. He said, "Friday, the president was in good shape domestically. Now the Soviets see that he is, in their mind, non-functional." Kissinger saw that the Soviet strategy was "one of throwing détente on the table" during a "moment of maximum U.S. weakness." Moorer quotes him as saying: "We must prevent them from getting away with this…. When you decide to use force, you must use plenty of it."[78]

6. The Failure to Avoid a Superpower Confrontation

The committee opted for drastic action. The group decided to issue a DEFCON III military alert, Defense Condition 3, which is short of full military readiness, but higher than a normal alert (DEFCON IV). It places on readiness the Strategic Air Command (SAC) and the North American Air Defense Command (NORAD), thereby involving strategic nuclear forces. Other measures were also taken. The 82nd Airborne Division was placed on high alert, B-52s positioned in Guam were returned to the United States, the aircraft carrier *Franklin Delano Roosevelt* was moved to join the carrier *Independence* south of Crete, and the carrier *John F. Kennedy* was moved into the Mediterranean.[79]

The move was, as Jeremi Suri writes, use of what became known as the "madman" strategy, employing the threat of irrationally applying disproportionate force—including the use of limited nuclear warfare—in order to make adversaries more accommodating to American needs.[80] The term came from a conversation between Nixon and H.R. "Bob" Haldeman during the 1968 campaign for the presidency. Nixon said, "I call it the madman theory, Bob. I want the North Vietnamese to believe I've reached the point where I might do *anything* to stop the war."[81] A participant in the events, cited by Blechman and Hart, noted that the alert fit well with Kissinger's approach to crisis management. Kissinger's tactic was to do something dramatic that would get the attention of Soviet decision makers, rather than do things "tit for tat." Pursuing a course that was unmistakably above the noise level would make unambiguously clear the gravity of the situation and the risks of not reaching accommodation. Furthermore, the changes in U.S. communications patterns would be detected immediately by Soviet intelligence systems.[82]

John Scherer suggests the possibility that Kissinger "might have used the alert to broaden American diplomatic options," not just during the Yom Kippur War but in future, potential crises. He cites Kissinger's 1957 book, *Nuclear Weapons and Foreign Policy*, in which Kissinger argues that the threat to use nuclear weapons has to be real in order to be effective. Scherer writes, "This was a chance to give credence to the nuclear deterrent with little risk.... [The alert] introduced unpredictability into affairs. Kissinger had sent troops into Cambodia late in the war and may have thought the worldwide nuclear alert would similarly confuse the Kremlin."[83] While Scherer's view is extreme, it is true that both Kissinger and Schlesinger believed that Watergate required a show of American strength and determination.

Among the most scathing critiques of Kissinger's performance was that of his biographer, Roger Morris. "With Haig and the assortment of senior bureaucrats acting as his rump NSC," he writes, "Henry Kissinger became for the night an unelected, unconfirmed, unacknowledged president, by default ordering American forces to the uncertain edges of war with an authority the constitution has specifically reserved only for the elected chief executive.[84]

Peter Rodman later defended the considerations behind the U.S. actions:

> It is absolutely impermissible that the Soviet Union even contemplated unilateral military intervention in the Middle East in a war to make itself—to make Soviet arms the arbiter of an Arab-Israeli conflict. That was totally impermissible. It threatened an American vital interest. We had absolutely a requirement to prevent it.... I personally think we would have and should have been willing to go to war to prevent it or at least to put American forces there to interpose in such a case.[85]

Speaking on behalf of the Israeli government, Golda Meir also later defended the alert in a press bulletin issued on November 13, 1973. The bulletin stated: "We are convinced that thanks to the alert declared by the President of the United States ... undesirable developments were averted. The result was that the U.S.S.R. preferred to cooperate with the United States in order to prevent a deterioration of the situation which would surely have been brought about by the unilateral Soviet measures."[86]

At 11:25 p.m. Kissinger spoke with Dinitz, who had a reply from Meir. She said that Israel would be prepared to move all forces to the east of the Canal if Egypt agreed to move all its forces west of the Canal, in essence creating two demilitarized strips which international observers would occupy. "They'll never agree to that, I'll tell you that right away," Kissinger responded.[87] Of the Israeli proposal, Kissinger wrote:

> It was an impossible scheme. Sadat would consider it an insult to be asked to vacate territory that not even the Israelis challenged as Egyptian. Nor could he end the war by withdrawing ten kilometers from where he had started it. And it was too complicated to negotiate in time to head off a Soviet intervention if indeed one was imminent. It might even accelerate the move if Sadat was sufficiently infuriated by it to insist on great power participation. I told Dinitz that I would discuss the proposal with my colleagues but that I knew it would not work.[88]

At 11:41 p.m. Moorer issued the alert, which was quickly picked up by Soviet intelligence and provoked an emergency meeting of the Politburo. The Soviet leadership was shocked by the realization that the Soviet Union and United States were moving toward a major confrontation. According to Israelyan, all saw the alert as a drastic and dangerous overreaction on the part of the Americans. Israelyan writes:

6. The Failure to Avoid a Superpower Confrontation

Using strong language and characterizing Nixon's decision as irresponsible, everyone at the meeting expressed indignation at the news that the Americans were preparing their troops for military action. Some saw no reason for such an action and were plainly taken by surprise. Others saw it in orthodox Marxist-Leninist terms as part of the class struggle in the international arena. Some wondered, "The Americans say we threaten them, but how did they get that into their heads?" And several believed that the Soviet Union's decisive role in maintaining peace and strengthening international security was making the American imperialists furious.

He continues:

> Very few indeed guessed that the pretext for Washington's decision was Brezhnev's latest message to Nixon. "What has this to do with the letter I sent to Nixon?" asked Brezhnev, who believed the emphasis in the letter was on joint Soviet-American action in accordance with the understanding reached during Kissinger's visit to Moscow. Brezhnev once again reminded everyone of Nixon's earlier message, in which the American president had suggested that the two leaders exert their influence to bring an end to the hostilities by putting pressure on their respective clients.
>
> "The Americans had no right to put their troops on alert all over the world, including their nuclear forces. It is a gross violation of the Soviet-American treaty on the prevention of nuclear war signed in 1972," stated [Defense Minister Andrei] Grechko.
>
> "Who could have imagined that the Americans would be so easily frightened?" asked [Chairman of the Soviet Presidium Nikolai] Podgorny, astonished. Sharp critique of Kissinger continued. Kosygin said: Kissinger lied to us when he was here. He preferred to fraternize with the Israelis." "He is not playing by the rules," grumbled [Chairman of State Security Yuri] Andropov.[89]

Immediately after issuing the alert, Kissinger dispatched a message to Sadat in Nixon's name: "I ask you to consider the consequences for your country if the two great nuclear countries were thus to confront each other on your soil."[90] Kissinger wrote in his memoirs that the letter was an attempt to "close off Moscow's diplomatic options by inducing Cairo to withdraw its invitation to the Soviets to send in troops."[91]

Kissinger then drafted a reply to Brezhnev in Nixon's name, which was approved during the meeting. Significantly, it was conciliatory, and thereby offered the Soviets a way out. The message was delivered to the Soviet Embassy at 5:40 a.m. on October 25.

> It is clear that the forces necessary to impose the ceasefire terms on the two sides would be massive and would require closest coordination so as to avoid bloodshed. This is not only clearly infeasible but is not appropriate to the situation. In this situation, the Security Council requires accurate infor-

> mation about what is occurring so that it each of us can exert maximum influence in Cairo and Tel Aviv, respectively, to ensure compliance with the terms of the ceasefire.
>
> To this end, I am prepared to join with you at once to augment the present truce supervisory force by additional men and equipment. I would be prepared to see included in such augmented truce supervisory units a number of American and Soviet personnel, though not combat forces. It would be understood that this is an extraordinary and temporary step, solely for the purpose of providing adequate information concerning compliance by both sides with the terms of the ceasefire. If this is what you mean by contingents, we will consider it.
>
> You must know, however, that we could in no event accept unilateral action. This would be in violation of our understandings of the agreed Principles we signed in Moscow in 1972 and of Article II of the Agreement on Prevention of Nuclear War. As I stated above, such action would produce incalculable consequences which would be in the interest of neither of our countries and which would end all we have striven so hard to achieve.[92]

That morning, at 6:30 a.m., Kissinger awoke after three hours of sleep and discovered that the American public had already learned of the alert, which was all over the morning news, with TV footage of the U.S. preparing for war, soldiers returning from leave, B-52s and war ships. What was especially shocking for most Americans was that they had gone to sleep the night earlier with no idea of possible Soviet preparations for intervention in the Middle East. Write Blechman and Hart:

> In the political atmosphere that had resulted from, first, years of increasingly strained efforts to present a favorable picture of the war in Vietnam and, second, the revelations of presidential misdeeds associated with Watergate, the U.S. military activity was viewed, if not cynically, at least skeptically. Indeed, by the time the Special Action Group reconvened in the morning of October 25, its primary task was to prove that the crisis was real and not an outrageous attempt to distract attention from Watergate.[93]

"I was shocked," Kissinger wrote of the public reaction. According to some stories, a reservist in Florida, who had been rushing to his post when he was called up for duty, was stopped by a policeman for speeding, when he leaked the news. Kissinger wrote that "the unexpected publicity would inevitably turn the event into an issue of prestige with Moscow, unleashing popular passions at home and seriously complicating the prospects of a Soviet retreat."[94]

Soon thereafter he delivered a nationally broadcast news conference, and took a "tough and conciliatory stance" toward the Soviet Union. He warned the Soviets not to send troops into the Middle East and not to expect the United States to join them in a joint peacekeeping force in the region.

6. The Failure to Avoid a Superpower Confrontation 159

"We possess, each of us, nuclear arsenals capable of annihilating humanity," he said. "We, both of us, have a special duty to see to it that the confrontations are kept within bounds that do not threaten civilized life. Both of us, sooner or later, will have to come to realize that the issues that divide the world today, and foreseeable issues, do not justify the unparalleled catastrophe that a nuclear war would represent." Yet he also extended the olive branch. "We do not consider ourselves in a confrontation with the Soviet Union," he added. "We are not talking of a missile-crisis-type confrontation."[95]

Kissinger then laid out a justification for the alert:

> The United States does not favor and will not approve the sending of a joint Soviet-United States force into the Middle East. The United States believes that what is needed in the Middle East above all is a determination of the facts, a determination where the lines are, and a determination of who is doing the shooting, so that the Security Council can take appropriate action. It is inconceivable that the forces of the great powers should be introduced in the numbers that would be necessary to overpower both of the participants. It is inconceivable that we should transplant the great-power rivalry into the Middle East or, alternatively, that we should impose a military condominium by the United States and the Soviet Union.
>
> The United States is even more opposed to the unilateral introduction by any great power, especially by any nuclear power, of military forces into the Middle East in whatever guise those forces should be introduced. And it is the ambiguity of some of the actions and communications and certain readiness measures that were observed that caused the President at a special meeting of the National Security Council last night, at 3 a.m., to order certain precautionary measures to be taken by the United States.[96]

During the same press conference, Kissinger was besieged with questions as to whether the crisis was manufactured to detract attention away from Watergate. Kissinger gave a testy response:

> We are attempting to conduct the foreign policy of the United States with regard for what we owe not just to the electorate but to future generations. And it is a symptom of what is happening to our country that it could even be suggested that the United States would alert its forces for domestic reasons.... It is up to you, ladies and gentlemen, to determine whether this is the moment to try to create a crisis of confidence in the field of foreign policy as well.... There has to be a minimum of confidence that the senior officials of the American government are not playing with the lives of the American people.[97]

Nixon held a press conference the following day, October 26, at 7:00 p.m. which was carried live on radio and television. It was his first press conference since October 4, and the Middle East crisis hardly topped the list of what the press—and the American public—wanted addressed; ostensibly the president was going to explain his abolishment of the office of the special Watergate prosecutor, the departure of the top two officials in the Justice Department and his decision two days earlier to turn over Watergate tape recordings to United States District Judge John J. Sirica. The prior Monday night, on route to Camp David, Nixon was inundated with automobiles "honking for impeachment," part of the anti–Nixon demonstrations along Pennsylvania Avenue. That same week, George Meany, president of the AFL-CIO and formerly one of Nixon's staunchest supporters, also called for impeachment. The labor leader stated to the press: "The events of the last several days prove the dangerous emotional instability of the president. We firmly believe there must be a complete independent investigation of the scandal in this administration.... The president has so destroyed the people's confidence in government that he should resign or be impeached."[98]

Nixon, his face "showing fatigue and his voice displaying occasional hurt and anger," as described by reporter John Herbers, began the press conference with a statement on the Middle East crisis: "We obtained information," Nixon said, "which led us to believe that the Soviet Union was planning to send a very substantial force into the Middle East—a military force."[99] He also suggested that no other leader could have dealt as successfully with the Russians as he did in bringing about a ceasefire. "It's because he [Brezhnev] and I know each other and it's because we have had this personal contact that ... result in a settlement rather than a confrontation," he boasted.[100]

Nixon went on to state that he would be appointing a new special prosecutor to replace Archibald Cox. At that point, he was ambushed by a question from Dan Rather. "Mr. President," Rather asked, "I wonder if you could share your thoughts, tell us what goes through your mind when you hear people, people who love this country and people who believe in you, say reluctantly that perhaps you should resign or be impeached." Nixon gave a shrug and replied, "Well, I am glad we don't take the vote of this room, let me say." He continued: "The events of this past week, I know for example, in your head office [CBS TV] in New York, some thought that it was simply a blown-up exercise; there wasn't a real crisis. I wish it had been that. It was a real crisis."[101] He then detonated:

> I have never heard or seen such outrageous, vicious, distorted reporting in twenty-seven years of public life.... And yet I should point out that even in this week, when many thought that the President was shell-shocked, unable

6. The Failure to Avoid a Superpower Confrontation   161

to act, the President acted decisively in the interest of peace, in the interests of the country, and I can assure you that whatever shocks gentleman of the press may have, or others, political people, these shocks will not affect me in doing my job.[102]

Nixon was asked how he was bearing up emotionally. "I have a quality," he responded, "which is—I guess I must have inherited it from my Midwestern mother and father—which is that the tougher it gets, the cooler I get." He acknowledged that terrible things had been said about him. "[But] I have learned to expect it. It has been my lot throughout my political life, and I suppose because I have been through so much, that may be one of the reasons that when I have to face an international crisis, I have what it takes," he said. Robert Pierpoint of CBS TV asked what it was about the television coverage "that has so aroused your anger." Nixon snapped back: "Don't get the impression that you arouse my anger.... You see, one can only be angry with those he respects." Nixon's biographer, Stephen Ambrose, writes that the president "did himself much harm" at the news conference. "He had let the reporters get to him, and aroused their wolfpack instincts. At issue now was.... Nixon's judgment, his sudden mood switches, his stability, his anger, perhaps his capacity to govern."[103]

A message arrived from Sadat, via Ismail, at 1:20 p.m. which demonstrated Sadat's acceptance of the U.S. proposal, and the withdrawal of his request for troops. It stated:

> We would like to inform the United States that we agree to the presence of international forces composed of units from non-permanent members of the Security Council as long as it is backed by the full support of the permanent members and in particular the U.S. and the U.S.S.R. ... We consider that the immediate and most urgent task of this force is to supervise and observe the implementation of the Security Council Resolution of 23 October 1973, i.e., the pullback of Israeli troops to the positions they held on the coming into effect of 22 October resolution. We expect the force to be immediately dispatched to the area to assume its function before any delay results in incalculable and far-reaching consequences.[104]

At 2:40 p.m. Dobrynin called Kissinger to read a message to the president from Brezhnev. "Is it going to calm me down or make me go into orbit again?" Kissinger asked. "No, not orbit," Dobrynin replied. He proceeded to read the contents of the message. Kissinger's allegation that the firing had ceased contradicted the facts, Brezhnev said. When the message was received, the Israelis were bombing the city of Ismailia and the fighting continued in the city of Suez. In response to Sadat's request, Moscow was sending seventy Soviet representatives to supervise the ceasefire, who would meet with U.S. observers whom he assumed Washington would be sending. The Soviet observers were instructed to "get into contact immediately" with the American observers and cooperate in a "businesslike operation" as soon as they arrive in Egypt. Brezhnev added: "We are ready to cooperate with the American side in taking other measures which will be dictated by the situation, to ensure immediate and strict implementation of the Security Council resolution of the 22nd and 23rd of October."

Kissinger asked Dobrynin if he had seen his press conference that morning. Dobrynin had. "Oh no," Kissinger responded. "At 4:00 in the morning I didn't try to be gentle. I thought you were threatening us. Don't. I take threats very badly. We will talk about it some time." Dobrynin replied that then was not the time.[105]

A potential crisis had been averted, but as Admiral Zumwalt makes clear in his memoirs, the alert had put the American and Soviet navies in a precariously close situation. "I doubt," writes Zumwalt, "that major units of the U.S. Navy were ever in a tenser situation since World War II ended than the Sixth Fleet in the Mediterranean was for the week after the alert was declared." He cites Admiral Dan Murphy's account of the situation:

> The U.S. Sixth Fleet and the Soviet Mediterranean Fleet were, in effect, sitting in a pond in close proximity and the stage for the hitherto unlikely "war at sea" scenario was set. This situation prevailed for several days. Both fleets were obviously in a high readiness posture for whatever might come next, although it appeared that neither fleet knew exactly what to expect.[106]

The final phase of the crisis played out over the next three days. On October 26, the Americans lifted the alert, and the Soviets relaxed their measures as well, though they had not included nuclear forces. The Israelis, however, did not return to the October 22 line, and they were reluctant to permit the resupply of the surrounded Third Army. While Kissinger rejected the Defense Department's suggestion of a U.S. airlift to relieve the beleaguered Egyptian troops, the Israelis felt the pressure. That same day, they allowed a convoy of supplies to pass through the lines. Checkpoints were established between the two armies, and a U.N. peacekeeping forces commanded by Finnish General Ensio Siilasvuo was put into place. On October 28, Major General Aharon Yariv of Israel and General Mohamed abdel–Gamasi Alghani of Egypt conducted direct talks, marking the first time in twenty-five years that military representatives of Egypt and Israel met to discuss the disengagement of forces.[107]

The Kalb brothers write that the alert "was clearly not Kissinger's finest hour, but he has insisted that it was one of those necessary exercises in big-power politics, which firmed up the U.S. position in the Middle East and opened the door to a direct U.S. role in mediating the dangerous Arab-Israeli conflict."[108] Yet many, such as Lebow and Stein, disagree. They argue that the history of the Cold War suggests that nuclear deterrence should be viewed as powerful but very dangerous medicine, analogous to the former use of arsenic to treat syphilis or chemotherapy to treat cancer. "In 1973, the United States did not see war as a likely possibility," they write, "but Soviet leaders worried actively about war.... Soviet leaders feared not only nuclear war but any kind of Soviet-American war. Their fear translated into self-deterrence; Brezhnev ruled out the commitment of Soviet forces on Egypt's behalf before the United States practiced deterrence."[109]

In his memoirs, Anatoly Dobrynin denies that there was any threat to the United States implicit in Soviet intentions, implying that the confrontation was a misplayed overreaction on the part of the administration. He writes:

> Many American historians describe the Middle East War as the deadliest crisis in our postwar relations, comparable to the Cuban crisis. While it was a indeed a serious political crisis, which made a rather unpleasant impact on our relations, there was no threat of a direct military clash between us.... That was and is Moscow's assessment. We took no measures to put our armed forces on high combat alert even in response to the American move, and we certainly did not alert our strategic forces as the Americans did. One cannot help but think that the myth of the Middle East being saved from a Soviet armed invasion was consequently put into circulation by the high American participants in the events in order to justify their rather unseemly role in the course of the crisis.[110]

Certainly, the alert, with or without the approval of the president, succeeded in facilitating an end to hostilities. Sadat withdrew his plea for superpower assistance, the Soviets backed down, and Israel abandoned its dismantling of the Egyptian Third Army. Kissinger's gamble had paid off. However, by using the threat of nuclear force as a strategic weapon, he put the United States, indeed the world, unnecessarily close to peril's door.

While the American public, with much prodding from the press, erroneously viewed the alert as a means to detract attention from Watergate, the alert was hardly a political ploy. Yet Kissinger's perception that the Soviets were emboldened by a weakened Administration played a large factor in his decision to roll the dice. Importantly, Kissinger had come, justifiably or not, to doubt the president's ability to lead in a decisive and lucid manner, a point which is seldom emphasized adequately in the literature. Though Nixon took credit for the alert, it will forever remain uncertain how he might have acted, had not critical decisions been made in his absence. In many ways, the alert, and its potentially devastating consequences, are part of the legacy of Watergate.

CHAPTER 7

Aftermath

While ostensibly an Israeli triumph, and an oft-offered example of Kissinger's foreign policy acumen, the consequences of the October war were multifarious and far-reaching. Any illusions, held by world opinion or among Israelis themselves, of Israeli invulnerability were vanquished, and Anwar Sadat emerged from the war as a leader on the world stage. Kissinger, who had been named, along with Nixon, as *Time's* "Man of the Year" in 1972, cemented his reputation as diplomat-in-chief. Yet the possibility of achieving one of his principal goals, rapprochement with the Soviet Union, lay in shambles after what had been a potentially catastrophic superpower confrontation.

The war shattered basic assumptions of U.S. policy in the Middle East. William Quandt names three. Firstly, Israeli military power had not ensured stability, as had been the prevailing assumption after the 1967 War. Secondly, détente with the Soviet Union had not served to minimize the danger of regional conflicts. Thirdly, the war challenged the prevailing view of the Arab World held by policy makers; contrary to beliefs about Arab ineptitude, they had fought well, exhibited remarkable solidarity, effectively used the oil weapon and shown restraint in private and public communications.[1] The result was a shift in U.S. policy from an inactive, status quo oriented approach to a new strategy aimed at bringing about substantial change.

Steven Spiegel concurs that the war resulted in a change in U.S. thinking regarding the Middle East. He writes that the war strengthened the position of those within the diplomatic and intelligence community who had been warning that another Mideast war would take place unless drastic diplomatic steps were taken. They now enjoyed greater credibility, and "their belief that the national interest demanded closer ties with the Arabs, even if it mean forcing Israeli concessions, gained greater acceptance throughout the bureaucracy." In fact, Spiegel writes that many of the officials who had been overly supportive of the Israelis had been removed from their positions, especially in the intelligence community, because it was believed that their prediction that there would be no hostilities revealed that they had been overly influenced by the Israelis.[2]

Following the war, writes Quandt, "for the first time, the United States committed its top diplomatic resources to a sustained search for a settlement of the Arab-Israeli conflict."[3] However, the elusiveness of such a settlement over the past four decades, and the fact that the issue of Palestinian sovereignty remains unresolved, betray the continued inadequacy of American efforts in the Middle East, and arguably, bestow a dubious legacy to Kissinger's efforts during the October War.

In Israel, the war proved to be a difficult and painful victory. The nation had suffered cataclysmic loss of lives, and the myth of its imperviousness to Arab attack was shattered, both internally, and throughout the world. It emerged from the war humbled, scarred and sobered. Politically, the war was a devastating blow to Golda Meir, who resigned as prime minister in June 1974; in 1977, her Labor Party lost power to the right-wing Likud Party of Menachem Begin. Yet the election was less an expression of support for the Likud's policy of expansionism that it was a vote of no confidence for the Labor Party's perceived ineptness. At the time, three out of four Israelis were ready to trade part or all of the occupied territories for peace.

However as Simcha Dinitz would later state, one result of the war was that it ultimately paved the way for peace between Israel and Egypt. Said Dinitz, "The Yom Kippur War, with all its agony and all its pain.... I think will enter into the annals of history as the war that brought the peace. If not an overall peace, at least it opened the peace process or charted the direction of peace."[4]

For the Arabs, the war had restored dignity and self-esteem, six years after its humiliating defeat in the Six-Day War. Sadat had managed to effect Arab unity to a degree never before achieved. He had successfully engineered and executed a surprise attack that accomplished its specific and limited objective, namely to force the beginning of the end to the status quo of an Israeli-occupied Sinai and make Middle East peace talks a primary focus of the United States. Significantly, he did so by employing the help of the Soviet Union, while at the same time, extricating Egypt from its over-handed influence. Under his leadership, the Sinai would be restored to Egyptian hands just five years after the war.

In terms of the Soviet Union, the war produced negligible to no gains. As Galia Golan notes, in accepting a ceasefire proposal which effectively ignored Arab demands for Israeli withdrawal to the borders of June 4, 1967, and by evading an explicit commitment to Palestinian rights, the Soviet Union effectively negated the benefits which it hoped to gain from the conflict. At the same time, its efforts to preserve détente and avoid a confrontation with the United States were "seriously jeopardized" by its simultaneous efforts to protect and recoup Soviet interests with the Arabs.[5] In the ensuing years, the Soviet reaction to the absence of any substantive success in the Middle East was an increasingly anti–American, pro-radical orientation in the region.[6]

The war's effects on the United States were far reaching. American relations with its allies had been severely damaged and the energy crisis wreaked havoc on the American economy. Importantly, as a consequence of the DEFCON III alert, détente took a severe beating. According to Robert Litwak, "The perceived failure of the Soviet Union to comply fully to the spirit and letter of the Moscow-Washington accords ... created a very serious crisis of confidence within the SALT forum. Though no explicit link was drawn between the two issues, the DEFCON III episode contributed to the promotion of a political atmosphere within the United States in which the questions of SALT verification and 'trust' in Soviet intentions became intertwined."[7]

Kissinger, despite mistakes, effectively ensured the exclusion of the Soviets from future negotiations in the Middle East peace process, and the dependence of the Israelis on the United States for arms and financial support, two consequences that when seen from a post–Cold War perspective, seem dubious accomplishments. In the eight months that followed the war, Kissinger made the Middle East his top priority, and his well-touted "shuttle diplomacy," what Kalb and Kalb call a "personal *tour de force*," cast him in the role of peacemaker.[8] Ultimately his efforts laid the foundation for the Camp David Accords, brokered by President Jimmy Carter and signed between Sadat and Israeli prime minister Menachem Begin in September 1978. However, as Seymour Hersh notes, the fundamental flaw of Kissinger's Middle East negotiations was that they "never came to grips with the real issue at stake: a future homeland for the Palestinians."[9] Although Sadat was willing to sidestep the issue in the interests of reacquiring the Sinai, the plight of the Palestinians continues to haunt us today. Additionally, Sadat's peace with Israel came at the price of the occupation of Syrian and Palestinian lands.

Regarding the ensuing oil crisis, there is some debate as to how serious the impact was on the United States. According to Dankwart Rustow, its impact was minimal, "largely hidden behind the popular melodrama of ... gasoline queues." He writes that in January and February 1974, U.S total energy supplies were reduced by only 2.4 percent, as compared to 2.8 percent for Japan and 5.6 percent for West Germany. Rather, he adds, "the severest losses were suffered by Third World countries that produce neither oil nor other essential raw materials, notably India, Pakistan,

Israeli prime minister Golda Meir at the White House in September 1969. She resigned six months after the war following the public outrage that ensued over Israel's failure to anticipate the attacks.

Bangladesh, Sri Lanka, and the poorer countries of Latin America," which also suffered from higher oil prices.[10] Interestingly, one of the beneficiaries was the Soviet Union, which was able to sell petroleum at higher prices, including exports of $40 million to the United States and $135.6 million to the Netherlands.[11] Additionally, the embargo's impact on American foreign policy was minimal. As Schlesinger later said, "I indicated at that time that we were prepared, if necessary to move military forces to the [Persian] Gulf to take over whatever country it was necessary to supply our oil."[12]

Still, the economic impact of the rise in crude oil prices from $2.41 a barrel in 1973 to a high of $11.59 in 1974 can hardly be underestimated.[13] As Kissinger put it in January 1974, "We are now living in a never-never land, I am certain, in which tiny, poor and weak nations can hold up for ransom some of the industrialized world."[14] In the words of historian Daniel J. Sargent, the "costly and divisive" oil crisis of 1973–74 "threatened the unity and prosperity of the West." Calling it "one of the seventies' seismic events," he writes that the oil crisis shifted the balance of power in the world economy away from the importing nations and toward oil exporters." Yet Sargent observes that the crisis had "sneaked up quietly on American leaders, who, until, proclamation of the embargo, had failed to perceive their own vulnerability—despite the warnings of oil economists who analyzed the rise of 'oil power' and warned of its consequences.... Despite clear warnings, the Nixon Administration failed to anticipate the power of petroleum as a political weapon."[15]

Additionally, the oil embargo caused ordinary Americans to realize that Israel and oil were inextricably linked. As Camille Mansour notes: "Prior to October, the Americans, with the exception of a few experts, had considered the link between oil and the Israeli-Arab conflict as mere rhetoric. For the United States, there were—and had to be—two separate strategic zones in the Middle East: that of the Israeli-Arab conflict and the oil zone.... After October 1973, the two zones could no longer be separated because the United States' own friends decided to engage in the oil embargo and reduce production in order to pressure it into modifying its attitude toward the conflict."[16]

In terms of the U.S.-Israeli relationship, the war, ironically under the stewardship of Richard Nixon, a president constantly at odds with the American Jewish community, ushered in an era whereby Israel became the recipient of about $3 billion annually in economic and military aid. Aid receipts at that level have given Israel unprecedented economic power to influence the governmental decisions of the United States. Elizabeth Stephens has noted that the Yom Kippur War transformed the very nature of the special relationship, as Israel changed from being a moral obligation and strategic asset into more of an economic investment.[17] Yet the emergence of conservative Christians as among the most ardent supporters of Israel in the United States demonstrate that a bond of kinship between the United States and Israel is alive and well in the twenty-first century. Additionally, Israel's tenacity in holding on to occupied territory and its treatment of the Palestinians has undercut any moral authority that it once possessed. With the Cold War at an end, its value as a strategic asset has been severely undermined; in fact, as the first Gulf War demonstrated, and the current situation in Iran may as yet confirm, Israel can be a strategic liability. When considering Kissinger's legacy, this reality can hardly be ignored.

Still, the special relationship holds strong. Today, few aspiring politicians get far in American politics if they are overtly critical of Israel, and being an active supporter of Israel could be said to a necessary part of any successful American politician's curriculum vitae. Though the number of Americans vocally critical of Israel has increased dramatically in the last decade, a March 2013 Gallup poll revealed that the percentage of Americans sympathetic to Israel has matched an all-time high.[18]

For Kissinger, the crisis, particularly the much publicized nuclear alert, marked a kind of "coming out," as Jeremi Suri has called it, of Kissinger as an international statesman. Following the war, he emerged as a celebrity, oft seen in the company of the Hollywood elite and jetsetters. He became known for his witticisms. "The nice thing about being a celebrity," he once characteristically said, "is that when you bore people, they think it's their fault." Perhaps his most telling—and most famous—quote was "Power is the ultimate aphrodisiac," quoted in the *New York Times* just days after the October War. In 1974, there was even talk of amending the constitutional requirement that a president be born in the United States, so that Kissinger might run for the nation's highest office.[19] In the view of many Americans, Kissinger's apparent success in the Middle East compensated for the U.S. failure in Vietnam, a failure in which he shoulders a great share of the burden.

Alistair Horne writes, "Few people (certainly not Americans) can be neutral about Henry Kissinger; they either hate him or love him."[20] The 2002 film *The Trials of Henry Kissinger*, based on the book by Christopher Hitchens by the same title, argues that Kissinger should be charged as a war criminal, based on his role in countries such as Cambodia, Chile, and Indonesia. His biographer, Walter Isaacson, writes that "Kissinger's realpolitik was ill-suited to an open and democratic society, where it is difficult to invoke distant ends to justify unpalatable means." Yet even Isaacson submits that "the structure of peace that Kissinger designed places him with Henry Stimson, George Marshall, and Dean Acheson atop the pantheon of American statesmen."[21] Others have referred to him as "Super K," and compared him to Metternich, Talleyrand, Bismarck, Machiavelli, Castlereagh, or a Lonesome Cowboy.[22] Former secretary of state George Shultz surely put it best: "There's only one Henry Kissinger. They broke the mold after they made him."[23]

Kissinger's conduct during the October War demonstrates the same ambiguity. At time duplicitous, a consummate flatterer, and willing to go to the brink of nuclear war on a gamble, Kissinger's brilliance and relentless focus on achieving his strategic objectives shine forth in every action, every conversation. In the end, as was often the case, with ruthlessness, Kissinger achieved his stated objectives.

In a 1981 article for the *Journal of Palestine Studies*, Kissinger asks the question "What was our strategy in '73?" He continues: "First, we sought to break up the Arab United Front. Also we wanted to ensure that the Europeans and Japanese did not get involved in the diplomacy; and of course, we wanted to keep the Soviets out of the diplomatic arena. Finally, we sought a situation which would enable Israel to deal with each of its neighbors."[24]

If judged on those terms, Kissinger was only partly successful in achieving his objectives. He did achieve the breakup of the Arab united front—Egypt did sign a separate peace with Israel in 1978; however, the other Arab countries hardly followed suit. Additionally, though the Soviet Union would go on to play a much diminished role in the Arab-Israeli conflict, Sadat had already begun the process when he ejected the Soviets from Egypt. It may only be Sadat who could lay claim to the war being anything close to a categorical success. The Egyptians had fought well and the war restored their dignity following the humiliating defeat of 1967. Sadat broke the diplomatic stalemate and jolted the U.S. into pursuing a decidedly more active role. Yet even here, qualification is required. Sadat and Egypt paid a heavy price for the 1978 peace accords. Sadat's "betrayal" of the Arab cause was arguably the most important factor triggering the rise of radical Islamism in Egypt. It also cost him his life.

According to Sadat's biographer, Raphael Israeli, Sadat came to view the war as a triumph, but he grew disappointed that other Egyptians did not share his conception of its glory. In an address in October 1976, he lamented that Egyptian literature had fallen short in its portrayal of the war, and neglected to treat it as an event of major world import, "since the post–October world is different from the pre–October one." Sadat complained that the war had not inspired any great work of art or literature, and he summoned the film star Omar Sharif, who is of Egyptian origin, to attempt to convince him to produce a movie like *The Longest Day*, which portrayed the Allies landing in Normandy in World War II, to honor the Egyptian capture of Israeli-occupied territory.[25]

It would be unfair to judge Kissinger's efficacy solely from the vantage point of twenty-first century hindsight. Yet the archival evidence paints a vivid picture of a secretary of state willing to circumvent the aims of a U.S. president, albeit a beleaguered one, by pursuing his own strategy and objectives, one willing to roll the dice in an explosive Cold War environment when an error in judgment could have had catastrophic consequences. In the words of Trotsky, "The end may justify the means as long as there is something that justifies the end." However, given the ensuing oil crisis, the rupture in relations with the Soviet Union, and the enduring and vehement anti–American sentiment of the Muslim world, as embodied in the Iranian Revolution of 1979 and the terrorism of recent years, the legacy of the October War is, for Kissinger, a questionable one.

Chapter Notes

Chapter 1

1. Yaacov Bar-Siman-Tov, "The United States and Israel since 1948: A 'Special Relationship?'" *Diplomatic History* 22, no. 2 (1998): 231.

2. Marvin C. Feuerwerger, *Congress and Israel: Foreign Aid Decision-Making in the House of Representatives, 1969–1976* (Westport, CT: Greenwood Press, 1979), 9.

3. James Petras, *The Power of Israel in the United States* (Atlanta: Clarity Press, 2006), 41.

4. John J. Mearsheimer and Stephen M. Walt, *The Israel Lobby and U.S. Foreign Policy* (New York: Farrar, Straus and Giroux, 2007), 40.

5. Bar-Siman-Tov, 232.

6. Douglas Little, *American Orientalism: The United States and Middle East Since 1945* (Chapel Hill: University of North Carolina Press, 2008), 5.

7. Henry Kissinger, *White House Years* (Boston: Little, Brown, 1979), 564.

8. See William B. Quandt, Decades of Decisions: American Policy Toward the Arab-Israeli Conflict: 1967–1976 (Berkeley: University of California Press, 1977) and Abraham Ben-Zvi, The United States and Israel: The Limits of the Special Relationship (New York: Columbia University Press, 1993).

9. Mearsheimer and Walt, 355.

10. Peter L. Hahn, "The View from Jerusalem: Revelations about U.S. Diplomacy from the Archives of Israel," *Diplomatic History* 22, no. 4 (Fall 1998): 509.

11. Bernard Reich, *Securing the Covenant: United States-Israel Relations After the Cold War* (Westport, CT: Praeger, 1995), 74.

12. *Washington Post*, November 13, 1974, A9.

13. Ibid., November 14, 1974, A1.

14. Steven L. Spiegel, *The Other Arab-Israeli Conflict: Making America's Middle East Policy, from Truman to Reagan* (Chicago: University of Chicago Press, 1985), 221.

15. Nadav Safran, *Israel the Embattled Ally* (Cambridge: Belknap Press of Harvard University Press, 1978), 572.

16. Dan Raviv and Yossi Melman, *Friends in Deed: Inside the U.S.-Israel Alliance* (New York: Hyperion, 1994), 157.

17. Michelle Mart, *Eye on Israel: How America Came to View Israel as an Ally* (Albany: State University of New York Press, 2006), 35.

18. Elizabeth Stephens, *U.S. Policy Towards Israel: The Role of Political Culture in Defining the "Special Relationship"* (Sussex: Sussex Academic Press, 2006), 70.

19. Abraham Ben-Zvi, *The United States*

and Israel: The Limits of the Special Relationship (New York: Columbia University Press, 1993), 15.

20. Reich, 74.

21. Feuerwerger, 9.

22. Harry S. Truman, *Memoirs by Harry S. Truman: Years of Trial and Hope* (New York: Smithmark, 1996), 161.

23. Michael J. Cohen, "Truman and the State Department: The Palestine Trusteeship Proposal," *Jewish Social Studies* 43, no. 2 (1981): 167.

24. David Schoenbaum, *The United States and the State of Israel* (New York: Oxford University Press, 1993), 92.

25. Douglas Little, "The Making of a Special Relationship: The United States and Israel, 1957–68," *International Journal of Middle East Studies* 25, no. 4 (1993): 567.

26. Ibid., 573.

27. William B. Quandt, "Lyndon Johnson and the June 1967 War: What Color Was the Light?" *Middle East Journal* 46, no. 2 (1992): 200.

28. Lyndon B. Johnson, *The Vantage Point: Perspectives of the Presidency, 1963–1969* (New York: Holt, Rinehart and Winston, 1971), 290

29. U.S. Department of State, National Security File, Country File, Middle East Crisis, CIA Intelligence Memoranda, 5/67–7/67, Office of the Historian, http://www.state.gov.

30. Johnson, 293.

31. Abba Eban, *Personal Witness: Israel Through My Eyes* (New York: G.P. Putnam's Sons, 1992), 389.

32. Quandt, "Lyndon Johnson and the June 1967 War," 214.

33. Eban, 405.

34. William B. Quandt, *Peace Process: American Diplomacy and the Arab-Israeli Conflict since 1967* (Berkeley: University of California Press, 1993), 47.

35. George Lenczowski, *American Presidents and the Middle East* (Durham: Duke University Press, 1990), 115.

36. Quandt, *Peace Process*, 60.

37. Richard Nixon, *RN: The Memoirs of Richard Nixon* (New York: Grosset & Dunlap, 1978), 481.

38. Ibid.

39. Ibid.

40. Kissinger, *White House Years*, 564.

41. Lenczowski, 121.

42. Nixon, *RN*, 484.

43. Noam Kochavi, *Nixon and Israel: Forging a Conservative Partnership* (Albany: State University of New York Press, 2009), 2.

44. Ibid.

45. Seymour M. Hersh, *The Price of Power: Kissinger in the Nixon White House* (New York: Summit Books, 1983), 117.

46. *The Washington Post*, June 9, 1973, A15.

47. Ibid.

48. Joan Hoff, *Nixon Reconsidered* (New York: Basic Books, 1995), 155.

49. Lawrence R. Jacobs and Robert Y. Shapiro, "The Rise of Presidential Polling: The Nixon White House in Historical Perspective," *The Public Opinion Quarterly* 59, no. 2 (1995): 165.

50. George Lardner, Jr., and Michael Dobbs, "New Tapes Reveal Depth of Nixon's Anti-Semitism," *Washington Post*, October 6, 1999, A31.

51. Douglas Brinkley and Luke A. Nichter, *The Nixon Tapes: 1971–1972* (New York: Houghton, Mifflin, Harcourt, 2014), 359.

52. Conrad Black, *Richard M. Nixon: A Life in Full* (New York: Public Affairs, 2007), 840.

53. Kissinger, *White House Years*, 564.

54. Salim Yaqub, "The Politics of Stalemate," in *The Cold War in the Middle East: Regional Conflict and the Superpowers, 1976–1973*, ed. Nijel J. Ashton (New York: Routledge, 2007), 37.

55. Nixon Presidential Materials, "Conversation Between President Nixon and The President's Assistant for National Security Affairs," White House Tapes, Oval Office, Conversation 771–2, http://www.history.state.gov/historicaldocuments/frus1969–76ve01/d93 (accessed October 20, 2010).

56. Ibid.

57. Kissinger Telcon, "Nixon / Kissinger," October 15, 1973, 11:46 a.m., http://foia.state.gov/Search/Results.aspx?collection=KISSINGER&searchText=

58. Little, *American Orientalism*, 106.

59. Jeremy Sharp, "U.S. Foreign Aid to Israel," Congressional Research Service, April 11, 2013, http://www.fas.org/sgp/crs/mideast/RL33222.pdf.

60. Asaf Siniver, *Nixon, Kissinger, and U.S. Foreign Policy Making: The Machin-*

ery of Crisis (Cambridge: Cambridge University Press, 2008): 187.
61. Jussi Hanhimäki, *The Flawed Architect: Henry Kissinger and American Foreign Policy* (Oxford: Oxford University Press, 2004), xviii.
62. Richard Ned Lebow and Janice Gross Stein, *We All Lost the Cold War* (Princeton: Princeton University Press, 1995); Raymond L. Garthoff, *Détente and Confrontation: American-Soviet Relations from Nixon to Reagan* (Washington, D.C.: The Brookings Institution, 1994).

Chapter 2

1. Quandt, *Peace Process*, 58.
2. Ibid., 56.
3. Hersh, 117.
4. Quandt, 61.
5. Henry Kissinger, *Years of Upheaval* (New York: Simon & Schuster, 1982), 202.
6. Brinkley and Nichter, *The Nixon Tapes*, 16.
7. John P. Burke, *Honest Broker? The National Security Advisor and Presidential Decision Making* (College Station: Texas A&M University Press, 2009), 120.
8. H.R. Haldeman, *The Haldeman Diaries: Inside the Nixon White House* (New York: GP Putnam's Sons, 1994), 83.
9. Ibid., 136.
10. Ibid., 176.
11. Ibid., 181.
12. Ibid., 182.
13. Ibid., 192.
14. Brinkley and Nichter, 37.
15. David A. Korn, "US-Soviet Negotiations of 1969 and the Rogers Plan," *Middle East Journal* 44, no. 1 (1990): 39.
16. Ibid.
17. Ibid., 43.
18. Yitzhak Rabin, *The Rabin Memoirs* (Berkeley: University of California Press, 1996), 147.
19. William P. Rogers, Rogers Plan Speech, December 9, 1969, In *Arab-Israeli Conflict and Conciliation: A Documentary History*, ed. Bernard Reich (Westport, CT: Praeger, 1995), 102.
20. Craig Daigle, *The Limits of Détente: The United States, The Soviet Union, and the Arab-Israeli Conflict, 1969–1973* (New Haven: Yale University Press, 2012), 67.
21. Ibid.

22. Don Peretz, "The United States, the Arabs and Israel: Peace Efforts of Kennedy, Johnson, and Nixon," *Annals of the American Academy of Political and Social Science* 401 (1972), 124.
23. Little, 286.
24. Hersh, 220.
25. Rabin, 161.
26. Ibid., 162.
27. Little, 286.
28. Quandt, *Decades of Decisions*, 92.
29. Nixon, 479.
30. Quandt, *Peace Process*, 75.
31. Ibid., 77.
32. Nixon, *RN*, 483.
33. Quandt, *Peace Process*, 80.
34. Rabin, 187.
35. Kissinger, *Years of Upheaval*, 624.
36. Rabin, 189.
37. Joseph Finklestone, *Anwar Sadat: Visionary Who Dared* (Portland: Frank Cass, 2003), 70.
38. Anwar Sadat, *Those I Have Known* (New York: Continuum International, 1984), 82.
39. Finklestone, 76.
40. Quandt, *Peace Process*, 101.
41. Steven L. Spiegel, *The Other Arab-Israeli Conflict: Making America's Middle East Policy, from Truman to Reagan* (Chicago: University of Chicago Press, 1985), 205.
42. Kissinger, *Years of Upheaval*, 376.
43. Spiegel, 209.
44. Hersh, 402.
45. Barry Rubin, "U.S. Policy, January-October 1973," *Journal of Palestine Studies* 3, no. 2 (Winter 1974), 99.
46. *New York Times*, November 23, 1973, 1.
47. Spiegel, 210.
48. Ibid., 211.
49. Quandt, *Peace Process*, 94.
50. Nixon, *RN*, 920.
51. Walter J. Boyne, *The Two O'Clock War* (New York: Thomas Dunne, 2002), 1.
52. Elbridge Colby, Avner Cohen, William McCants, and Bradley Morris, *The Israeli "Nuclear Alert" of 1973: Deterrence and Signaling in Crisis* (Alexandria: CNA, 2013), 16, https://www.cna.org/sites/default/files/research/DRM-2013-U-004480-Final2.pdf, accessed November 2, 2014.
53. Anwar el-Sadat, *The Public Diary of President Sadat: The Road to War, Octo-*

ber 1970—October 1973 (Leiden: Brill Academic, 1997), 82.

54. Anwar el–Sadat, *In Search of Identity: An Autobiography* (New York: Harper and Row, 1978), 226.

55. Ibid., 228.

56. Foy D. Kohler, Leon Gouré, and Mose L. Harvey, *The Soviet Union and the October 1973 Middle East War: The Implications for Détente* (Miami: University of Miami Center for Advanced International Studies, 1974), 32.

57. Ibid, 33.

58. Ibid., 32.

59. Daigle, 195.

60. Isabella Ginor and Gideon Remez, "The Origins of a Misnomer," in *The Cold War in the Middle East: Regional Conflict and the Superpowers, 1976–1973*, ed. Nijel J. Ashton (New York: Routledge, 2007), 139.

61. Ibid.

62. Sadat, *In Search of Identity*, 231.

63. Barry Rubin, "Soviet Policy in the Middle East," in *Crucible: Studies on the Arab-Israeli War of October 1973*, edited by Naseer H. Aruri (Wilmette, IL: Medina University Press International, 1975), 301.

64. Kissinger, *Years of Upheaval*, 206.

65. Hassan el–Badri, Taha el–Magdoub, and Mohammed Dia el Din Zohdy, *The Ramadan War, 1973* (New York: Hero Books, 1978), 15.

66. Raphael Israeli, *Man of Defiance: A Political Biography of Anwar Sadat* (Totowa, NJ: Barnes & Noble Books, 1985), 106.

67. Memorandum from Richard T. Kennedy of the National Security Council Staff to Kissinger, Library of Congress, Manuscript Division, Kissinger Papers, Box CL 168, Geopolitical File, May 15, 1972-May 7, 1973, Secret, Sensitive, *Foreign Relations*, 1.

68. Message from Dobrynin to Kissinger, undated, National Archives, Nixon Presidential Materials, NSC Files, Kissinger Office Files, Box 70, Country Files, Europe, USSAR, Exchange of Notes between Dobrynin and Kissinger, Vol. 5, note "Handed to Kissinger by Dobrynin," *Foreign Relations*, 19.

69. Nixon, *RN*, 786.

70. Ibid.

71. Memorandum for the president's files by Kissinger, February 6, 1973, National Archives, Nixon Presidential Materials, NSC Files, Kissinger Office Files, Box 137, Country Files, Middle East, Iran—Oil to JORDAN/RIFAI, January 3, 1973, Secret, Sensitive, *Foreign Relations*, 31.

72. Kissinger, *Years of Upheaval*, 219.

73. *The Washington Post*, February 12, 1973, A12.

74. Ibid., February 22, 1973, A1.

75. Ibid., February 23, 1973, A18.

76. Kissinger, *Years of Upheaval*, 213.

77. Janice Gross Stein, "The Failures of Deterrence and Intelligence," in Richard B. Parker, *The October War: A Retrospective* (Gainesville: University Press of Florida, 2001), 81.

78. Mohamed Heikal, *The Road to Ramadan* (New York: The New York Times Book Co., 1975), 202.

79. Conversation between Nixon and Kissinger, *Foreign Relations of the United States, 1969–1976, Volume XXV, Arab-Israeli Crisis and War, 1973*, Document 24, http://history.state.gov/historicaldocuments/frus1969–76v25/d24.

80. Memorandum from Kissinger to Nixon, *Foreign Relations of the United States, 1969–1976, Volume XXV, Arab-Israeli Crisis and War, 1973*, Document 25, http://history.state.gov/historicaldocuments/frus1969–76v25/d25#fnref2.

81. Daigle, 196.

82. Ibid.

83. Ibid.

84. *New York Times*, April 2, 1973, 1.

85. David A. Korn, *Assassination in Khartoum* (Bloomington: Indiana University Press, 1973), 148.

86. Kissinger, *Years of Upheaval*, 223.

87. State Department Telegram 51645 to the U.S. Interests Section in Cairo, National Archives, Nixon Presidential Materials, NSC Files, Kissinger Office Files, Box 638, Country Files, Middle East, Arab Republic of Egypt, IX, January-October 1973, *Foreign Relations*, 121.

88. Memorandum from Kissinger to Nixon, March 30, 1973, National Archives, Nixon Presidential Materials, NSC Files, Box 1171, Harold H. Saunders Files, Middle East Negotiations Files, Middle East—Jarring Talks, April 1–30, 1973, Secret, *Foreign Relations*, 123.

89. "The Battle Is Now Inevitable," Sadat interview with Arnaud de Borchgrave, *Newsweek*, April 9, 1973, 44.

90. Memorandum from Schlesinger to Kissinger, April 16, 1973, National Archives,

Nixon Presidential Materials, NSC Files, Kissinger Office Files, Box 135, Country Files, Middle East, Rabin/Dinitz Sensitive Memcons, 1973, Sensitive, *Foreign Relations*, 149.

91. Steven E. Ambrose, *Nixon: The Triumph of a Politician, 1962–1972* (New York: Simon & Schuster, 1989), 458.

92. See M.A. Adelman, "The Oil Cartel Will Get Us If We Don't Watch Out," *New York Times*, April 21, 1973, 21.

93. Tim Jon Semmerling, *"Evil" Arabs in American Popular Film: Orientalist Fear* (Austin: University of Texas Press, 2006), 10.

94. R.S. Zaharna, "The Palestinian Leadership and the American Media: Changing Images, Conflicting Results," in *The U.S. Media and the Middle East: Image and Perception*, ed. Yahya R. Kamalipour (Westport, CT: Praeger, 1995), 42.

95. *New York Times*, April 15, 1973, 13.

96. Ibid., April 17, 1973, 2.

97. Ibid., April 20, 1973, 7.

98. Donald Neff, *Warriors Against Israel: How Israel Won the Battle to Become America's Ally, 1973* (Brattleboro, VT: Amana Books, 1988), 112.

99. *Sarasota Herald Tribune*, April 20, 1973, 3A.

100. Neff, 113.

101. Memorandum of Conversation, May 3, 1973, National Archives, Nixon Presidential Materials, NSC Files, Kissinger Office Files, Box 135, Country Files, Middle East, Rabin/Dinitz Sensitive Memcons, 1973, Top Secret, Sensitive, *Foreign Relations*, 149.

102. Memorandum from Schlesinger to Kissinger, May 5, 1973, National Archives, Nixon Presidential Materials, NSC Files, Box 647, Country Files, Middle East (General), Vol. #9, 1972 – Aug. 1974, Secret, Sensitive, *Foreign Relations*, 154.

103. Memorandum of Conversation, May 7, 1973, National Archives, Nixon Presidential Materials, NSC Files, Kissinger Office Files, Box 75, Country Files, Europe, USSR, Kissinger Conversations at Zavidovo, May 5–8, 1973, Top Secret, Sensitive, *Foreign Relations*, 155.

104. *New York Times*, May 16, 1973, 6.

105. President's Wednesday Briefing, "Inter-Arab Military Movements," May 16, 1973, Richard Nixon Presidential Library and Museum, Central Intelligence Agency.

President Nixon and the Role of Intelligence in the 1973 Arab-Israeli War. Yorba Linda, CA, 2013, Kindle edition, location 742.

106. National Archives, Nixon Presidential Materials, Henry Kissinger Office Files, box 132, Egypt/Ismail, Vol. VII, May 20-Sept. 23, 1972, The National Security Archive, ed. William Burr, October 7, 2003, "The October War and U.S. Policy," http://www.gwu.edu/~nsarchiv/NSAEBB/NSAEBB98/, Document 2A, http://www.gwu.edu/~nsarchiv/NSAEBB/NSAEBB98/octwar-02a.pdf. Note: Future citations will henceforth appear as "Burr," with the URL address and original, archived document's physical location.

107. Memorandum from Kissinger to Nixon, "Meeting with Hafiz Ismail on May 20," June 2, 1973, National Archives, Nixon Presidential Materials, Henry Kissinger Office Files, Box 132, Egypt/Ismail Vol. VII, May 20-Sept., Burr, Document 2B. http://www.gwu.edu/~nsarchiv/NSAEBB/NSAEBB98/octwar-02b.pdf.

108. Burr, notes, page 8. http://www.gwu.edu/~nsarchiv/NSAEBB/NSAEBB98/.

109. This memorandum has not been found but it is quoted in a December 20 paper prepared by the Intelligence Community staff, "The Performance of the Intelligence Community Before the Arab-Israeli War of October 6, 1973: A Preliminary Post-Mortem Report," *Foreign Relations*, 193.

110. Intelligence Memorandum Prepared in the Central Intelligence Agency, Central Intelligence Agency, Directorate of Intelligence, Office of Current Intelligence, Job 79-T00861A, Box 16, Folder 40, Secret, *Foreign Relations*, 195.

111. Nixon, *RN*, 884.

112. Kissinger, memorandum for the president's files, President's Meeting with General Secretary Leonid Brezhnev on Saturday, June 23, 1973 at 10:30 p.m. at the Western White House, San Clemente, California, HENRY KISSINGER OFFICE FILES, Box 75, Brezhnev visit, June 18–25, 1973, Memcons, Burr, Document 3. http://www.gwu.edu/~nsarchiv/NSAEBB/NSAEBB98/octwar-03.pdf.

113. Kissinger, *Years of Upheaval*, 298.

114. Daigle, 244.

115. *New York Times*, July 27, 1973, 1.

116. Telegram 2193 from Cairo, July 23, National Archives, RG 59, Central Foreign Policy Files, *Foreign Relations*, 246.

117. http://unispal.un.org/UNISPAL.NSF/0/D359EEC4EB0E3EA50525652900785400.

118. http://www.jewishvirtuallibrary.org/jsource/UN/usvetoes.html.

119. Memorandum from Harold Saunders to Kissinger, National Archives, Nixon Presidential Materials, NSC Files, Box 1172, Harold H. Saunders Files, Middle East Negotiations Files, M.E. Jarring Talks, Aug. 1, 1973-Aug. 31, 1973, Secret, *Foreign Relations*, 250.

120. Kurt Waldheim, *In the Eye of the Storm: A Memoir* (Bethesda: Adler & Adler, 1986), 58.

121. *New York Times*, August 10, 1973, 1.

122. Ibid., September 6, 1973, 26.

123. "Memorandum of Conversation," National Archives, Nixon Presidential Materials, Henry Kissinger Office Files, Box 135, Rabin/Dinitz, Sensitive Memcons, Burr, Document 5. http://www.gwu.edu/~nsarchiv/NSAEBB/NSAEBB98/octwar-05.pdf.

124. "Briefing Memorandum from Cline to Kissinger," National Archives, Nixon Presidential Materials, NSC Files, Box 1173, Harold H. Saunders Files, Middle East Negotiations Files, 1973 Middle East War, file 1, October 6, 1973, top secret, *Foreign Relations*, 278.

125. "Telegram from U.S. Embassy in Israel to the Department of State," National Archives, RG 59, Central Foreign Policy Files, secret, immediate, *Foreign Relations*, 280.

126. "Telegram the Department of State to the U.S. Embassy in Israel," National Archives, RG 59, Central Foreign Policy Files, secret, priority, *Foreign Relations*, 281.

127. Lebow and Stein, *We All Lost the Cold War*, 176.

128. "Message from Meir to Kissinger," National Archives, Nixon Presidential Materials, NSC Files, Kissinger Office Files, Box 136, Country Files, Middle East, Dinitz, June 4-October 31, 1973, *Foreign Relations* 284.

129. Henry Kissinger, *Crisis: The Anatomy of Two Major Foreign Policy Crises* (New York: Simon & Schuster, 2003), 13.

130. Golda Meir, *My Life: The Autobiography of Golda Meir* (London: Futura Publications, 1975), 357.

131. Alistair Horne, *Kissinger: 1973, The Crucial Year* (New York: Simon & Schuster, 2009), 238.

132. Brecher and Raz, 492.

133. Ibid., 496.

134. Michael Brecher, *Decisions In Crisis: Israel, 1967 and 1973* (Berkeley: University of California Press, 1980), 183.

135. Department of State, Operations Center, Middle East Task Force, Situation Room #8, "Situation in the Middle East, as of 2300 Hours," October 7, 1973, National Archives, Nixon Presidential Materials, NSC Files, Box 1173, 1973 War, file no. 2, Burr, Document 19, http://www.gwu.edu/~nsarchiv/NSAEBB/NSAEBB98/octwar-19.pdf.

136. "Minutes of Cabinet Meeting," October 18, 1973, Ford Library, National Security Adviser, Memoranda of Conversation, Box 2, Secret, 3:09 p.m. *Foreign Relations*, 588.

137. Moshe Dayan, *Story of My Life* (New York: William Morrow, 1976), 376.

138. Brecher, *Decisions in Crisis*, 185.

139. Parker, *The October War*, 127.

140. Kissinger, *Years of Upheaval*, 467.

141. Michael Brecher and Mordechai Raz, "Images and Behavior: Israel's Yom Kippur Crisis, 1973," *International Journal* 32, no. 3 (Summer 1977): 480.

142. Kissinger, *Years of Upheaval*, 466.

143. Ibid., 467.

144. Interview with Harold P. Ford, April 2, 1987, *President Nixon and the Role of Intelligence in the 1973 Arab-Israeli War* (Yorba Linda, CA: Richard Nixon Presidential Library and Museum, 2013), 19.

145. William Colby, Memorandum to Henry Kissinger, "Critique of Middle East Crisis," October 27, 1973, *President Nixon and the Role of Intelligence in the 1973 Arab-Israeli War*, 18.

146. Ibid.

147. Memorandum to the Director of Central Intelligence prepared by the Intelligence Community Staff, *The Performance of the Intelligence Community Before the Arab-Israeli War of October 1973: A Preliminary Post-Mortem Report*, December 20, 1973, 2. http://www.foia.cia.gov/sites/default/files/document_conversions/89801/DOC_0001331429.pdf.

148. Ibid., 3.
149. Ibid., 4.
150. Kissinger, *Years of Upheaval*, 464.

Chapter 3

1. U.S. Embassy Israel, Cable 7766 to Department of State, October 6, 1973, "*GOI Concern About Possible Syrian and Egyptian Attack Today*," National Archives, Nixon Presidential Materials Project, National Security Council Files, box 1173, 1973 War (Middle East), October 6, 1973, File No. 1. http://www.gwu.edu/~nsarchiv/NSAEBB/NSAEBB98/octwar-09.pdf.
2. Kissinger Telcon, "Dobrynin / Kissinger," October 6, 1973, 6:40 a.m., http://foia.state.gov/documents/Kissinger/0000C202.pdf.
3. Ibid.
4. Anatoly Dobrynin, *In Confidence: Moscow's Ambassador to America's Six Cold War Presidents* (New York: Random House, 1995), 295.
5. Kissinger Telcon, "Shalev / Kissinger," October 6, 1973, 6:55 a.m., http://foia.state.gov/documents/Kissinger/0000C203.pdf.
6. Kissinger Telcon, "Zayad / Kissinger," October 6, 1973, 7:00 a.m., http://foia.state.gov/documents/Kissinger/0000C204.pdf.
7. Kissinger, *Crisis*, 17.
8. Kissinger, *Years of Upheaval*, 454.
9. Ibid.
10. U.S. Department of State Cable 199583 to U.S. Embassies Jordan and Saudi Arabia, "Message from Secretary to King Faisal and King Hussein," National Archives, Nixon Presidential Files, NSC Files, box 1173, 1973 War (Middle East), October 6, 1973, File No. 1. http://www.gwu.edu/~nsarchiv/NSAEBB/NSAEBB98/octwar-12.pdf.
11. Haig claims in his memoirs that the White House Situation Room had informed him at approximately 6:00 a.m. that hostilities had begun and that he immediately informed the president. Haig, *Inner Circles*, 411.
12. Kissinger, *Years of Upheaval*, 454.
13. Message from Secretary Kissinger, New York, to White House Situation Room, National Archives, Nixon Presidential Materials, NSC Files, Box 664, Middle East War Memos & Misc. October 1 – October 17, 1973, Burr, Document 10, http://www.gwu.edu/~nsarchiv/NSAEBB/NSAEBB98/octwar-10.pdf.
14. Kissinger Telcon, "Scowcroft / Kissinger," October 6, 1973, 8:50 a.m., http://foia.state.gov/documents/Kissinger/0000C210.pdf.
15. Melvin and Bernard Kalb, *Kissinger* (Boston: Little, Brown, 1974), 458.
16. Ibid., 459.
17. Kissinger Telcon, "Scowcroft / Kissinger," October 6, 1973, 8:50 a.m., http://foia.state.gov/documents/Kissinger/0000C210.pdf.
18. Minutes of WSAG Meeting, October 6, 1973, 9:01 a.m., National Archives, Nixon Presidential Materials, NSC Files, NSC Institutional Files (H-Files), Box H–117, WSAG Meeting Minutes, Originals, 1973, top secret, *Foreign Relations*, 294.
19. Raphael Israeli, *Man of Defiance: A Political Biography of Anwar Sadat* (Totowa, NJ: Barnes & Noble Books, 1985), 106.
20. Kissinger Telcon, "Dobrynin / Kissinger," October 6, 1973, 9:20 a.m., http://foia.state.gov/documents/Kissinger/0000C214.pdf.
21. Kissinger Telcon, "Nixon / Kissinger," October 6, 1973, 9:25 a.m., National Archives, Nixon Presidential Materials, Kissinger Telephone Conversations, Telcons, Chronological File, Box 22, *Foreign Relations*, 306,
22. Kissinger, *Years of Upheaval*, 470.
23. Victor Israelyan, *Inside the Kremlin During the Yom Kippur War* (University Park: Pennsylvania State University Press, 1995), 37.
24. Andrei Gromyko, *Memoirs* (New York: Doubleday, 1989), 281.
25. John L. Scherer, "Soviet and American Behavior During the Yom Kippur War," *World Affairs* 141, no. 1 (Summer 1978): 10.
26. William B. Quandt, "Soviet Policy in the October Middle East War—I," *International Affairs* (Royal Institute of International Affairs 1944-) 53, No. 3 (July 1977), 387.
27. Kissinger Telcon, "Dobrynin / Kissinger," October 6, 1973, 9:35 a.m., http://foia.state.gov/documents/Kissinger/0000C215.pdf.
28. Kissinger, *Crisis*, 32.
29. Memorandum to Kissinger, ini-

tialed "LSE" (Lawrence S. Eagleburger), October 6, 1973, RG 59, SN 70–73, Pol 27–14, Arab Israeli War, Burr, Document 16. http://www.gwu.edu/~nsarchiv/NSAEBB/NSAEBB98/octwar-16.pdf.

30. Kissinger Telcon, "Haig / Kissinger," October 6, 1973, 12:45 p.m. http://foia.state.gov/documents/Kissinger/0000C21D.pdf.

31. Ibid.

32. Alexander M. Haig, Jr., *Inner Circles: How America Changed the World: A Memoir* (New York: Warner Books, 1992), 411.

33. "Message from the Soviet Leadership to Nixon and Kissinger," National Archives, Nixon Presidential Materials, NSC Files, Kissinger Office Files, Europe, USSR, Dobrynin/Kissinger, Vol. 19, July 13-October 11, Top Secret, *Foreign Relations*, 314.

34. Niall Ferguson, *The Shock of the Global: The 1970's in Perspective* (Cambridge: Belknap Press of Harvard University Press, 2010), 224.

35. Saliba Sarsar, "The Question of Palestine and United States Behavior at the United Nations," *International Journal of Politics, Culture and Society* 17, no. 3 (2004), 458.

36. Francis Fukuyama, *The End of History and the Last Man* (New York: Free Press, 2006), 282.

37. Lawrence S. Finkelstein, "The United States and the United Nations Proper Prudence—Or a New Failure of Nerve," *Korea Journal* 35, no. 1 (1995): 63.

38. B.K. Shrivastava, "The United States and the United Nations," *India Quarterly* 32, no. 2 (1976), 221.

39. Waldheim, 111.

40. Robert Alden, "Bush Leaving U.N. Post is Fearful of Bloc Voting," *New York Times*, December 20, 1972.

41. Randall G. Holcombe and Russell S. Sobel, "The Stability of International Coalitions in United Nations Voting from 1946 to 1973," *Public Choice* 86, no. 1/2 (1996), 21.

42. Kissinger Telcon, "Dobrynin / Kissinger, October 6, 1973, 3:50 p.m. http://foia.state.gov/documents/Kissinger/0000C222.pdf.

43. Kissinger, *Years of Upheaval*, 474.

44. Transcript of Telephone Conversation between Scowcroft and Dobrynin," October 6, 1973, 5:45 p.m. National Archives, Nixon Presidential Materials, Kissinger Office Files, Europe, USSR, Dobrynin/Kissinger, Vol. 19, July 13-October11, Top Secret, *Foreign Relations*, 317.

45. Kissinger, *Years of Upheaval*, 474.

46. Israelyan, 37.

47. Memorandum from William Quandt and Donald Stukel, "WSAG Meeting—Middle East, Saturday, October 6, 1973, 3:00 p.m. National Archives, Nixon Presidential Materials, NSC Files, Box H-94, WSAG Meeting, Middle East, October 6, 1973, 7:30 p.m. folder 1, Burr, Document 15, http://www.gwu.edu/~nsarchiv/NSAEBB/NSAEBB98/octwar-15.pdf.

48. Minutes of WSAG Meeting, October 6, 1973, 7:22 p.m. National Archives, Nixon Presidential Materials, NSC Files, Kissinger Office Files, Box 129, Country Files, Middle East, Nodis/Cedar/Plus, 1971–74, Top Secret, *Foreign Relations*, 324.

49. Kissinger Telcon, "Zayyat / Kissinger," October 6, 1973, 8:45 p.m. http://foia.state.gov/documents/Kissinger/0000C232.pdf.

50. Memcon between Kissinger and Ambassador Huang Zhen, PRC Liaison Office, October 6, 1973, 9:10–9:30 p.m. RG 59, Records of the Policy Planning Staff, Director's Files (Winston Lord), 1969–1977, box 328, Chinese Exchanges July 10-October 31, 1973, Burr, Document 17, http://www.gwu.edu/~nsarchiv/NSAEBB/NSAEBB98/octwar-17.pdf.

51. Kissinger Telcon, "Haig / Kissinger," October 7, 1973, 9:35 p.m. http://foia.state.gov/documents/Kissinger/0000C23B.pdf.

52. Mario Del Pero, *The Eccentric Realist: Henry Kissinger and the Shaping of American Foreign Policy* (Ithaca: Cornell University Press, 2010), 136.

53. *The Washington Post*, February 8, 1973, A26.

54. Del Pero, 9.

55. Kissinger Telcon, "Nixon / Kissinger," October 7, 1973, 2:07 p.m. http://foia.state.gov/documents/Kissinger/0000C244.pdf.

56. Kissinger Telcon., "Haig / Kissinger," October 7, 1973, 3:10 p.m. http://foia.state.gov/documents/Kissinger/0000C245.pdf.

57. Kissinger Telcon, "Dobrynin / Kissinger, October 7, 1973, 3:25 p.m.

http://foia.state.gov/documents/Kissinger/0000C246.pdf.
58. Kissinger, *Years of Upheaval*, 481.
59. Anatoly Dobrynin, *In Confidence: Moscow's Ambassador to America's Six Cold War President* (New York: Times Books, 1995), 295.
60. Kissinger, *Crisis*, 101.
61. Kissinger Telcon, "Eban / Kissinger," October 7, 1973, 5:08 p.m. http://foia.state.gov/documents/Kissinger/0000C251.pdf.
62. Kissinger, *Years of Upheaval*, 481.
63. Kissinger, *Crisis*, 111.
64. Kissinger Telcon, "Nixon / Kissinger," October 7, 1973, 10:30 p.m. http://foia.state.gov/documents/Kissinger/0000C2BA.pdf.
65. Richard Reeves, *President Nixon* (New York: Simon & Schuster, 2001), 13.
66. http://www.inaugural.senate.gov/swearing-in/address/address-by-richard-m-nixon-1969.
67. "Transcript of Telephone Conversation between Haig and Rogers," September 5, 1972, 10:55 p.m. *Black September*, CD-ROM, BACM Research.
68. Ibid.
69. Department of State, Operations Center, Middle East Task Force, Situation Report #8, "Situation in the Middle East, as of 2300 Hours (EDT, October 7, 1973), National Archives, Nixon Presidential Materials, NSC Files, Box 1173, 1973, Burr, Document 19, 1973 file no. 2, http://www.gwu.edu/~nsarchiv/NSAEBB/NSAEBB98/octwar-19.pdf.
70. Kissinger Telcon, Dinitz / Kissinger, October 8, 1973, 1:14 p.m. http://foia.gov/documents/Kissinger/0000C28A.pdf.
71. Kissinger, *Crisis*, 112.
72. Quandt, *Decades of Decisions*, 174.
73. Kissinger to Egyptian Foreign Minister Al-Zayyat, October 8, 1973, enclosing "Message for Mr. Hafiz Ismail from Dr. Kissinger," National Archives, Nixon Presidential Materials, Henry Kissinger Office Files, Box 132, Egypt/Ismail, Vol. VII, October 1–21, 1973, Burr, Document 20, http://www.gwu.edu/~nsarchiv/NSAEBB/NSAEBB98/octwar-20.pdf.
74. Kissinger, *Crisis*, 114.
75. Kissinger, *Years of Upheaval*, 488. *Crisis*, 118, 121, 126 and 127.
76. Kissinger Telcon, Dinitz / Kissinger, October 9, 1973, 5:40 p.m. National Archives, Nixon Presidential Materials,

Kissinger Telephone Conversations, Chronological File, Box 22, *Foreign Relations*, 279.
77. Kalb and Kalb, 466.
78. Kissinger, *Years of Upheaval*, 489.
79. Kalb and Kalb, 466.
80. Kissinger, *Years of Upheaval*, 491.
81. Kalb and Kalb, 466.
82. Kissinger Telcon, "The president / Kissinger," October 8, 1973, 7:08 p.m. http://foia.state.gov/documents/Kissinger/0000C276.pdf.
83. Kissinger Telcon, "Dinitz / Kissinger," October 9, 1973, 1:45 a.m., http://foia.state.gov/documents/Kissinger/0000C279.pdf.
84. Memcon between Dinitz and Kissinger, October 9, 1973, 8:20–8:40 a.m., RG 59, Records of Henry Kissinger, Box 25, CAT C Arab-Israeli War, Burr, Document 21A, http://www.gwu.edu/~nsarchiv/NSAEBB/NSAEBB98/octwar-21a.pdf.
85. Kissinger, *Crisis*, 146.
86. Walter Isaacson, *Kissinger: A Biography* (New York: Simon & Schuster, 2005), 518.
87. William Quandt to Kissinger, "Middle Eastern Issues, October 9, 1973," National Archives, Nixon Presidential Materials, NSC Files, Box 664, Middle East War Memos and Misc. October 6-October 17, 1973, Burr, Document 22, http://www.gwu.edu/~nsarchiv/NSAEBB/NSAEBB98/octwar-22.pdf.
88. Kissinger, *Years of Upheaval* 494.
89. Ibid., 147.
90. Kohlher, Gouré, and Harvey, 64.
91. Kalb and Kalb, 467.
92. Kissinger Telcon, "Dobrynin / Kissinger," October 9, 1973, 11:29 a.m., http://foia.state.gov/documents/Kissinger/0000C17B.pdf.
93. Kissinger Telcon., "Dobrynin / Kissinger," October 9, 1973, 12:32 p.m. http://foia.state.gov/documents/Kissinger/0000C17D.pdf.
94. http://cdn.geraldrfordfoundation.org/memcons/1552617.pdf.
95. Memcon between Dinitz and Kissinger, October 9, 1973, 6:10–6:35 P.M.,RG 59, SN 70–73, Pol Isr-US.
96. Kissinger Telcon, "Dinitz / Kissinger," October 9, 1973, 7:25 p.m. http://foia.state.gov/documents/Kissinger/0000C27F.pdf.

97. Kissinger, *Years of Upheaval*, 497. *Crisis*, 169.
98. Kissinger Telcon, "Dobrynin / Kissinger," October 10, 1973, 8:35 a.m., http://foia.state.gov/documents/Kissinger/0000C17E.pdf.
99. Kissinger, *Years of Upheaval*, 498.
100. Ibid., 499.
101. Kalb and Kalb, 468.
102. Ibid.
103. Kissinger Telcon, "Scali / Kissinger," October 10, 1973, 12:15 p.m. http://foia.state.gov/documents/Kissinger/0000C286.pdf.Kissinger. Note that the original documents says "Hoveda, the Israeli Ambassador." Kissinger correctly writes "Iranian Ambassador" in *Crisis*, 170.
104. Kissinger, *Years of Upheaval*, 501.
105. Kalb and Kalb, 469.
106. Memcon between Deputy Secretary of State Kenneth Rush and Petroleum Company Executives, "The Middle East Conflict and U.S. Oil Interests," October 10, 1973, RG 59, SN 70–73, POL 27 Arab-Isr, Burr, Document 26, http://www.gwu.edu/~nsarchiv/NSAEBB/NSAEBB98/octwar-26.pdf.
107. Kalb and Kalb, 470.
108. Kissinger Telcon, "Waldheim / Kissinger," October 10, 1973, 8:27 p.m. http://foia.state.gov/documents/Kissinger/0000C291.pdf.
109. Kissinger, *Crisis*, 175.
110. Kalb and Kalb, 471.
111. Kissinger, *Years of Upheaval*, 504.
112. Kissinger Telcon, "Nixon / Kissinger," October 11, 1973, 11:00 a.m., http://foia.state.gov/documents/Kissinger/0000C29A.pdf.
113. Kissinger, *Years of Upheaval*, 504.
114. Kissinger, *Crisis*, 182.
115. Kissinger Telcon, "Sisco / Kissinger," October 11, 1973, 2:40 p.m. http://foia.state.gov/documents/Kissinger/0000C29E.pdf.
116 Kissinger, *Crisis*, 183.
117. Kalb and Kalb, 472.
118. Kissinger Telcon, "Dinitz / Kissinger," October 11, 1973, 3:05 p.m. http://foia.state.gov/documents/Kissinger/0000C2A0.pdf.
119. Kissinger Telcon, "Sisco / Kissinger," October 11, 1973, 5:35 p.m. http://foia.state.gov/documents/Kissinger/0000C2A9.pdf.
120. Memcon. Kissinger and Brent Scowcroft, October 11, 1973, 5:55 p.m. Source: Nixon Presidential Materials Project, Henry A. Kissinger Telephone Conversations Transcripts, Chronological File, Box 22, File 10, 089, http://www.gwu.edu/~nsarchiv/NSAEBB/NSAEBB123/Box%2022,%20File%2010,%20Scowcroft%20-%20Kissinger%20oct%2011%2073%205,55%20pm%20089.pdf.
121. Kissinger Telcon, "Heath / Kissinger," October 11, 1973, 8:00 p.m. http://foia.state.gov/documents/Kissinger/0000D99E.pdf.
122. Kissinger Telcon, "Dinitz / Kissinger," October 11, 1973, 8:10 p.m. http://foia.state.gov/documents/Kissinger/0000C2AB.pdf.
123. Department of State, Operations Center, Middle East Task Force, Situation Report #22, "Situation Report in the Middle East, as of 0600 EDT, October 12, 1973, National Archives, Nixon Presidential Materials, NSC Files, Box 1174, 1973 Middle East War – 12 October 1973, file no. 7, Burr, Document 27, http://www.gwu.edu/~nsarchiv/NSAEBB/NSAEBB98/octwar-27.pdf.
124. Kalb and Kalb, 471.
125. Kissinger Telcon, "Dinitz / Kissinger," October 12, 1973, 8:35 a.m., http://foia.state.gov/documents/Kissinger/0000C6E2.pdf.
126. Kissinger, *Years of Upheaval*, 506.
127. Kalb and Kalb, 472.
128. Kissinger Telcon, "Nixon / Kissinger," October 12, 1973, 8:38 a.m., http://foia.state.gov/documents/Kissinger/0000C6E3.pdf.
129. Kissinger Telcon, "Dinitz / Kissinger," October 12, 1973, 11:04 a.m., http://foia.state.gov/documents/Kissinger/0000C6E6.pdf.
130. Kissinger, *Years of Upheaval*, 507.
131. Ibid.
132. Kalb and Kalb, 473.
133. Kissinger, *Years of Upheaval*, 508.
134. Kalb and Kalb, 474.
135. Kissinger Telcon, "Vorontsov / Kissinger," October 12, 1973, 7:00 p.m. http://foia.state.gov/documents/Kissinger/0000C731.pdf.
136. Kissinger, *Years of Upheaval*, 509.
137. Kissinger, *Years of Upheaval*, 510. Kissinger Telcon, "Lord Cromer / Kissinger," October 12, 1973, 8:15 p.m. http://

foia.state.gov/documents/Kissinger/0000C733.pdf.
138. Kissinger, *Years of Upheaval*, 511. Kissinger, Crisis, 209.
139. Kissinger Telcon, "Lord Cromer / Kissinger," October 12, 1973, 9:33 p.m. http://foia.state.gov/documents/Kissinger/0000C735.pdf.
140. Kissinger, *Crisis*, 211.
141. Kissinger, *Years of Upheaval*, 512.
142. Kalb and Kalb, 475.
143. Ibid.
144. Kissinger, *Crisis*, 212.
145. Ibid., 215.
146. Lebow and Stein, 190, interview with Peter Rodman, April 24, 1991.
147. Ibid., 191, interview with Joseph Sisco, April 17, 1991.
148. Spiegel, 251.
149. Asaf Siniver, *Nixon, Kissinger and U.S. Foreign Policy Making: The Machinery of Crisis*, interview with Quandt (Cambridge: Cambridge University Press, 2008), 201.
150. Quandt, *Decades of Darkness*, 204.
151. Edward R. F. Sheehan, "How Kissinger Did It: Step by Step in the Middle East," in *Dynamics of Third Party Intervention: Kissinger in the Middle East*, ed. Jeffrey Z. Rubin (New York: Praeger, 1983), 51.
152. Mario Del Pero, *The Eccentric Realist: Henry Kissinger and the Shaping of American Foreign Policy* (Ithaca: Cornell University Press, 2010), 136.
153. Haig, *Inner Circles*, 411.
154. Parker, 256.
155. Kissinger, *Years of Upheaval*, 513.
156. Kissinger Telcon, "Haig / Kissinger," October 13, 1973, 9:35 a.m., http://foia.state.gov/documents/Kissinger/0000C73D.pdf.
157. Kissinger Telcon, "Haig / Kissinger," October 13, 1973, 9:37 a.m., http://foia.state.gov/documents/Kissinger/0000C744.pdf.
158. Kissinger Telcon, "Douglas-Home / Kissinger," October 13, 1973, 9:38 a.m., http://foia.state.gov/documents/Kissinger/0000C744.pdf. Note: Original Telcon incorrectly says conversation was with "Hume" and not "Douglas-Home."
159. Kissinger, *Years of Upheaval*, 514.
160. Kalb and Kalb, 477.
161. Memorandum of Conversation," Special WSAG Meeting, Ford Library, National Security Adviser, Memoranda of Conversation, Box 2, Secret, *Foreign Relations*, 482.
162. Kissinger, *Crisis*, 228.
163. Kissinger Telcon, "Dobrynin / Kissinger," October 13, 1973, 1:40 p.m. http://foia.state.gov/documents/Kissinger/0000C754.pdf.
164. Kissinger Telcon, "Douglas-Home / Kissinger," October 13, 1973, 3:35 p.m. http://foia.state.gov/documents/Kissinger/0000C75A.pdf.
165. Kissinger Telcon, "Scowcroft / Kissinger," October 13, 1973, 4:05 p.m. http://foia.state.gov/documents/Kissinger/0000C75C.pdf.
166. Kissinger Telcon, "Dobrynin / Kissinger," October 13, 1973, 4:25 p.m. http://foia.state.gov/documents/Kissinger/0000C75E.pdf.
167. Kissinger Telcon, "Cromer / Kissinger," October 13, 1973, 4:35 p.m. http://foia.state.gov/documents/Kissinger/0000C75F.pdf.
168. Kissinger Telcon, "Dobrynin / Kissinger," October 13, 1973, 7:55 p.m. http://foia.state.gov/documents/Kissinger/0000C78F.pdf. Also, Kissinger, *Crisis*, 241.
169. Memcon: "Nixon / Secretary Kissinger," October 14, 1973, 9:04 a.m., National Security Archive collection, http://www.gwu.edu/~nsarchiv/NSAEBB/NSAEBB265/19731014a.pdf.
170. Asaf Siniver, 203.
171. Peter Rodman, *Presidential Command: Power, Leadership, and the Making of Foreign Policy from Richard Nixon to George W. Bush* (New York: Alfred A. Knopf, 2009), 73.

Chapter 4

1. "Transcript of telephone conversation between President Nixon and Secretary of State Kissinger," October 14, 1973, 9:04 a.m., National Archives, Nixon Presidential Materials, Kissinger Telephone Conversations, Transcripts (Telcons), Chronological Fire, Box 23, *Foreign Relations*, 495.
2. Ibid., 496.
3. Ibid., 498.
4. Kissinger, *Crisis*, 254.
5. Ibid., 256.
6. State Department Cable 203672

to U.S. Embassy, Saudi Arabia, "Message to the King from the Secretary," October 14, 1973, National Archives, Nixon Presidential Materials, NSC Files, Box 1174, 1973 Middle East War 15, file no. 9, Burr, Document 29A, http://www.gwu.edu/~nsarchiv/NSAEBB/NSAEBB98/octwar-29a.pdf.

7. U.S. Embassy Saudi Arabia, Cable 45491 to State Department, "U.S. Arms to Israeli: Saudis Sorrowful: King May Send Another Message," October 14, 1973, National Archives, Nixon Presidential Materials, NSC Files, Box 1174, 1973 Middle East War 15, file no. 11, Burr, Document 29B, http://www.gwu.edu/~nsarchiv/NSAEBB/NSAEBB98/octwar-29b.pdf.

8. Ibid., 522.

9. Kissinger, *Years of Upheaval*, 525.

10. "Situation Report in the Middle East as of 12:00 EDT, October 15, 1973," Middle East Task Force, Situation Report #32, National Archives, Nixon Presidential Materials, NSC Files, NSCF, box 1174, 1973 Middle East War, October 15, File #10, Burr, Document 30, http://www.gwu.edu/~nsarchiv/NSAEBB/NSAEBB98/octwar-30.pdf.

11. "Jackson Bids U.S. Speed Israel Aid: Speech by Senator Appears to Open Policy Battle," *New York Times*, October 15, 1973, 21.

12. "Minutes of WSAG Meeting," October 15, 1973, 10:08 a.m., National Archives, Nixon Presidential Materials, NSC Institutional Files, Box H-117, WSAG Meeting Minutes, Originals, 1973, Top Secret, *Foreign Relations*, 525.

13. "Minutes of the Secretary of State's Staff Meeting," October 15, 1973, 3:15 p.m. National Archives, RG 59, Transcripts of Sec. of State Kissinger's Staff Meetings, 1973–77: lot 78 D 443, box 1, Secret, *Foreign Relations*, 537.

14. "Backchannel Message from Kissinger to Ismail, undated, National Archives, NSC Files, Kissinger Office files, Box 132, Country Files, Middle East Egypt/Ismail, Vol. VII, October 1–31, 1973, Attached to a transmittal memorandum from Scowcroft on October 15. *Foreign Relations*, 541.

15. "Kissinger and Tho Win Nobel Prize for Vietnam Pact," Special to *New York Times*, October 16, 193, 1.

16. "NATO Implications of the Middle East Conflict: NAC Meeting of October 16, 1973," NATIONAL ARCHIVES, NIXON PRESIDENTIAL MATERIALS, NSCF, Box 1174, 1973 Middle Eastern War, October 16, File No. 11, Burr, Documents 32A and 32B, http://www.gwu.edu/~nsarchiv/NSAEBB/NSAEBB98/octwar-32a.pdf, http://www.gwu.edu/~nsarchiv/NSAEBB/NSAEBB98/octwar–32b.pdf.

17. "Situation Report in the Middle East as of 18:00 EDT, October 16, 1973," Middle East Task Force, Situation Report #36, NATIONAL ARCHIVES, NIXON PRESIDENTIAL MATERIALS, NS7CF, box 1174, 1973 Middle East War, October 16, File #11, Burr, Document 33, http://www.gwu.edu/~nsarchiv/NSAEBB/NSAEBB98/octwar-33.pdf.

18. Alistair Horne, *Kissinger: 1973, The Crucial Year* (New York: Simon & Schuster, 2009), 349.

19. Ragaei el Mallakh, "Arab Oil and the World Economy," in *Middle East Crucible: Studies on the Arab-Israeli War of October 1973*, ed. Naseer H. Aruri (Wilmette, IL: Medina University Press International, 1975), 329.

20. "Minutes of WSAG Meeting, October 16, 1973, 10:08 a.m. National Archives, NSC Files, NSC Institutional Files, Box H-117, Minutes Files (1969–74), Top Secret, *Foreign Relations*, 545.

21. "Backchannel Message from Kissinger to Ismail, October 16, 1973, 9:07 a.m. National Archives, NSC Files, Kissinger Office files, Box 132, Country Files, Middle East Egypt/Ismail, Vol. VII, October 1–31, 1973, Secret, *Foreign Relations*, 543.

22. Kissinger, *Crisis*, 271.

23. *Foreign Relations*, 586. Also cited from *Foreign Relations* is Telegram 3790; National Archives, Nixon Presidential Materials, NSC Files, Box 1175, Harold H. Saunders File, Middle East Negotiation Files, 1973 Middle East War, October 18, 1973.

24. Kissinger, *Years of Upheaval*, 873.

25. Central Intelligence Agency, DI/OER Files, Job 80-T01315A, Box 36, Folder 2. From *Foreign Relations*, 587.

26. Farouk A. Sankari, "Western Europe: From Belligerency to Neutrality," in *Middle East Crucible: Studies on the Arab-Israeli War of October 1973*, ed. Naseer H. Aruri (Wilmette, IL: Medina University Press International, 1975), 278.

Notes—Chapter 4

27. Ibid.
28. Telcon, "Nixon / Kissinger," October 17, 1973, 8:44 a.m., National Archives, Kissinger Telephone Conversations, Chronological File, Box 23, *Foreign Relations*, 556.
29. Telcon, "Dobrynin / Kissinger," October 17, 1973, 9:42 a.m., National Archives, Kissinger Telephone Conversations, Dobrynin File, Box 28, *Foreign Relations*, 560.
30. "Message from Brezhnev to Nixon," National Archives, NSC Files, Kissinger Office Files, Box 69, Country Files, Europe, USSR, Dobrynin/Kissinger, Vol. 20, October 12-Nov. 21, 1973, *Foreign Relations*, 562.
31. Memorandum of Conversation, National Archives, Nixon Presidential Materials, NSC Files, Box 664, Country Files, Middle East, Middle East War, Memos and Misc., October 6–17, 1973, Top Secret, *Foreign Relations*, 565.
32. Kissinger Telcon, "Nixon / Kissinger," October 17, 1973, 1:40 p.m. http://foia.state.gov/documents/Kissinger0000 C7F2.pdf.
33. Minutes of WSAG Meeting, October 17, 1973, 3:05 p.m. National Archives, NSC Files, NSC Institutional Files (H-Files), Box H-117, WSAG Meetings Minutes, 1093, *Foreign Relations*, 575.
34. Memorandum of Conversation, National Archives, Nixon Presidential Materials, NSC Files, NSC Institutional Files (H-Files), Box H-92, Meeting Files, WSAG Meetings, Middle East, October 17, 1973, Secret, *Foreign Relations*, 585.
35. Kissinger Telcon, "Dinitz / Kissinger," October 17, 1973, 5:20 p.m. http://foia.state.gov/documents/Kissinger0000 C7F5.pdf.
36. *The Washington Post*, March 30, 1973, A15.
37. http://www.cfr.org/trade/jackson-vanik-amendment/p18844.
38. "Minutes of Cabinet Meeting," October 18, 1973, Ford Library, National Security Adviser, Memoranda of Conversation, Box 2, Secret, 3:09 p.m. *Foreign Relations*, 588.
39. Kissinger Telcon, "Dobrynin / Kissinger," October 18, 1973, 8:45 p.m. http://foia.state.gov/documents/Kissinger/0000C7FC.pdf.
40. Kissinger Telcon, "Nixon / Kissinger," October 18, 1973, 9:35 p.m. http://foia.state.gov/documents/Kissinger/0000 C7FE.pdf. Also, Kissinger, *Crisis*, 289.
41. "Message from Nixon to Brezhnev," October 18, 1973, National Archives, Nixon Presidential Materials, NSC Files, Kissinger Office Files, Box 70, Country Files, Europe, USSR, Exchange of Notes between Dobrynin & Kissinger, Vol. 7, *Foreign Relations*, 594.
42. Kissinger Telcon, "Scowcroft / Kissinger," October 18, 1973, 10:45 p.m. http://foia.state.gov/documents/Kissiner/0000C800.pdf.
43. "Message from Dinitz to Kissinger," October 18, 1973, National Archives, Nixon Presidential Materials, NSC Files, Kissinger Office Files, Box 136, Country Files, Middle East, Dinitz, June 4-October 31, 1973, *Foreign Relations*, 599.
44. Minutes of WSAG Meeting, October 19, 1973, 10:04 p.m. National Archives, NSC Files, NSC Institutional Files (H-Files), Box H-117, WSAG Meetings Minutes, 1973, *Foreign Relations*, 602.
45. Kissinger Telcon, "Dobrynin / Kissinger," October 19, 1973, 11:04 a.m., http://foia.state.gov/documents/Kissinger/0000C802.pdf.
46. Kissinger Telcon, "Dobrynin / Kissinger," October 19, 1973, 11:38 a.m., *Foreign Relations*, 615.
47. Victor Israelyan, *Inside the Kremlin During the Yom Kippur War* (University Park: Pennsylvania State University Press, 1995), 122.
48. Kissinger, *Crisis*, 293.
49. Kissinger Telcon, "Dobrynin / Kissinger," October 19, 1973, 11:38 a.m., Memorandum of Conversation, National Archives, Nixon Presidential Materials, Kissinger Telephone Conversations, Dobrynin File, Box 28, *Foreign Relations*, 615.
50. Kissinger Telcon, "Dobrynin / Kissinger," October 19, 1973, 1:35 p.m. http://foia.state.gov/documents/Kissinger/0000C805.pdf.
51. Kissinger, *Crisis*, 295.
52. Kissinger Telcon, "Haig / Kissinger," October 19, 1973, 3:20 p.m. http://foia.state.gov/documents/Kissinger/0000 C807.pdf.
53. Kissinger, *Crisis*, 298, Telcon, "Haig / Kissinger," October 19, 1973, 3:35 p.m.
54. Kalb and Kalb, 483.
55. Kissinger Telcon, "Dinitz / Kissinger," October 19, 1973, 7:09 p.m. http://

foia.state.gov/documents/Kissinger/0000C810.pdf.

56. Memorandum of Conversation, National Archives, Nixon Presidential Materials, NSC Files, Box 1027, Presidential/HAK Memcons, April-Nov. 1973, Secret, *Foreign Relations*, 621.

57. Kissinger, *Crisis*, 302.

Chapter 5

1. Telegram from Kissinger to Scowcroft, 1315Z,National Archives, Nixon Presidential Materials, Kissinger Office Files, Box 39, Kissinger Trip Files, HAK Trip—Moscow, Tel Aviv, London, HAKTO, SECTO, TOSEC, Misc., October 20–23, 2973, Secret, Sensitive, *Foreign Relations*, 624.

2. Telegram from Kissinger to Scowcroft, 1545Z,National Archives, Nixon Presidential Materials, Kissinger Office Files, Box 39, Kissinger Trip Files, HAK Trip—Moscow, Tel Aviv, London, HAKTO, SECTO, TOSEC, Misc., October 20–23, 2973, Secret, Sensitive, *Foreign Relations*, 625.

3. Message from Nixon to Brezhnev, National Archives, Nixon Presidential Materials, NSC Files, Kissinger Office Files, Box 70, Country Files, Europe, USSR, *Foreign Relations*, 626.

4. "Message from Kissinger to Scowcroft," HAKTO 06, NATIONAL ARCHIVES, NIXON PRESIDENTIAL MATERIALS, HENRY KISSINGER OFFICE FILES, box 39, HAK Trip—Moscow, Tel Aviv, London—October 20–23, 1973, HAKTO, SECTO, TOSEC, Burr, 48, http://www.gwu.edu/~nsarchiv/NSAEBB/NSAEBB98/octwar-48.pdf.

5. Telegram from Scowcroft to Kissinger, 1755Z, National Archives, Nixon Presidential Materials, Kissinger Office Files, Box 39, Kissinger Trip Files, HAK Trip—Moscow, Tel Aviv, London, TOHAK, Misc., October 20–23, 2973, Secret, Sensitive, *Foreign Relations*, 627.

6. Kissinger, *Years of Upheaval*, 547.

7. Kalb and Kalb, 484.

8. Victor Israelyan, "The October 1973 War: Kissinger in Moscow," *Middle East Journal* 49, no. 2 (Spring 1995), 254.

9. Israelyan, 438.

10. "Memcon between Brezhnev and Kissinger," RG 59, SN 70–73, POL 7 U.S./Kissinger, Burr, Document 46, http://www.gwu.edu/~nsarchiv/NSAEBB/NSAEBB98/octwar-46.pdf.

11. Kissinger, *Years of Upheaval*, 552.

12. Ibid.

13. Telegram from Scowcroft to Kissinger, 1538Z, National Archives, Nixon Presidential Materials, Kissinger Office Files, Box 39, Kissinger Trip Files, HAK Trip—Moscow, Tel Aviv, London, TOHAK, Misc., October 20–23, 2973, Secret, Sensitive, *Foreign Relations*, 643.

14. Kissinger, *Years of Upheaval*, 553.

15. Israelyan, 129.

16. Kissinger, *Years of Upheaval*, 553.

17. Andrei Gromyko, *Memoirs* (New York: Doubleday, 1989), 287.

18. "Memcon between Brezhnev and Kissinger," October 21, 1973, RG 59, SN 70–73, POL 7 U.S./Kissinger, Burr, Document 49, http://www.gwu.edu/~nsarchiv/NSAEBB/NSAEBB98/octwar-49.pdf.

19. Garthoff, 418.

20. "Letter from Nixon to Meir," National Archives, Nixon Presidential Materials, NSC Files, Kissinger Office Files, box 136, Country Files, Middle East, Dinitz, June 4-October 31, 1973, *Foreign Relations*, 648. Note: Telegram Tohak 70, October 22, 0338Z informed Kissinger that Israel had accepted the resolution, but needed clarification on a number of questions.

21. Telegram from Kissinger to Scali, 1813Z, National Archives, Nixon Presidential Materials, Kissinger Office Files, Box 39, Kissinger Trip Files, HAK Trip—Moscow, Tel Aviv, London, HAKTO, SECTO, TOSEC, Misc., October 20–23, 2973, Top Secret, *Foreign Relations*, 645.

22. "U.S. Embassy Soviet Union Cable 13148 to Department of State," October 21, National Archives, Nixon Presidential Materials, Kissinger Office Files, Xox 39, HAK Trip—Moscow, Tel Aviv, London—October 20–23, Burr, Document 51, http://www.gwu.edu/~nsarchiv/NSAEBB/NSAEBB98/octwar-51.pdf.

23. "Memcon between Kissinger and Western Ambassadors," October 21, RG 59, SN 70–73, POL 7 U.S./Kissinger, Burr, Document 50, http://www.gwu.edu/~nsarchiv/NSAEBB/NSAEBB98/octwar-50.pdf.

24. Kissinger, *Years of Upheaval*, 556.

25. Ibid.

26. Department of State Operations Center, Middle East Task Force Situation Report #52, "Situation Report in the Middle East as of 1830 EDT, 10/21/73," NATIONAL ARCHIVES, NIXON PRESIDENTIAL MATERIALS, NSCF, box 1175, 1973 Middle East War, October 21, 1973, file no. 16, Burr, Document 52, http://www.gwu.edu/~nsarchiv/NSAEBB/NSAEBB98/octwar-52.pdf.

27. "Memcon between Gromyko and Kissinger," October 22, 1973, RG 59, SN 70–73, POL U.S.-USSR, Burr, Document 53, http://www.gwu.edu/~nsarchiv/NSAEBB/NSAEBB98/octwar-53.pdf.

28. Matti Golan, *The Secret Conversations of Henry Kissinger: Step-by-Step Diplomacy in the Middle East* (New York: Quandrangle, 1976), 77.

29. Israelyan, 143.

30. Ibid., 144.

31. Abba Eban, *Personal Witness: Israel Through My Eyes* (New York: G.P. Putnam's Sons, 1992), 537.

32. Jussi Hanhimäki, 312.

33. Elinor Burkett, *Golda* (New York: HarperCollins, 2008), 334.

34. Ibid., 344.

35. "Memcon between Meir and Kissinger," October 22, 1973, RG 59, SN 70–73, POL 7 U.S./Kissinger, Burr, Document 54, http://www.gwu.edu/~nsarchiv/NSAEBB/NSAEBB98/octwar-54.pdf.

36. Garthoff, 418.

37. "Memcon of Luncheon for Kissinger's Party," RG 59, SN 70–73, POL 7 U.S./Kissinger, Burr, Document 55, http://www.gwu.edu/~nsarchiv/NSAEBB/NSAEBB98/octwar-55.pdf.

38. Kissinger, *Years of Upheaval*, 561.

39. Isaacson, 528.

40. Lebow and Stein, 216.

41. Ibid., Interview with Sisco in Washington, D.C., April 17, 1991.

42. Ibid., Interview with Kissinger in New York, June 19, 1991.

43. Ibid., 217, Kissinger interview.

44. Ibid., 218, interview with senior officer of the Israel Defense Forces, April 1988.

45. Ibid.

46. Kissinger, *Years of Upheaval*, 567.

47. Ibid.

48. Ibid.

49. Barry M. Blechman and Douglas M. Hart, "The Political Utility of Nuclear Weapons: The 1973 Middle East Crisis," *International Security* 7, no. 1 (Summer 1982), 136.

Chapter 6

1. See *Parker's The October War: A Retrospective*, 160–230, for an analysis by Bernard Reich and a panel discussion of the DEFCON III alert.

2. Ibid., 568.

3. "Conversation with Prime Minister Meir," U.S. Embassy Cable 8513 to State Department, National Archives, Nixon Presidential Materials, NSC Files, Box 1175, 1973 Middle East War, October 23, 1973, file no. 18, Burr, Document 58, http://www.gwu.edu/~nsarchiv/NSAEBB/NSAEBB98/octwar-58.pdf.

4. Kissinger, *Years of Upheaval*, 569.

5. Ibid.

6. Department of State Operations Center, Middle East Task Force Situation Report #57, "Situation Report in the Middle East as of 12:00 EDT, October 23," National Archives, Nixon Presidential Materials, NSC Files, Box 1175, 1973 Middle East War, October 23, 1973, file #18, Burr, Document 59, http://www.gwu.edu/~nsarchiv/NSAEBB/NSAEBB98/octwar-59.pdf.

7. Message from Brezhnev to Kissinger, National Archives, Nixon Presidential Materials, NSC Files, Kissinger Office File, Box 69, Country Files, Europe, USSR, Dobrynin/Kissinger, Vol. 2, October 12-Nov. 21, 1973, *Foreign Relations*, 676.

8. Ibid., Foreign Relations, 677.

9. Kissinger, *Years of Upheaval*, 570.

10. Transcript of Telephone Conversation between Kissinger and Dinitz, National Archives, Nixon Presidential Materials, Kissinger Telephone Conversations, Telcons, Chronological File, Box 23, Foreign Relations, 678.

11. Kissinger, *Years of Upheaval*, 571.

12. Hoff, *Nixon Reconsidered*, 155.

13. Transcript of Telephone Conversation between Kissinger and Vorontsov, National Archives, Nixon Presidential Materials, Kissinger Telephone Conversations, Telcons, Chronological File, Dobrynin File, Box 28, *Foreign Relations*, 679.

14. Transcript of Telephone Conversation between Kissinger and Dinitz, National Archives, Nixon Presidential

Materials, Kissinger Telephone Conversations, Telcons, Chronological File, Box 23, *Foreign Relations*, 682.

15. Kissinger, *Years of Upheaval*, 571.

16. Hotline Message from Brezhnev to Nixon, National Archives, Nixon Presidential Materials, NSC Files, Kissinger Office Files, Box 69, Country Files, Europe, USSR, Dobrynin/Kissinger, Vol. 20, October 12 – Nov. 21, Top Secret, *Foreign Relations*, 684. Note: Kissinger notes the time the message was received in *Years of Upheaval*, 572.

17. Kissinger, *Crisis*, 312.

18. Hotline Message from Nixon to Brezhnev, National Archives, Nixon Presidential Materials, NSC Files, Kissinger Office Files, Box 69, Country Files, Europe, USSR, Dobrynin/Kissinger, Vol. 20, October 12 – Nov. 21, Top Secret, *Foreign Relations*, 685.

19. Kissinger Telcon, "Dobrynin / Kissinger," October 23, 1973, 1:35 p.m. http://foia.state.gov/documents/Kissinger/0000C829.pdf.

20. Kissinger Telcon, "Dobrynin / Kissinger," October 23, 1973, 1:40 p.m. http://foia.state.gov/documents/Kissinger/0000C82B.pdf.

21. "Hotline Message from Brezhnev to Nixon," NATIONAL ARCHIVES, NIXON PRESIDENTIAL MATERIALS, HENRY KISSINGER OFFICE FILES, Box 69, Dobrynin/Kissinger, Vol. 20, October 12-Nov. 27, Burr, Document 58, http://www.gwu.edu/~nsarchiv/NSAEBB/NSAEBB98/octwar-58.pdf.

22. Kissinger, *Crisis*, 314.

23. Ibid.

24. Backchannel Message from Sadat to Nixon, National Archives, Nixon Presidential Materials, NSC Files, Kissinger Office Files, Middle East, Egypt/Ismail, Vol. 7, October 1–31, Secret, Sensitive, *Foreign Relations*, 687.

25. Backchannel Message from Nixon to Sadat, National Archives, Nixon Presidential Materials, NSC Files, Kissinger Office Files, Box 132, Country Files, Middle East, Egypt/Ismail, Vol. 7, October 1-October 31, *Foreign Relations*, 702.

26. Kissinger Telcon, "Dinitz / Kissinger," October 23, 1973, 8:30 p.m. http://foia.state.gov/documents/Kissinger/0000C842.pdf.

27. Blechman and Douglas M. Hart, "The Political Utility of Nuclear Weapons: The 1973 Middle East Crisis, *International Security* 7, no. 1 (Summer 1982): 134.

28. Kissinger, *Years of Upheaval*, 575.

29. Kissinger Telcon, "Dinitz / Kissinger," October 24, 1973, 9:22 a.m., http://foia.state.gov/documents/Kissinger/0000C845.pdf.

30. Kissinger Telcon, "Dinitz / Kissinger," October 24, 1973, 9:32 a.m., http://foia.state.gov/documents/Kissinger/0000C846.pdf.

31. Kissinger Telcon, "Dobrynin / Kissinger," October 24, 1973, 9:45 a.m., http://foia.state.gov/documents/Kissinger/0000C19E.pdf.

32. Backchannel Message from Nixon to Sadat, National Archives, Nixon Presidential Materials, NSC Files, Kissinger Office Files, Box 132, Country Files, Middle East, Egypt/Ismail, Vol. 7, October 1-October 31, Secret, Sensitive, *Foreign Relations*, 708.

33. Kissinger Telcon, "Dobrynin / Kissinger," October 24, 1973, 10:19 a.m., http://foia.state.gov/documents/Kissinger/0000C84D.pdf.

34. Ibid.

35. Minutes of Washington Special Actions Group Meeting, National Archives, Nixon Presidential Materials, NSC Files, Kissinger Office Files, Box H-117, WSAG Meetings Minutes, Originals, 1973, Top Secret, *Foreign Relations*, 711.

36. Ibid.

37. Backchannel Message from Kissinger to Sadat, National Archives, Nixon Presidential Materials, NSC Files, Kissinger Office Files, Box 132, Country Files, Middle East, Egypt/Ismail, Vol. 7, October 1-October 31, *Foreign Relations*, 720.

38. Kissinger Telcon, "Schlesinger / Moorer / Colby / Scowcroft / Kissinger, October 24, 1973, 1:05 p.m. http://www.fordlibrarymuseum.gov/library/document/0314/1552626.pdf.

39. Bruno Pierri, "A Chess Game in the Middle East: Dr. Kissinger's Diplomacy against the USSR during the Yom Kippur War," *Rivista di Studi Politici Internazionali* 76, no. 3 (303) (July—September 2009), 369.

40. Message from Brezhnev to Nixon, National Archives, Nixon Presidential Materials, NSC Files, Kissinger Office Files, Box 69, Country Files, Europe,

USSR, Dobrynin/Kissinger, Vol. 20, October 12 – Nov. 21, *Foreign Relations*, 727.

41. Kissinger Telcon, "Dinitz / Kissinger," October 24, 1973, 3:40 p.m. http://foia.state.gov/documents/Kissinger/0000C852.pdf.

42. Golda Meir, *My Life*, 375.

43. Kissinger Telcon, "Schlesinger / Kissinger," October 24, 1973, 4:25 p.m. http://foia.state.gov/documents/Kissinger/0000C856.pdf.

44. Briefing memorandum from Colby to Kissinger, National Archives, RG 59, Central Files 1970–73, POL 27–14, ARAB-ISR, Secret, *Foreign Relations*, 729.

45. Kissinger, *Years of Upheaval*, 581.

46. Ibid., 582.

47. Kissinger Telcon, "Dobrynin / Kissinger," October 24, 1973, 7:15 p.m. http://foia.state.gov/documents/Kissinger/0000C85E.pdf.

48. Kissinger Telcon, "Scali / Kissinger," October 24, 1973, 7:25 p.m. http://foia.state.gov/documents/Kissinger/0000C860.pdf.

49. Kissinger Telcon, "Dobrynin / Kissinger," October 24, 1973, 7:25 p.m. http://foia.state.gov/documents/Kissinger/0000C85F.pdf.

50. Kissinger Telcon, "Dinitz / Kissinger," October 24, 1973, 7:35 p.m. http://foia.state.gov/documents/Kissinger/0000C863.pdf.

51. Kissinger Telcon, "Dobrynin / Kissinger," October 24, 1973, 8:02 p.m. http://foia.state.gov/documents/Kissinger/0000C864.pdf.

52. Kissinger Telcon, "Dobrynin / Kissinger," October 24, 1973, 8:25 p.m. http://foia.state.gov/documents/Kissinger/0000C866.pdf.

53. Israelyan, 167.

54. Kissinger, *Crisis*, 341.

55. "Backchannel message from Nixon through Ismail to Sadat," October 24, 1973, RG 59, SN 70–73, POL 27–14, Arab-Isr, Burr, Document 59, http://www.gwu.edu/~nsarchiv/NSAEBB/NSAEBB98/octwar-59.pdf. Note: Kissinger states that he drafted the message in Nixon's name in *Years of Upheaval*, 583.

56. Kissinger, *Years of Upheaval*, 583.

57. Message from Brezhnev to Nixon, National Archives, Nixon Presidential Materials, NSC Files, Kissinger Office Files, Box 69, Country Files, Europe, USSR, Dobrynin/Kissinger, Vol. 20, October 12 – Nov. 21, *Foreign Relations*, 734.

58. Kissinger, *Years of Upheaval*, 583.

59. Kissinger, *Crisis*, 343.

60. Kissinger, *Years of Upheaval*, 585.

61. Kissinger Telcon, "Dinitz / Kissinger," October 24, 1973, 10:00 p.m. http://foia.state.gov/documents/Kissinger/0000C869.pdf.

62. Kissinger, *Years of Upheaval*, 585.

63. Israelyan, 174.

64. Ibid., 586.

65. Ray Cline, "Policy without Intelligence," *Foreign Policy* 17 (Winter 1974–75), p. 128, in *Foreign Relations*, 737.

66. Patrick Tyler, *A World of Trouble: The White House and the Middle East—From the Cold War to the War on Terror* (New York: Farrar, Straus and Giroux), 172.

67. Elmo R. Zumwalt, Jr., *On Watch* (New York: The New York Times Book Co., 1976), 448.

68. Helmut Sonnenfeldt, *The Nixon Presidency: Twenty-two Intimate Perspectives of Richard M. Nixon*, ed. Kenneth W. Thompson (Lanham, MD: University Press of America, 1987), 325.

69. Kalb and Kalb, 492.

70. Interview with Harold P. Ford, March 31, 1988, *President Nixon and the Role of Intelligence in the 1973 Arab-Israeli War* (Yorba Linda, CA: Richard Nixon Presidential Library and Museum, 2013), electronic book, location 320.

71. Rodman, 74.

72. Haig, Jr., *Inner Circles*, 415.

73. Nixon, *RN*, 938.

74. Roger Morris, *Uncertain Greatness: Henry Kissinger & American Foreign Policy* (New York: Harper & Row, 1977), 248.

75. "Memorandum for the Record," October 26, National Archives, RG 218, Records of Admiral Thomas Moorer, Diary, October 1973, top secret, sensitive—hold close, *Foreign Relations*, 738.

76. Blechman and Hart, 137.

77. Moorer, "Memorandum for the Record," 738. Note: Kissinger writes that there were eight Soviet An-22 transport planes activated in *Years of Upheaval*, 589.

78. Ibid., 739.

79. Garthoff, 379.

80. Jeremi Suri, *Henry Kissinger and the American Century* (Cambridge: Belknap Press of Harvard University Press), 260.

See also William Burr, "The Nixon Administration the 'Horror Strategy' and the Search for Limited Nuclear Options, 1969–1972: Prelude to the Schlesinger Doctrine," *Journal of Cold War Studies* 7, no. 3 (2005): 38.

81. Allen J. Matusow, "Nixon as Madman," *Reviews in American History* 27, no. 4 (1999): 623.

82. Blechman and Hart, 145.

83. John L Scherer, "Soviet and American Behavior during the Yom Kippur War," *World Affairs* 141, no. 1 (Summer 1978): 18.

84. Morris, 249.

85. Bernard Reich, "Crisis Management," in *The October War*: A Retrospective, ed. Richard B. Parker (Gainesville: University Press of Florida, 2001), 168.

86. Ibid. Original source: Israel Government Press Office Weekly News Bulletin, November 13–19, 1973, supplement, S2.

87. Kissinger Telcon, "Dinitz / Kissinger," October 24, 1973, 11:25 p.m. http://foia.state.gov/documents/Kissinger/0000C86C.pdf

88. Kissinger, *Years of Upheaval*, 588.

89. Israelyan, 179.

90. "Backchannel Message from Kissinger to Sadat," National Archives, Nixon Presidential Materials, NSC Files, Kissinger Office Files, Box 132, Country Files, Middle East, Egypt/Ismail, Vol. 7, October 1—October 31. *Foreign Relations*, 744.

91. Kissinger, *Years of Upheaval*, 588.

92. "Message from Nixon to Brezhnev," National Archives, Nixon Presidential Materials, NSC Files, Kissinger Office Files, Box 70, Country Files, Europe, USSR, Exchange of Notes between Dobrynin & Kissinger, Vol. 8, *Foreign Relations*, 747.

93. Blechman and Hart, 142.

94. Kissinger, *Years of Upheaval*, 589.

95. Press conference of October 26, 1973, in Department of State Bulletin LXIX, No. 1795, http://archive.org/stream/departmentofstatb6973unit/departmentofstatb6973unit_djvu.txt.

96. Ibid.

97. Kissinger, *Years of Upheaval*, 596.

98. *New York Times*, October 25, 1973, 1.

99. Kalb and Kalb, 498.

100. *New York Times*, October 27, 1973, 1.

101. Steven E. Ambrose, *Nixon: Ruin and Recovery, 1973–1990* (New York: Touchstone, 1991), 257.

102. Nixon, *RN*, 942.

103. Ambrose, 258.

104. "Backchannel Message from Ismail to Kissinger," National Archives, Nixon Presidential Materials, NSC Files, Kissinger Office Files, Box 132, Country Files, Middle East, Egypt/Ismail, Vol. 7, October 1 – October 31, Secret, Sensitive, *Foreign Relations*, 749.

105. Kissinger Telcon, "Dobrynin / Kissinger," October 25, 1973, 2:40 p.m. http://foia.state.gov/documents/Kissinger/0000C1A0.pdf.

106. Zumwalt, 447.

107. Walter J. Boyne, *The Two O'Clock War: The 1973 Yom Kippur Conflict and the Airlift That Saved Israel* (New York: Thomas Dunne, 2002), 267.

108. Kalb and Kalb, 499.

109. Richard Ned Lebow and Janice Gross Stein, "Deterrence and the Cold War," *Political Science Quarterly* 110, no. 2 (Summer 1995): 168.

110. Dobrynin, *In Confidence*, 305.

Chapter 7

1. Quandt, *Decades of Darkness*, 200.

2. Spiegel, *The Other Arab-Israeli Conflict*, 221.

3. Ibid., 202.

4. Parker, 244.

5. Galia Golan, *Yom Kippur and After: The Soviet Union and the Middle East Crisis* (Cambridge: Cambridge University Press, 1977), 128.

6. Ibid., 250.

7. Robert S. Litwak, *Détente and the Nixon Doctrine: American Foreign Policy and the Pursuit of Stability, 1969–1976* (Cambridge: Cambridge University Press, 1984), 165.

8. Kalb and Kalb, 545.

9. Seymour M. Hersh, *The Price of Power: Kissinger in the Nixon White House* (New York: Summit Books, 1983), 637.

10. Dankwart A. Rustow, "Who Won the Yom Kippur and Oil Wars?" *Foreign Policy* 17 (Winter 1974–1975): 167.

11. Scherer, "Soviet and American Behavior," 19.

12. Bernard Reich, "Crisis Manage-

ment," in *The October War*: A Retrospective, ed. Richard B. Parker (Gainesville: University Press of Florida, 2001), 168.

13. P.G.K. Paniker, "Oil: From Crisis to Crisis," *Economic and Political Weekly* 26, no. 9/10 (March 2–9, 1991): 479.

14. Foreign Relations of the United States, 1969–1976, Volume XXXV, National Security Policy, 1973–1976, Document 29, Minutes of the Secretary of State's Staff Meeting, January 7, 1974, 12:10–1:02 p.m. http://history.state.gov/historicaldocuments/frus1969-76v35/d29.

15. Daniel J. Sargent, "The United States and Globalization in the 1970s," in *The Shock of the Global: The 1970s in Perspective*, ed. Niall Ferguson, Charles S. Maier, Erez Manela and Daniel J. Sargent (Cambridge: Belknap Press of Harvard University Press, 2010), 49.

16. Camille Mansour, *Beyond Alliance: Israel and U.S. Foreign Policy* (New York: Columbia University Press, 1994), 114.

17. Stephens, *U.S. Policy towards Israel*, 162.

18. http://www.gallup.com/poll/161387/americans-sympathies-israel-match-time-high.aspx.

19. Horne, *Kissinger*, 396.

20. Ibid., 400.

21. Isaacson, *Kissinger*, 767.

22. Scherer, "Soviet and American Behavior," 5.

23. Referenced in in Jussi M. Hanhimäki, "'Dr. Kissinger' or 'Mr. Henry'? Kissingerology, Thirty Years and Counting, *Diplomatic History* 27, no. 5 (November 2003): 637.

24. Henry Kissinger, "Conversations with Kissinger," *Journal of Palestine Studies* 10, no. 3 (Spring 1981): 188.

25. Raphael Israeli, *Man of Defiance: A Political Biography of Anwar Sadat* (Totowa, NJ: Barnes & Noble Books, 1985), 128.

Bibliography

Ambrose, Steven E. *Nixon: The Triumph of a Politician, 1962–1972*. New York: Simon & Schuster, 1989.

Bar-Siman-Tov, Yaacov. "The United States and Israel since 1948: A 'Special Relationship?'" *Diplomatic History* 22, no. 2 (1998): 231–262.

Ben-Zvi, Abraham. *The United States and Israel: The Limits of the Special Relationship*. New York: Columbia University Press, 1993.

Black, Conrad. *Richard M. Nixon: A Life in Full*. New York: Public Affairs, 2007.

Blechman, Barry M., and Douglas M. Hart. "The Political Utility of Nuclear Weapons: The 1973 Middle East Crisis." *International Security* 7, no. 1 (Summer 1982): 132–156.

Boyne, Walter J. *The Two O'Clock War: The 1973 Yom Kippur Conflict and the Airlift That Saved Israel*. New York: Thomas Dunne, 2002.

Brecher, Michael. *Decisions in Crisis: Israel, 1967 and 1973*. Berkeley: University of California Press, 1980.

———, and Mordechai Raz. "Images and Behavior: Israel's Yom Kippur Crisis, 1973." *International Journal* 32, no. 3 (Summer 1977): 475–500.

Brinkley, Douglas, and Luke A. Nichter. *The Nixon Tapes: 1971–1972*. New York: Houghton, Mifflin, Harcourt, 2014.

Bundy, William. *A Tangled Web: The Making of Foreign Policy in the Nixon Presidency*. New York: Hill and Wang, 1998.

Burke, John P. *Honest Broker? The National Security Advisor and Presidential Decision Making*. College Station: Texas A&M University Press, 2009.

Burkett, Elinor. *Golda*. New York: HarperCollins, 2008.

Burr, William. "The Nixon Administration the 'Horror Strategy' and the Search for Limited Nuclear Options, 1969–1972: Prelude to the Schlesinger Doctrine," *Journal of Cold War Studies*, 7, no. 3 (2005): 34–78.

———. *The October War and U.S Policy*, 2003. http://www2.gwu.edu/~nsarchiv/NSAEBB/NSAEBB98/.

Clarke, Duncan L. "U.S. Security Assistance to Egypt and Israel: Politically Untouchable?" *Middle East Journal* 51, no. 2 (1997): 200–214.

Cohen, Michael J. "Truman and the State Department: The Palestine Trusteeship Proposal," *Jewish Social Studies* 43, no. 2 (1981): 165–178.

Colby, Elbridge Avner Cohen, William McCants, and Bradley Morris. *The Israeli "Nuclear Alert" of 1973: Deterrence and Signaling in Crisis*. Alexandria: CNA, 2013. https://www.cna.org/sites/default/files/research/DRM-2013-U-004480-Final2.pdf. Accessed November 2, 2014.

Bibliography

Daigle, Craig. *The Limits of Détente: The United States, The Soviet Union, and the Arab-Israeli Conflict, 1969–1973.* New Haven: Yale University Press, 2012.

Dayan, Moshe. *Story of My Life.* New York: William Morrow, 1976.

Del Pero, Mario. *The Eccentric Realist: Henry Kissinger and the Shaping of American Foreign Policy.* Ithaca: Cornell University Press, 2010.

Dobrynin, Anatoly. *In Confidence.* New York: Times Books, 1995.

Eban, Abba. *Personal Witness: Israel Through My Eyes.* New York: G.P. Putnam's Sons, 1992.

El-Badri, Hassan, Taha el–Magdoub, and Mohammed Dia el Din Zohdy. *The Ramadan War, 1973.* New York: Hero Books, 1978.

El Mallakh, Ragaei. "Arab Oil and the World Economy." In *Middle East Crucible: Studies on the Arab-Israeli War of October 1973.* Edited by Naseer H. Aruri. Wilmette, IL: Medina University Press International, 1975.

Ferguson, Niall. *The Shock of the Global: The 1970's in Perspective.* Cambridge: Belknap Press of Harvard University Press, 2010.

Feuerwerger, Marvin C. *Congress and Israel: Foreign Aid Decision-Making in the House of Representatives, 1969–1976.* Westport, CT: Greenwood Press, 1979.

Finkelstein, Lawrence S. "The United States and the United Nations Proper Prudence—Or a New Failure of Nerve." *Korea Journal* 35, no. 1 (1995): 17–34.

Finklestone, Joseph. *Anwar Sadat: Visionary Who Dared.* Portland: Frank Cass, 2003.

Fukuyama, Francis. *The End of History and the Last Man.* New York: Free Press, 2006.

Garthoff, Raymond L. *Détente and Confrontation: American-Soviet Relations from Nixon to Reagan.* Washington, D.C.: The Brookings Institution, 1994.

Ginor, Isabella, and Gideon Remez. "The Origins of a Misnomer." In *The Cold War in the Middle East: Regional Conflict and the Superpowers, 1976–1973.* Edited by Nijel J. Ashton. New York: Routledge, 2007.

Golan, Galia. *Yom Kippur and After: The Soviet Union and the Middle East Crisis.* Cambridge: Cambridge University Press, 1977.

Golan, Matti. *The Secret Conversations of Henry Kissinger: Step-by-Step Diplomacy in the Middle East.* New York: Quadrangle, 1976.

Gromyko, Andrei. *Memoirs.* New York: Doubleday, 1989.

Hahn, Peter L. "The View from Jerusalem: Revelations about U.S. Diplomacy from the Archives of Israel." *Diplomatic History* 22, no. 4 (Fall 1998): 509–532.

Haig, Alexander M., Jr. *Inner Circles: How America Changed the World: A Memoir.* New York: Warner Books, 1992.

Haldeman, H.R. *The Haldeman Diaries: Inside the Nixon White House.* New York: G.P. Putnam's Sons, 1994.

Hanhimäki, Jussi M. "'Dr. Kissinger' or 'Mr. Henry'? Kissingerology, Thirty Years and Counting, *Diplomatic History* 27, no. 5 (November 2003): 637–676.

———. *The Flawed Architect: Henry Kissinger and American Foreign Policy.* Oxford: Oxford University Press, 2004.

Heikal, Mohamed. *The Road to Ramadan.* New York: The New York Times Book Co., 1975.

Hersh, Seymour M. *The Price of Power: Kissinger in the Nixon White House.* New York: Summit Books, 1983.

Hoff, Joan. *Nixon Reconsidered.* New York: Basic Books, 1995.

Holcombe, Randall G., and Russell S. Sobel, "The Stability of International Coalitions in United Nations Voting from 1946 to 1973." *Public Choice* 86, no. 1/2 (1996): 17–34.

Horne, Alistair. *Kissinger: 1973, The Crucial Year.* New York: Simon & Schuster, 2009.

Isaacson, Walter. *Kissinger: A Biography.* New York: Simon & Schuster, 2005.

Israeli, Raphael. *Man of Defiance: A Political Biography of Anwar Sadat.* Totowa, NJ: Barnes & Noble Books, 1985.

Israelyan, Victor. *Inside the Kremlin During the Yom Kippur War.* University Park: Pennsylvania State University Press, 1995.

———. "The October 1973 War: Kissinger in Moscow." *Middle East Journal* 49, no. 2 (Spring 1995): 248–268.

Jacobs, Lawrence R., and Robert Y. Shapiro. "The Rise of Presidential Polling: The Nixon White House in Historical Perspective." *The Public Opinion Quarterly* 59, no. 2 (1995): 163–195.

Johnson, Lyndon B. *The Vantage Point: Perspectives of the Presidency, 1963–1969.* New York: Holt, Rinehart and Winston, 1971.

Kalb, Melvin, and Bernard Kalb. *Kissinger.* Boston: Little, Brown, 1974.

Kissinger, Henry. "Conversations with Kissinger," Journal of Palestine Studies, vol. 10, no. 3 (Spring, 1981): 186–195.

———. *Crisis: The Anatomy of Two Major Foreign Policy Crises.* New York: Simon & Schuster, 2003.

———. *White House Years.* Boston: Little, Brown, 1979.

———. *Years of Upheaval.* New York: Simon & Schuster, 1982.

Kochavi, Noam. *Nixon and Israel: Forging a Conservative Partnership.* Albany: State University of New York Press, 2009.

Kohler, Foy D., Leon Gouré, and Mose L. Harvey. *The Soviet Union and the October 1973 Middle East War: The Implications for Détente.* Miami: University of Miami Center for Advanced International Studies, 1974.

Korn, David A. *Assassination in Khartoum.* Bloomington: Indiana University Press, 1973.

———. "U.S.-Soviet Negotiations of 1969 and the Rogers Plan," *Middle East Journal* 44, no. 1 (1990): 37–50.

Lebow, Richard Ned, and Janice Gross Stein. "Deterrence and the Cold War." *Political Science Quarterly*, vol. 110, no. 2 (Summer 1995): 157–181.

———, and ———. *We All Lost the Cold War.* Princeton: Princeton University Press, 1994.

Lenczowski, George. *American Presidents and the Middle East.* Durham: Duke University Press, 1990.

Little, Douglas. *American Orientalism: The United States and the Middle East since 1945.* Chapel Hill: University of North Carolina Press, 2008.

———. "The Making of a Special Relationship: The United States and Israel, 1957–68." *International Journal of Middle East Studies* 25, no. 4 (1993): 563–585.

Litwak, Robert S. *Détente and the Nixon Doctrine: American Foreign Policy and the Pursuit of Stability, 1969–1976.* Cambridge: Cambridge University Press, 1984.

Mansour, Camille. *Beyond Alliance: Israel and U.S. Foreign Policy.* New York: Columbia University Press, 1994.

Mart, Michelle. *Eye on Israel: How America Came to View Israel as an Ally.* Albany: State University of New York Press, 2006.

Matusow, Allen J. "Nixon as Madman." *Reviews in American History* 27, no. 4 (1999): 623–629.

McAlister, Melani. *Epic Encounters: Culture, Media and U.S. Interests in the Middle East since 1945.* Berkeley: University of California Press, 2005.

Mearsheimer, John J., and Stephen M. Walt. *The Israel Lobby and U.S. Foreign Policy.* New York: Farrar, Straus and Giroux, 2007.

Meir, Golda. *My Life: The Autobiography of Golda Meir.* London: Futura Publications, 1975.

Morris, Roger. *Uncertain Greatness: Henry Kissinger & American Foreign Policy.* New York: Harper & Row, 1977.

Naftali, Timothy. *Blind Spot: The Secret History of American Counterterrorism.* New York: Basic Books, 2005.

Neff, Donald. *Warriors Against Israel: How Israel Won the Battle to Become America's Ally, 1973.* Brattleboro, VT: Amana Books, 1988.

Nixon, Richard. *RN: The Memoirs of Richard Nixon.* New York: Grosset & Dunlap, 1978.

Paniker, P.G.K. "Oil: From Crisis to Crisis." *Economic and Political Weekly* 26, no. 9/10 (March 2–9, 1991): 479–481.

Parker, Richard B. *The October War: A Retrospective.* Gainesville: University Press of Florida, 2001.

Peretz, Don. "The United States, the Arabs and Israel: Peace Efforts of Kennedy, Johnson, and Nixon." *Annals of the American Academy of Political and Social Science* 401 (1972): 116–125.

Petras, James. *The Power of Israel in the United States.* Atlanta: Clarity Press, 2006.

Pierri, Bruno. "A Chess Game in the Middle East: Dr. Kissinger's Diplomacy Against the USSR During the Yom Kippur War." *Rivista di Studi Politici Internazionali* 76, no. 3 (July–September 2009): 351–380.

Quandt, William B. *Decade of Decision: American Policy Toward the Arab-Israeli Conflict, 1967–76*. Berkeley: University of California Press, 1978
———. "Lyndon Johnson and the June 1967 War: What Color Was the Light?" *Middle East Journal* 46, no. 2 (1992): 198–228.
———. *Peace Process: American Diplomacy and the Arab-Israeli Conflict since 1967*. Berkeley: University of California Press, 2005.
———. "Soviet Policy in the October Middle East War—I." *International Affairs* 53, no. 3 (July 1977): 377–389.
Rabin, Yitzhak. *The Rabin Memoirs*. Berkeley: University of California Press, 1979.
Raviv, Dan, and Yossi Melman. *Friends in Deed: Inside the U.S.-Israel Alliance*. New York: Hyperion, 1994.
Reeves, Richard. *President Nixon*. New York: Simon & Schuster, 2001.
Reich, Bernard. *Securing the Covenant: United States-Israel Relations after the Cold War*. Westport, CT: Praeger, 1995.
Rodman, Peter. *Presidential Command: Power, Leadership, and the Making of Foreign Policy from Richard Nixon to George W. Bush*. New York: Alfred A. Knopf, 2009.
Rogers, William P. "Rogers Plan Speech, December 9, 1969." In *Arab-Israeli Conflict and Conciliation: A Documentary History*. Edited by Bernard Reich. Westport, CT: Praeger, 1995.
Rubin, Barry. "Soviet Policy in the Middle East." In *Crucible: Studies on the Arab-Israeli War of October 1973*. Edited by Naseer H. Aruri. Wilmette, IL: The Medina University Press International, 1975.
Rustow, Dankwart A. "U.S. Policy, January-October 1973." *Journal of Palestine Studies* 3, no. 2 (Winter 1974): 98–113.
———. "Who Won the Yom Kippur and Oil Wars?" *Foreign Policy*, no. 17 (Winter, 1974–1975): 166–175.
Sadat, Anwar. *In Search of Identity: An Autobiography*. New York: Harper and Row, 1978.
———. *The Public Diary of President Sadat: The Road to War, October 1970—October 1973*. Leiden: Brill Academic, 1997
———. *Those I Have Known*. New York: Continuum International, 1984.
Safran, Nadav. *Israel: The Embattled Ally*. Cambridge: Belknap Press of Harvard University Press, 1978.

Sankari, Farouk A. "Western Europe: From Belligerency to Neutrality." In *Middle East Crucible: Studies on the Arab-Israeli War of October 1973*. Edited by Naseer H. Aruri. Wilmette, IL: Medina University Press International, 1975.
Sargent, Daniel J. "The United States and Globalization in the 1970s." In *The Shock of the Global: The 1970s in Perspective*. Edited by Niall Ferguson, Charles S. Maier, Erez Manela and Daniel J. Sargent. Cambridge: Belknap Press of Harvard University Press, 2010.
Sarsar, Saliba. "The Question of Palestine and United States Behavior at the United Nations." *International Journal of Politics, Culture and Society* 17, no. 3 (2004): 457–470.
Scherer, John L. "Soviet and American Behavior during the Yom Kippur War." *World Affairs* 141, no. 1 (Summer 1978): 3–23.
Schoenbaum, David. *The United States and the State of Israel*. New York: Oxford University Press, 1993.
Semmerling, Tim Jon. *"Evil" Arabs in American Popular Film: Orientalist Fear*. Austin: University of Texas Press, 2006.
Sheehan, Edward R. F. "How Kissinger Did It: Step by Step in the Middle East." In *Dynamics of Third Party Intervention: Kissinger in the Middle East*. Edited by Jeffrey Z. Rubin. New York: Praeger, 1983.
Shrivastava, B.K. "The United States and the United Nations." *India Quarterly*, 32, no. 2 (1976): 220–235.
Siniver, Asaf. *Nixon, Kissinger and U.S. Foreign Policy Making: The Machinery of Crisis*. Cambridge: Cambridge University Press, 2008.
Sonnenfeldt, Helmut. *The Nixon Presidency: Twenty-two Intimate Perspectives of Richard M. Nixon*. Edited by Kenneth W. Thompson. Lanham, MD: University Press of America, 1987.
Spiegel, Steven L. *The Other Arab-Israeli Conflict: Making America's Middle East Policy, from Truman to Reagan*. Chicago: University of Chicago Press, 1985.
Stephens, Elizabeth. *U.S. Policy Towards Israel: The Role of Political Culture in Defining the 'Special Relationship.'* Sussex: Sussex Academic Press, 2006.

Suri, Jeremi. *Henry Kissinger and the American Century*. Cambridge: Belknap Press of Harvard University Press, 2007.

Truman, Harry S. *Memoirs by Harry S. Truman: Years of Trial and Hope*. New York: Smithmark, 1996.

Tyler, Patrick. *A World of Trouble: The White House and the Middle East—From the Cold War to the War on Terror*. New York: Farrar, Straus and Giroux, 1996.

U.S. Central Intelligence Agency. Memorandum to the Director of Central Intelligence prepared by the Intelligence Community Staff. *The Performance of the Intelligence Community Before the Arab-Israeli War of October 1973: A Preliminary Post-Mortem Report*. December 20, 1973. http://www.foia.cia.gov/sites/default/files/document_conversions/89801/DOC_0001331429.pdf.

U.S. Department of State. *Foreign Relations of the United States, 1969–1976, Volume XXV, Arab-Israeli Crisis and War, 1973*. Washington, D.C.: United States Government Printing Office, 2011.

_____. *Henry Kissinger Telephone Transcripts*. Freedom of Information Act Document Collection. http://foia.state.gov/Search/Collections.aspx.

Waldheim, Kurt. *In the Eye of the Storm: A Memoir*. Bethesda: Adler & Adler, 1986.

Yaqub, Salim. "The Politics of Stalemate." In *The Cold War in the Middle East: Regional Conflict and the Superpowers, 1976–1973*. Edited by Nijel J. Ashton. New York: Routledge, 2007.

_____. "The Weight of Conquest: Henry Kissinger and the Arab-Israeli Conflict. In *"Nixon in the World: American Foreign Relations, 1969–1977*. Edited by Fredrik Logevall and Andrew Preston. New York: Oxford University Press, 2008.

Zaharna, R.S. "The Palestinian Leadership and the American Media: Changing Images, Conflicting Results." In *The U.S. Media and the Middle East: Image and Perception*. Edited Yahya R. Kamalipour. Westport, CT: Praeger, 1995.

Zumwalt, Elmo R., Jr. *On Watch*. New York: The New York Times Book Co., 1976.

Index

Numbers in **_bold italics_** indicate pages with illustrations.

Agnew, Spiro 3, 20, **_36_**, 72, 88
Akhbar al–Yom 39
Aleandrov, Andrei 123
AMAN (Israeli military intelligence organization) 57
Ambrose, Stephen 161
American Israel Public Affairs Committee (AIPAC) 6, 7
Andropov, Yuri 157
Anti-Ballistic Missile Treaty (1972) 70
Arab-Israeli conflict: Kissinger's strategy 171; Nixon's ability to handle 24; superpower confrontation 13; U.S. role in mediating 163, 166, 171
Arab oil embargo: American strategy in respect of 111; consequences 108, 168–169; impact on U.S. foreign policy 169; Kissinger on 169; possibility of 96, 103; as response to U.S. aid to Israel 108
Assad, Hafez al- 53
Atherton, Alfred 69, 123

Bar-Siman-Tov, Yaacov 5, 6
Begin, Menachem 4, 166, 167
Ben-Gurion, David 10
Benites, Leopoldo 82
Black, Conrad 17
Black September terrorist attack 31, 44
Blechman, Barry 135
Borchgrave, Arnaud de 45
Bork, Robert 20
Boumédiene, Houari 85
Brecher, Michael 58
Brezhnev, Leonid: on delay of Soviet military aid to Egypt 37; foreign policy of 38; on Israel's violation of ceasefire 139–140, 144, 146–147; on Israel's violation of Security Council decision 141–142; on Jewish emigration 112; negotiations in Moscow with Kissinger 48, 123–125; Nixon's communications with 51, 70, 109; position on Arab-Israeli war 78, 82; response to American military alert 157, 161–162; on Security Council Resolution 338 139–140; visit to Washington 50–51, **_67_**
Brown, George 7, 94
Burkett, Elinor 132
Bush, George H.W. 74
Butterfield, Alexander 54
Byroade, Henry 10

Camp David Accords 4, 60, 167
Carter, Jimmy 4, 167
ceasefire negotiations 81, 120, 129–130, 144, 146; *see also* Yom Kippur War
Central Intelligence Agency (CIA): analytical capabilities 61; on possibility of Arab-Israeli war 61–63; reliance on Israeli intelligence 64; report on effect of oil embargo 108
Clement, William 22, 94
Clements, William 87, 110, 152
Cline, Ray: anticipation of Arab-Israeli war 68–69; on Israel's violation of ceasefire 147; memorandum on possibility of war in Middle East 49–50; on Nixon's absence on "meeting of principals" 152; on Syrian military activity 55

Clinton, Bill 9
Cohen, Michael J. 10
Colby, William 61, 69, 116
Cox, Archibald 20, 54, 118, 124
Cromer, George Rowland Stanley Baring 92, 98

Daigle, Craig 38
Dayan, Moshe 55, 57, 58, 59, 89
DEFCON III military alert 4, 137, 155, 158, 163–164
Defense Intelligence Agency (DIA) 80
Del Pero, Mario 77, 95
détente 32, 76–77, 114
DiBona, Charles 111
Dinitz, Simcha: on demilitarization strip 156; on Israel's position on ceasefire 92; Kissinger's communications with 79, 85, 86, 90, 141, 143–144, 150; Kissinger's meetings with 55, 89; reaction on Brezhnev's threat of unilateral actions 150; on Soviet military aid to Arabs 56, 91; on Syrians military preparations 47; on U.S. military aid to Israel 83, 84, 91, 112
Dobrynin, Anatoly: on Arab pressure on Moscow during October war 78; on attack on Soviet merchant ship 92; invitation to Kissinger to visit Moscow 116–117; Kissinger's communications with 41, 66, 73, 98, 103, 161–162; meeting with Rogers 25; as message bearer in superpower confrontation 151, 161; on Middle East conflict settlement 41; Nixon and 27; secret meeting with Kissinger 35; on Security Council resolution for ceasefire 92, 114; on Soviet position on ceasefire 86, 98–99; on Soviet support of Egypt 29–30; on U.S.-Soviet relations and Middle East war 163
Dorsey, B.R. 88
Douglas-Home, Alec 96, 97, 130

Eagleburger, Lawrence 72, 129
Eban, Abba 12, 68, 72, 130, 131
Egypt: anti-Soviet rhetoric in media 39; ceasefire with Israel 30; closure of Straits of Tiran 11; consideration of peace agreement with Israel 87; defense treaty with Jordan 11; impact of Yom Kippur War on 166; losses in war 102, 104; population 36; position on ceasefire agreement 125–126; preparation for war with Israel 45; relations with Soviet Union 37, 42; Soviet military aid to 37, 50; state media on ceasefire agreement 139; withdrawal of Soviet troops from 39
Ehrlichman, John 20
Eid, Guy 44
Eilts, Herman 83
Eisenhower, Dwight D. 10

Elazar, David 58, 133
El Mallakh, Ragaei 106
Eshkol, Levi 11
Europe: impact of Arab oil embargo 108; tensions with U.S. 105
Evron, Eppie 12

Faisal, King of Saudi Arabia 47, 104
Fedayeen 46
Fedayeen militant group 30
Feuerwerger, Marvin C. 9
Finklestone, Joseph 32
Ford, Gerald 92, 112, 152
Fortas, Justice Abe 12–13
Fukuyama, Francis 73
Fulbright, J.W. 46

Gamasy, Mohamed abdel- 162
Garment, Leonard 29, 131
Garthoff, Raymond L. 22, 128
Gaulle, Charles de 27
Ginor, Isabella 39
Golan, Galia 167
Golan, Matti 130
Graham, Billy 17
Grechko, Andrei 131, 157
Gromyko, Andrei 71, 117, 123, 127, 130–131
Gur, Mordechai 83, 93

Habash, George 30
Hahn, Peter L. 7
Haig, Alexander: Kissinger's communication with 77–78; on Nixon's foreign policy amid Watergate scandal 152–153; portrait 85; positions in U.S. administration 31, 68; on public image of president 72; on relationship between Kissinger and Schlesinger 95; on Schlesinger's assessment of Israeli foreign policy 96
Haldeman, H.R. 16, 20, 25, 26, 155
Hanhimäki, Jussi 21
Harmon, Abe 13
Hart, Douglas 135
Heath, Edward 90
Heikal, Mohamed 43, 48–49
Herbers, John 160
Hersh, Seymour 15, 24, 29, 34, 167
Hitchens, Christopher 170
Horne, Alistair 57, 106, 170
Hussein, King of Jordan 30, 31, 90

Isaacson, Walter 83, 170
Ismail, Hafiz 40, 42, 43–44, 49, 78
Ismail, Mohammed Zakariya 68
Israel: border security 29; consequences of Yom Kippur War for 166; Lichud opposition on ceasefire agreement 139; losses in war 83; miscalculation of military strength 57–58; 1970 ceasefire with

Egypt and Jordan 30; plea for U.S. military aid 83; population 36; prospects of winning war against Arabs, 82; public appreciation of American airlift 112; in Six-Day War 36–37; "special relationship" with United States 2, 5, 7; U.S. aid to 5, 100, 169; violations of ceasefire 120, 138, 147
Israeli, Raphael 40, 69, 171
The Israeli Lobby and U.S. Foreign Policy (Mearsheimer and Walt) 7
Israelyan, Victor: on Brezhnev's foreign policy 70; on discussion in Kremlin on sending troops to Egypt 148–149; on Dobrynin's role in superpower crisis 151; on negotiations in Moscow 123; on reaction of Politburo on American military alert 157; on suggestion to invite Kissinger to Moscow 117
Izvestia 39

Jackson, Henry: accusation of U.S. administration in delaying help for Israel 89; on congressional investigation of national security system 98; as critic of Nixon 101; on emigration of Soviet Jews to Israel 76; as sponsor of vote on military credits for Israel 33, 34; as supporter of Israel 8, 22
Jackson-Vanik amendment 15, 22, 77, 95, 112
Jacobs, Lawrence R. 16
Jacobson, Eddie 7
Jamieson, Kenneth 88
Japan 108
Jarring, Gunnar 27, 30
Javits, Jacob 81
Johnson, Joseph 10
Johnson, Lyndon B. 11–12, 13
Jordan 11, 31–32
Jungers, Frank 47

Keating, Kenneth 55, 66, 138
Keegan, George 94
Kennedy, John F. 10, 11
Kennedy, Ted 81
Keyes, Paul 17
Kissinger, Henry: on American Jewish community 19; appointment as Secretary of State 54; Arab foreign ministers' meeting with 109–110; attempt to stop Jackson-Vanick amendment 95; backchannel communications with Sadat 144, 145–146; on Brezhnev's diplomacy 51, 56; on Brezhnev's three-point plan for peace settlement 126; on ceasefire proposal 96; celebrity status 170; as chief Middle East negotiator 23, 34; Chinese delegation's meeting with 75–76; on Chinese reaction on peace settlement 115; on CIA reports 63; Cold War thinking 21–22; concerns of Soviet threat 3–4; confidence in Israel's ability to withstand Arabs 64; conflict with Rogers 24–25, 26; considerations of post-war negotiations 146; conversation with Meir on ceasefire 147; criticism 22, 95, 155–156; Cromer's conversation on ceasefire resolution with 98; decision-making in foreign policy 21–22; demand of immediate military aid to Israel 97; on demilitarization strip 156; on détente 91; Dinitz's communications with 79, 85, 86, 89–90, 140–141, 143–144, 150; diplomacy of 1, 2, 66–68, 81, 88, 167; Dobrynin's communications with 35, 41, 66, 73, 98, 103, 161–162; on domestic reaction on U.S. military alert 158; dual position in Nixon administration 20–21; on exclusion of Soviets from peace negotiations 103; failure to predict Arab-Israeli war 60–61; as head of National Security Council 24; Heath's telephone conversation with 90; invitation to visit Egypt 107; Ismail's communications with 40, 43–44, 49, 78, 105; on Israel intervention in Jordan 31; on Israel preemptive attack 58–59; on Israel's complaints of delay of U.S. aid 93; on Israel's respect to ceasefire 138–139; King Faisal's communications with 104; King Hussein's meeting with 42; legacy 166, 171, 172; "Man of the Year" 165; at meeting with Nixon and Rogers *50*; message to Soviet Embassy after issuing military alert 157–158; on Middle East policy 2, 33–34, 66, 91; on military aid to Israel 84; mistakes 1–2; on Nixon's foreign policy 6–7, 14–15, 72; on Nixon's personality 141; as Nobel Peace Prize recipient 19, 105; on nuclear threat 155; on oil embargo 108, 169; order to Schlesinger not to resupply Israel 94; outcomes of Middle East diplomacy 167–168; outrage over *Newsweek* article 26; on peace settlement 102, 105, 109, 111; personality 127; political influence 20; on possibility of superpower confrontation 112–113; post-war goals 101–102; on power 170; press conference on justification of military alert 158–159; on public perception of Middle East conflict 55; Rabin's communications with 29, 31–32; on Rabin's personality 16; on relations with Egypt 44; on relations with Soviet Union 75; on responsibility of policy-makers 59; on Rogers Plan 28–29; on role of superpowers in Yom Kippur War 99; on roots of Soviet demarche 153–154; on Sadat's foreign policy 40, 45; on Schlesinger's delay of aid to Israel 95, 96; scholars on 170–

171; secret talks with North Vietnamese 32; secret visit to China 32; on Security Council Resolution 242, 113; self-confidence 145; Shalev's meeting with 89; sources of information 61; on Soviet position in Middle East crisis 78, 90; speech at press conference in 1974 *18*; strategy in Arab-Israeli conflict 86, 99, 171; on UN conference on Middle East 107; on U.S. goals in Arab-Israeli war 83–84, 107; on U.S. position on ceasefire 104; on U.S.-Soviet joint approach to Arab-Israeli war 72; visit to Israel 131–136, 138; visit to Moscow 117–129; Vorontsov's conversation with 141; warnings to Soviets 82, 144

Kochavi, Noam 15
Kornienko, Georgii 123
Kosygin, Alexei 105, 107, 109, 157
Kulikov, Viktor 149
Kuznetsov, Vasilii 117

Le, Duc Tho 105
Lebow, Richard Ned 22
Lee, James 88
Lenczowski, George 13, 15
Libyan Arab Airlines incident 42
Life 17
Little, Douglas 6
Litwak, Robert 167
Love, John 111
Luns, Joseph 106

"madman" strategy 155
Maher El-Sayed, Ahmad 49
Malik, Yakov 147, 148, 149
Mansfield, Mike 81, 107, 110
Mansour, Camille 169
Mart, Michelle 8
McGovern, George S. 16
Meany, George 160
Mearsheimer, John 7
Meir, Golda: on Arab interpretation of U.N. Resolution on ceasefire 115–116; on ceasefire agreement 130, 138; diplomacy 66; on Elazar's position on preemptive strike 58; on full-scale mobilization 57; Kissinger's communications with 140–141, 147; on Kissinger's personality 132; meeting of Kitchen Cabinet 58; resignation 166; on response to possible attack of Syria and Egypt 56; on Rogers Plan 29; on Senator Fulbright 46–47; on Soviet interference in Middle East affairs 15; Super Mirage aircraft deal and 43; on U.S. nuclear alert 156; on U.S.-Israel relations 11; Waldheim's meeting with 53–54; in White House *168*
Merrick, Roger 60

Middle East conflict: public view of 55; search for diplomatic solution of 26–27
Mills, Wilbur 77
Moore, George Curtis 44, 154, 156
Moorer, Thomas 69, 94, 105, 154
Morris, Roger 155
Mossad 57
Munich massacre 33
Murphy, Dan 162

Nasser, Gamal Abdel 10, 32
Neff, Donald 47
New York Times 17, 54
Newsweek 17, 45
Niles, David 7
Nixon, Richard: absence at "meeting of principals" 152; Agnew resignation and 3; anti-Semitism of 16–17, 19; Arab foreign ministers' meeting with 109–110; on Arab-Israeli conflict 24, 31; on Brezhnev's foreign policy 112; complaints about the pro–Israeli lobby 14; on comprehensive settlement between Arabs and Israel 100; détente policy 38; Dobrynin and *27*; foreign policy 13, 38, 85, 101; on Jewish control over media 17; on Jordan civil war 31; King Hussein's meeting with 42; Kissinger's relationship with 26, 41; on liberals and intellectuals 14; on "madman" strategy 155; media and 16–17; at meeting with Kissinger and Rogers *50*; Middle East policy 15, 41, 54–55, 99, 102, 103; on military aid to Israel 97, 99; negotiations with Brezhnev 50–51; news on imminent attack on Israel 36; October 26 press conference 159–161; on peace settlement 102, 110; personality 4, 79–80, 148, 160–161; pressure on Israel 43; Rabin's support of 16; re-election campaign 16; on Rogers 25; on Rogers Plan 30; Schlesinger's meeting with *21*; telegram to Kissinger on peace settlement 122; on threat of impeachment 148; on U.N. conference on Middle East 107; on U.N.'s inability to resolve Arab-Israeli conflict 80; on U.S. airlift 96, 100, 111; on U.S. foreign policy 14, 28; U.S.–Israeli relationship and 5, 13, 15, 89; visit to Egypt *87*; visit to Peking 35; visit to Soviet Union 38; Watergate scandal and 3, 54
Nixon-Brezhnev talks in Washington 51, 52
Nixon Doctrine 34
Noel, Cleo 44
Noyes, James 69
nuclear threats 163

Obama, Barack 112
October War *see* Yom Kippur War
Operation Red Sea Regatta 12

Index

Organization of Arab Petroleum Exporting Countries (OAPEC) 108
Organization of Petroleum Exporting Countries (OPEC) 108

Palestinian terrorism 44, 46
Pentagon 94
Petras, James 5
Pierpoint, Robert 161
Pierri, Bruno 146
Podgorny, Nikolai 157
Popular Front for the Liberation of Palestine (PFLP) 30
Portugal 98

Quandt, William 11, 20, 30, 71, 94, 165

Rabin, Yitzhak 15, 16, 28, 29, 31–32
Rather, Dan 160
Reeves, Richard 79
Reich, Bernard 7
Remez, Gideon 39
Richardson, Elliot 20, 32, 118, 124
Rifai, Zayd al- 40, 42
Rodman, Peter 83, 94, 100, 135, 152–153, 156
Rogers, William: appointment as Secretary of State 24; as chief negotiator in Middle East 33; conflict with Kissinger 24–25, 26; Dobrynin's meeting with 25; at meeting with Nixon and Kissinger 50; Middle East crisis and 23, 26, 27–28; on military aid to Israel 34–35; Nixon on 34; presentation of U.S. peace plan 28; resignation 20, 54; visit to Egypt 33
Rogers Plan 28, 29–30
Ruckelshaus, William 20, 118, 124
Rumsfeld, Donald 106
Rush, Kenneth 69, 88
Rusk, Dean 13
Rustow, Dankwart 168

Sabry, Ali 33
Sadat, Anwar: acceptance of U.S. proposal to withdraw troops 161; backchannel communications with Kissinger 144, 145–146; on ceasefire 125–126; collaboration with Assad 53; conflict with Soviet Union 37–38; criticism of United Nations 53; diplomacy of 39–40; disinformation plan on Egypt weaponry 40; foreign policy 35–36, 37, 45, 48; interview to *Newsweek* 45; Nixon's visit to Egypt and 87; personality 32–33, 60; preparation for war with Israel 40, 43; as president of Egypt 32; reaction to U.S.-Soviet talks on Middle East 38–39; reputation in Arab world 171; Rifai's meeting with 40–41; role in Egyptian politics 171–172; speech in United Nations 52–

53; threats to launch war against Israel 23; on use of SCUD missiles 131; on withdrawal of Soviet troops from Egypt 39; as world political leader 165
Safron, Nadav 8
SALT I *see* Strategic Arms Limitation Talks (SALT I)
Sargent, Daniel J. 169
Saturday Night Massacre 20, 124–125
Saudi Arabia: concern over U.S. aid to Israel 109; oil embargo announcement 123; oil production and politics 47; tensions with U.S. 103, 129; terrorist attack in Embassy in Khartoum 44
Saunders, Harold 53
Scali, John 52, 73, 87, 128
Scherer, John 71, 155
Schlesinger, James: on Arab pressure on U.S. and Israel 48; delay of military aid to Israel 87, 89, 95–96; on Egypt's preparation for war 45; at meeting with Nixon 21; role in Middle East conflict 22; scepticism of shortage of Israeli military supplies 93–94; on U.S. policy toward Israel 146; at WSAG meetings 69, 152
Scott, Hugh 81
Scowcroft, Brent 56, 68, 69, 115, 125
Semmerling, Tim Jon 46
Shalev, Mordechai 56, 66, 67, 68, 89
Shapiro, Robert Y. 16
Sharif, Omar 172
Sheehan, Edward 95
Shrivastava, B.K. 73
Shultz, George 112, 171
Siilasvuo, Ensio 162
Siniver, Asaf 20, 100
Sirica, John J. 160
Sisco, Joseph: Dinitz's conversation with 56; on economic interest between U.S. and Arab petroleum countries 106; Keating's telegram to 55; as mediator between Meir and Nasser 30, 35; at meeting with Soviet leaders in Moscow 123; news on Arab war with Israel 65–66; on Security Council resolution 110; on U.S. policy toward Israel 134; on use of civilian carriers to deliver military supplies to Israel 89
Six-Day War (1967) 11
Sonnenfeldt, Helmut 123, 152
Soviet Union: anti–Egyptian rhetoric in media 39; as beneficiary of Arab oil embargo 169; "diploma taxes" 112; Middle East policy 3–4, 38, 109, 116; military aid to Arab countries 50, 84, 86, 88; proposal of Security Council Resolution 114–115; relations with Egypt 38, 42; Watergate scandal in media 54; Yom Kippur War and 64–65, 81, 167

special relationship *see* U.S.-Israel special relationship
Spiegel, Steven 8, 165
Stein, Janice Gross 22
Stennis, John 124
Stephens, Elizabeth 9, 169
Stevenson, Adlai 10, 11
Stoddard, Philip 59, 60
Strategic Arms Limitation Talks (SALT I) 51, 70, 71, 167
Sudan 37
Suez Canal 42
superpower confrontation: assessments 162–163; avoidance of nuclear crisis 162; crisis of confidence 167; Israel's violation of ceasefire and 142; Kissinger's role in 151, 154, 157; Meir's rejection of Russian ultimatum 142; Nixon's televised news conference on 153; origin 137; role of Dobrynin in 151; scholars on 137; Soviet position on ceasefire enforcement 148; Soviet threat of unilateral actions 150, 151, 153–154; standoff of Soviet and U.S. fleet 162; U.S. military alert 156, 158; WSAG's "meeting of principals" 151–152
Suri, Jeremi 155, 170
Symington, Stuart 34
Syria 31–32, 37

Tal, Wasfi al- 33
Tanaka, Kakuei 82
terrorism 31, 44, 46
The Trials of Henry Kissinger 170
Truman, Harry S. 10

United Kingdom 92, 96–97
United Nations: Malik's speech in 149; Middle East conflict and 52, 81–82; non-aligned nations in 73–74; proposal of *Resolution 338* 139; Scali's speech on "tyranny of the majority" 73; Security Council *Resolution 242* 24, 52, 53, 102, 103, 113, 124; Security Council *Resolution 339* 143; Soviet initiatives 81, 114–115, 148; Waldheim on character of 73–74; Zayat's request for introduction of troops 148, 149
United Nations Emergency Force (UNEF) 11
United States: antipathy toward Arabs in 8, 46, 47; Arab-Israeli war and 64–65, 79, 81, 89, 90, 167; Azores military base 96, 97, 98; congressional resolution on creation of Israeli State 9; economic crisis 45–46; foreign policy 33, 106; interests of oil producers 88; interference in Soviet domestic policy 76–77; Jewish lobby 7; Middle East policy 30, 34–35, 55–56, 165; National Security Council 24; oil import 108; policy toward Israel 8–9; public support of Israel 93; relations with Europe 106; relations with Jordan 42; relations with Saudi Arabia 103; support of Israel in United Nations 6, 53; *see also* Arab oil embargo
U.S. aid for Israel: airlift of weapons and ammunition 96, 104; allocation of emergency funds 19–20, 118; amount 5, 107, 169; C-5As transports 97; military credits 33, 34–35; Nixon's demand for 97; three pint plan 96; WSAG meeting on 97
U.S.-Israel special relationship 5, 6, 7, 8, 169–170

Vanik, Charles 76
Vietnam War 32
Vinogradov, Vladimir 125, 131
Vorontsov, Yuli 91, 139, 142

Waldheim, Kurt 53–54, 73, 88, 139
Walt, Stephen 7
War Powers Act 92
The Washington Post 17, 42, 47
Washington Special Actions Group (WSAG) meetings: on Arab oil embargo 116; DEFCON III military alert 155; "madman" strateg, 155; "meeting of principals" 151–152, 153; on military aid to Israel 84, 102–103, 106–107, 145; origin and purpose 69; on response to Brezhnev's letter 150–151; on Security Council resolution 110–111; on sending attaché to the East Bank of Suez Canal 145; on Soviet influence in Middle East 75; on U.S. relations with Soviet Union 106–107; on U.S. strategy in Arab-Israeli war 78–79, 116
Watergate scandal: demonstrations and protests against Nixon 160; escalation 135; foreign affairs and 3, 88; impeachment proceedings 118, 135; legal action against Nixon 54; Saturday Night Massacre 20, 124–125; in Soviet media 54
Weizman, Ezer 57

Yamani, Ahmad Zaki 47
Yaqub, Salim 17
Yariv, Aharon 162
Yom Kippur War: approaches to ceasefire agreement 81; background 2–3; beginning 11, 64, 69–70, 73; conflict of interest between U.S. and Israel 146; consequences 165–167; diplomatic failure to prevent escalation 100; Egyptian and Syrian plans for 71–72; Egyptian attacks on Sinai Peninsula 86, 99, 104; Egyptian diplomacy 75; final phase 162; idea of joint Soviet-American action in Security Council on 74; Israeli advancement to Damascus 89, 91, 125; Israeli

losses 80, 83; Israeli military capabilities 80, 115; Jordan's intervention 86, 90; Kissinger's strategy 70, 71, 81; long-term outcomes 4, 22, 172; position of Egyptian Third Army 129, 133–134, 138, 141, 143–144; role of superpowers 1, 77, 99; situation on Golan Heights 86; Soviet aid to Syria and Egypt 84; Soviet diplomacy and 3, 71; U.S. diplomacy and 3, 66–68, 73, 74, 75, 76; U.S. Senate resolution on 81; U.S. strategy in 76, 79, 101–102; use of SCUD missiles 130–131; *see also* ceasefire negotiations

Zaharna, R.S. 46
Zayat, Mohamed El- 67, 68, 75, 87
Zumwalt, Elmo 94, 152, 162

www.ingramcontent.com/pod-product-compliance
Lightning Source LLC
Chambersburg PA
CBHW032058300426
44116CB00007B/789